Berlitz®
HAN
PERU
C000176917

Contents

Top 25 attractions

1 **Machu Picchu** The best-preserved Inca city, located in a dramatic mountaintop setting *(see p.141)*

2 **Cusco** The lively colonial city is among the most beautiful in the Americas *(see p.123)*

3 **Lake Titicaca** The world's highest navigable lake has unique, floating man-made islands offering a taste of local culture *(see p.156)*

4 **The Sacred Valley** Inca ruins, from temples to its fabled road, lie amid towns and markets *(see p.133)*

5 **Huascarán National Park** Hike or ski on one of the world's most beautiful mountain ranges *(see p.192)*

6 **Manu National Park** A protected Amazon forest noted for its wild animals and exotic plants *(see p.239)*

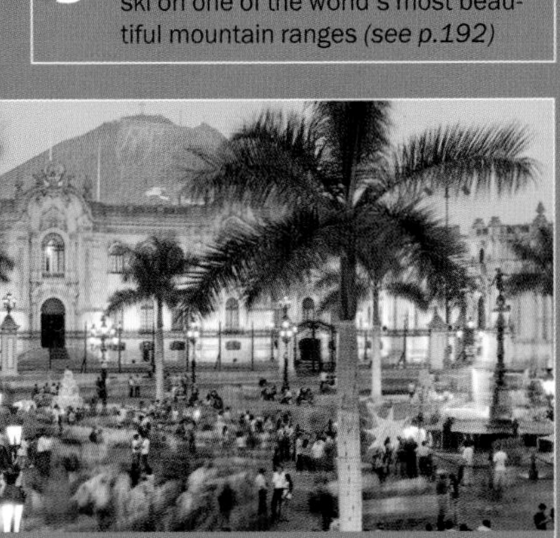

7 **Lima** Peru's vibrant capital, with a historic center and exceptional cuisine *(see p.64)*

8 **Colca and Cotahuasi Canyons** The world's deepest canyons boast condors and sports *(see p.111–2)*

9 **Surfing at Máncora** Ride the waves of Peru's most enjoyable tropical beach town *(see p.37)*

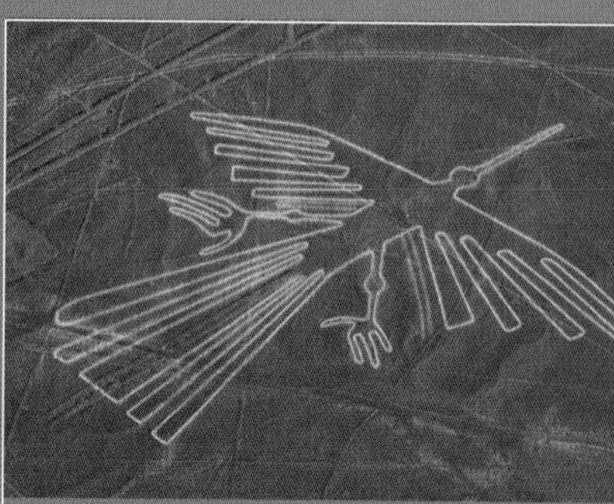

10 **Nazca** Fly over immense, unexplained indigenous art etched into the desert *(see p.104)*

11 **Iquitos** Sip cocktails alongside the world's mightiest river and visit Amazon lodges *(see p.231)*

12 **Huaca de la Luna** See striking, multicolored murals uncovered in an ancient pyramid *(see p.204)*

13 **Kuélap** Hike through sprawling ruins hidden away near the headwaters of the Amazon *(see p.222)*

14 **Train to the skies** Take an epic Andean journey on the world's second-highest railway *(see p.176)*

15 **Sandboarding at Cerro Blanco** Ride down the world's highest dunes *(see p.41)*

16 **Arequipa** Dare to sample the hot spices on offer in the remarkable 'White City' *(see p.106)*

17 **Chan Chan** Marvel at the world's largest adobe city, a dramatic sight in the desert *(see p.205)*

18 **Paracas** Stay near the beach and see spectacular marine wildlife, from seals to penguins *(see p.100)*

19 **Trujillo** A relaxed colonial city near the coast, close to the pyramids that make Peru the Egypt of the Americas *(see p.203)*

20 **Cajamarca** Visit a delightful colonial Andean town close to Inca baths and stately haciendas *(see p.213)*

21 Chiclayo See the witch doctor's market and visit nearby Sipán and Sicán museums *(see p.208)*

22 Chavín de Huantar Trek to the ruins of one of Peru's oldest Andean civilizations *(see p.194)*

23 Caral The oldest known city of the Americas emerged in the desert 4,600 years ago *(see p.85)*

24 Pongo de Manique Raft from the Andes to the Amazon through a beautiful jungle ravine *(see p.239)*

25 Laguna de Huacachina Relax at a palm-fringed desert oasis said to have curative waters *(see p.104)*

Peru fact file

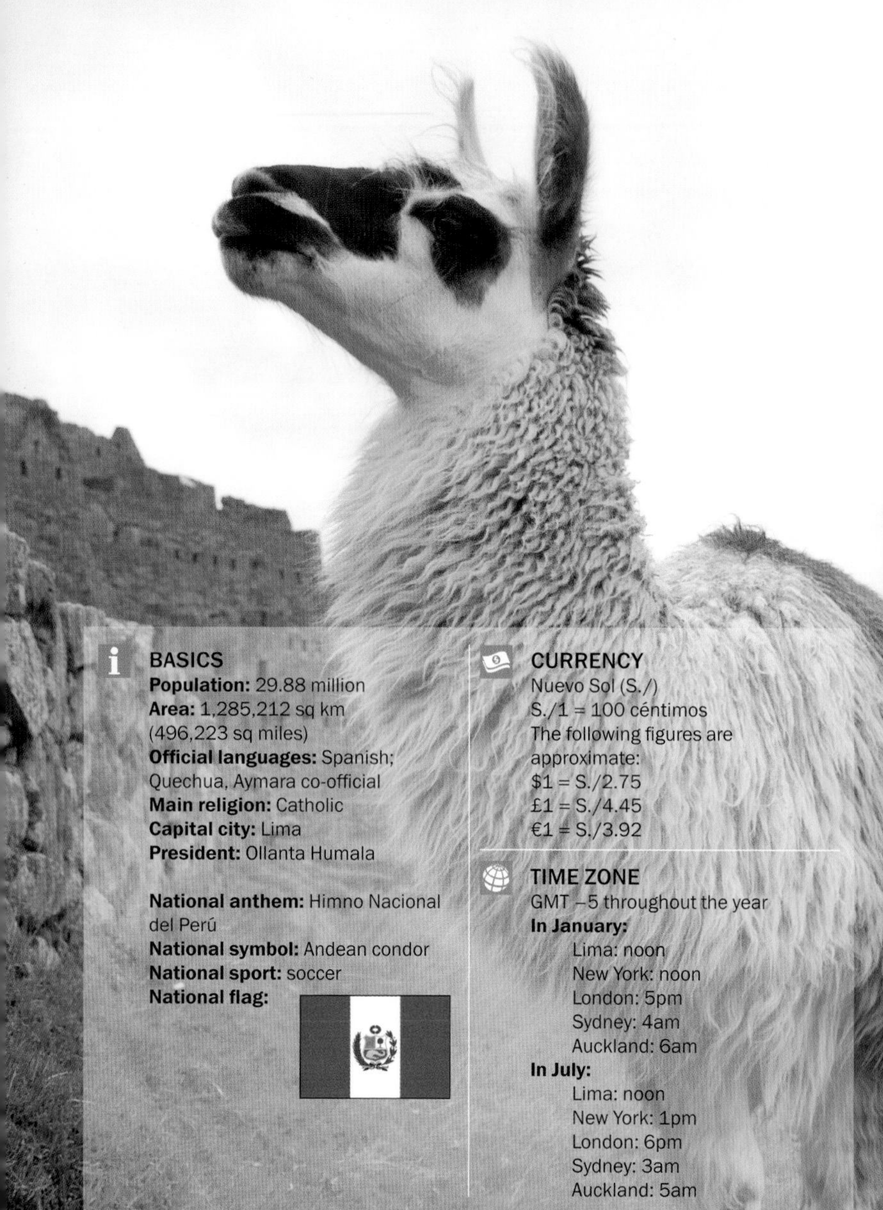

BASICS

Population: 29.88 million
Area: 1,285,212 sq km (496,223 sq miles)
Official languages: Spanish; Quechua, Aymara co-official
Main religion: Catholic
Capital city: Lima
President: Ollanta Humala

National anthem: Himno Nacional del Perú
National symbol: Andean condor
National sport: soccer
National flag:

CURRENCY

Nuevo Sol (S./)
S./1 = 100 céntimos
The following figures are approximate:
$1 = S./2.75
£1 = S./4.45
€1 = S./3.92

TIME ZONE

GMT –5 throughout the year

In January:
- Lima: noon
- New York: noon
- London: 5pm
- Sydney: 4am
- Auckland: 6am

In July:
- Lima: noon
- New York: 1pm
- London: 6pm
- Sydney: 3am
- Auckland: 5am

From coastal desert to snow-capped summits and torrid rainforest, Peru is a land of extraordinary diversity. While it has dozens of microclimates, it is geographically divided into a relatively narrow coast, a broad Andean mountain range, and nearly two-thirds which is Amazon jungle. A quarter of the population live in Lima, the capital and dominant city, and half of all Peruvians live along the Pacific coast. About 40 percent live in the cities and rural areas of the Andes, and just 11 percent in the Amazon Basin.

IMPORTANT TELEPHONE NUMBERS

Country code: +51
International calls: 00 + country code + number
Police: 105
Tourist police: 01-460-1060/ 01-460-0844
Ambulance: 470-5000
Fire: 116

AGE RESTRICTIONS

Driving: 18
Drinking: 18
Age of consent: 18
Smoking: Smoking is banned inside public buildings, including bars, pubs, and restaurants, and at places of work

ELECTRICITY

220 volts, 60 Hertz (Talara 110/220 volts; Arequipa 50 Hertz) 2- to 3-pin plug, American-style; sometimes European-style 2-pin plug

OPENING HOURS

Banks: Mon–Fri 9am–5pm
Shops: Mon–Sat 9am–5pm/6pm; many open Sun for shorter hours
Archeological sites: Most open during daylight hours around 7am–6pm
Museums: Most open Mon–Sat 9am–noon, 3–6pm

POSTAL SERVICE

Postal service: Serpost
Opening hours in major cities: Mon–Fri 8am–6pm
Postboxes: located inside post offices and retail outlets
Standard post: S./2.40
Airmail: S./6.60–S./9.00

Trip planner

WHEN TO GO

Climate

Peru is located in the tropics, but the high-altitude Andes create temperate and even cold climates in many areas. Additionally, foggy cloud cover – *garúa* – cools the coast for six months annually from April to November, which sours everyone's mood. The worst month for this is August, with temperatures around 13–17°C (55–62°F). The rest of the year, Lima enjoys sunshine and temperatures from 21–26°C (69–79°F).

Towns like Nazca on the western slopes of the Andes are dry and hot all year round, but the central Andes experience distinct wet and dry seasons. Snow is uncommon in inhabited areas, although the highest Andean peaks are covered in snow throughout the year. The best time to visit the highlands is between May and September. Although the days are bright and clear, nights can be bitterly cold, and temperatures can fall to 0°C (32°F). During the rest of the year, the weather is warmer but wetter, and the Andes are often obscured.

In the Amazon, the wet season lasts from January to April, when landslides and flooding are a constant problem. During the dry season, May to October, there might be short showers every day. Daytime temperatures average from

Public holidays

January 1	New Year's Day
May 1	Labor Day
June 29	St Peter's and St Paul's Day
July 28	Independence Day celebrations
August 30	St Rosa of Lima Day
October 8	Angamos Battle
November 1	All Saints' Day
December 8	Immaculate Conception
December 24	Christmas Eve (half-day)
December 25	Christmas Day

During Easter, Holy Week (Semana Santa), Maundy Thursday, and Good Friday are holidays.

Government offices and banks are closed during holidays, as are many small shops. Shopping centers remain open, as do main attractions and museums (except the Christmas and New Year holidays).

Changing of the guard at the Palacio de Gobierno, Lima

Traditional *caballitos de mar* at Huanchaco

27–32°C (81–90°F), with nighttime lows averaging 21–26°C (69–79°F).

High and low season

It is possible to visit Peru throughout the year, but it is most popular between May and September, as this coincides with the dry season in the highlands and the jungle. You'll find many more visitors at Machu Picchu, and other important sights and hiking trails, during the summer holidays for the Northern Hemisphere. High season for the beaches runs from Christmas to Feburary and also in September, when it can get crowded. It's necessary to book well ahead for domestic airline and bus tickets during these months and ahead of Peruvian holidays, especially the July independence celebrations – hotel and transportation costs can rise by 30 percent or more.

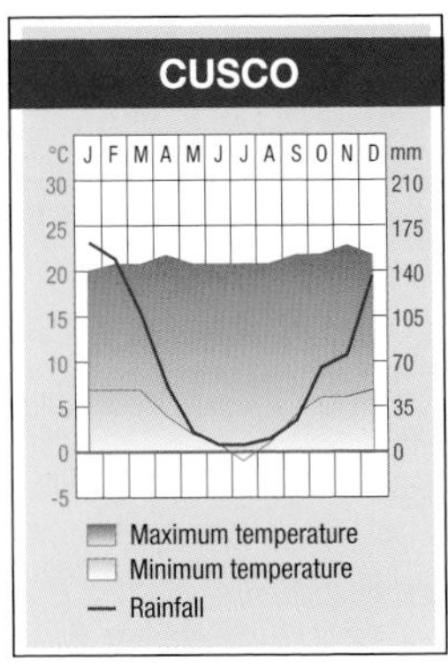

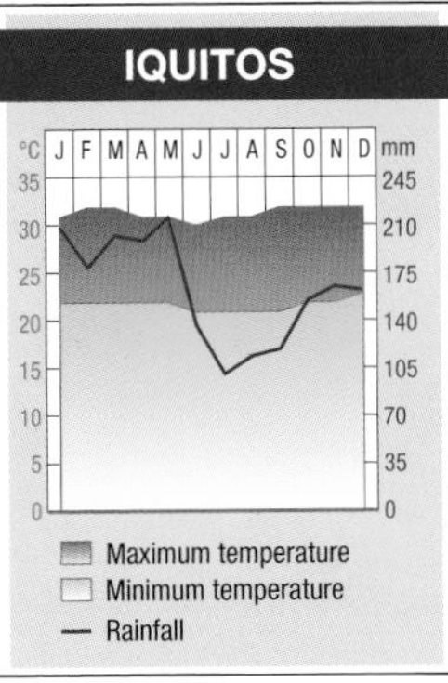

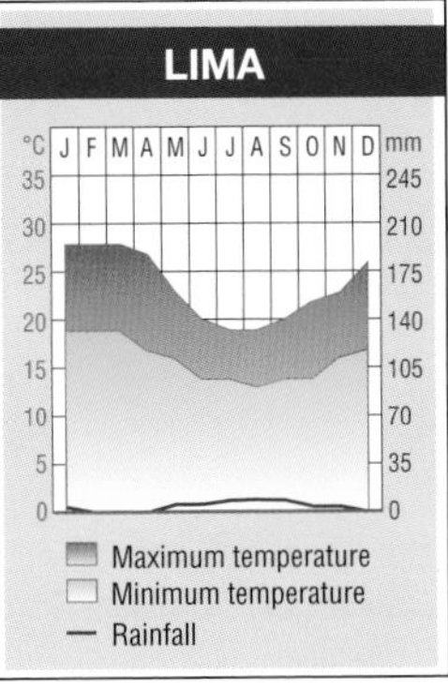

ESSENTIAL EVENTS

A lady performing a traditional dance at the Festival de la Marinera

January

Festival de la Marinera, end of January, Trujillo

Since 1960, Trujillo has hosted a *marinera* contest, celebrating the complex, flirty and highly traditional dance. There are also processions through the city and plenty of revelry in the Plaza de Armas.

February

La Virgen de la Candelaria, early February, Puno

More than 200 music and dance groups from around Lake Titicaca gather in Puno to celebrate the Candelaria Virgin or 'La Mamita Candicha' in an elaborate and very colorful two-week religious festival.

Carnival, mid-February to early March, Puno, Cajamarca, Ayacucho, and Huaraz

The main centers of Carnival festivities in Peru are in these areas. The event includes planting the *yunza*, a tree trunk laden with gifts. Note that there is frequent dousing of bystanders with water during the celebrations.

March

Fiesta de la Vendimia, early March, Ica

Celebration of the wine harvest includes the treading of the first vat by the beauty queen, parade floats and afro-Peruvian dances, particularly the *Festejo*.

Semana Santa, March–April

Ayacucho is the scene of religious celebrations during Easter Week. Numerous processions begin before Palm Sunday and continue through Easter Sunday, when the huge Lord of the Resurrection is carried through the main square before dawn.

April

National Paso Horse Contest, third week of April, Lima

The most important competitive *paso* horse event in the country is held at the Mamacona exhibition grounds in Pachacámac, 30km (19 miles) south of Lima. The event features horsemanship and horse dances.

May

Cruz Velacuy, May 2, Cusco
The crosses in all the churches are veiled, and festivities take place.

Las Cruces, May 3, Lima and the Andes
A pre-Hispanic festivity marking thanksgiving for the harvest; indigenous communities decorate and parade crosses from important churches.

June

Corpus Christi, mid-June, Cusco
One of the most beautiful displays of religious folklore, in which the Procession of the Consecrated Host is accompanied by statues of saints from churches all over Cusco.

Inti Raymi (Festival of the Sun), June 24, Cusco
Pushed back in colonial times to coincide with the day of St John the Baptist, the marking of the Andean winter solstice draws crowds to reenactments of Inca ceremonies at Sacsayhuamán thanking the sun god, Inti.

July

La Virgen del Carmen, Cusco
Festivities are held throughout the highlands and are especially colorful in Paucartambo, 255km (160 miles) from Cusco.

October

El Señor de los Milagros, October 18, 19, and 28, Lima
One of Latin America's largest religious processions, carrying the 2-ton litter of Lima's patron, the Lord of the Miracles, through the city for 24 hours. Bullfights are part of the festivities.

La Virgen de la Candelaria is a highlight of the Puno calendar

ITINERARIES

Peru has an array of fascinating destinations for culture, nature, and adventure lovers. Many of the stellar ruins, such as Chan Chan and Nazca, can be visited as part of trekking circuits or are close to the beach. Domestic flights are reasonably priced and can help you to cover a lot of ground quickly. Bear in mind that Peru is the third-largest country in South America, and poor roads make many areas difficult to access – Iquitos can only be reached by plane or riverboat.

Two-week cultural highlights tour

***Days 1–3:* Cusco.** Take it easy on arrival, ambling around the Plaza de Armas. On the second day, explore Cusco's churches and museums; on the third, take in Sacsayhuamán and other ruins close to Cusco.

***Days 4–5:* Sacred Valley and Machu Picchu.** Visit Pisac and stay overnight in Ollantaytambo, taking an early train to visit Machu Picchu. Return to Cusco.

***Days 6–8:* Lake Titicaca.** Travel overland to Puno via Andahuaylillas and Raqchi. Get up around dawn to head onto the lake and visit the Uros Islands and Taquile. Depart by air from Juliaca.

***Days 9–10:* Trujillo.** Tour the colonial town, Chan Chan, and the nearby pyramids of 'Peru's Egypt.' Catch the surf on a *caballito de totora* (traditional

A reed boat on Lake Titicaca

reed watercraft) at Huanchaco.
Days 11–12: **Chiclayo.** Visit the world-class Brüning Museum in Lambayaque, Sicán National Museum in Ferrañafe, and the famous witch doctor's market.
Days 13–14: **Lima.** See the historic center and art museums, then indulge in the cuisine and some last-minute craft shopping.

Three-week southern sporting adventure

Days 1–4: **Cusco.** Acclimatize by visiting the colonial gem, then bike the Sacred Valley.
Days 5–10: **Inca Trail.** Hike the spectacular Inca road or pick a less-traveled alternative route to Machu Picchu.
Days 11–14: **Lake Titicaca.** Visit the unique and surprisingly diverse island cultures on the world's highest lake by kayak.
Days 15–18: **Arequipa and Nazca.** Descend to the coast via colonial Arequipa and Nazca, where you can view the mysterious lines etched into the desert. Ride down the world's highest dunes and relax at the picture-perfect Huacachina desert oasis.
Days 19–21: **Paracas.** Marvel at the landscape and marine wildlife.

Five weeks for the Grand Tour

Days 1–4: **Trujillo.** Head north via Caral, the oldest ruin in the Americas, to Trujillo, visiting the nearby archeological sites and enjoying the beach at Huanchaco.
Days 5–6: **Chiclayo.** See the region's spectacular archeological finds in the Brüning and Sicán museums.

Colorful attire in the Sacred Valley

Days 7–10: **Northern Sierra.** Explore beautiful, colonial Cajamarca and its environs before viewing the vast Kuélap ruins and witnessing the Gocta waterfall, one of the world's tallest. Fly to Iquitos from Tarapoto.
Days 11–15: **Iquitos.** Experience the bustling Amazon city and the jungle in a lodge.
Days 16–18: **Paracas.** See the wildlife near Paracas and the Nazca lines from the air.
Days 19–22: **Arequipa.** Visit the colonial city and the great Colca Canyon, one of the world's deepest.
Days 23–25: **Lake Titicaca.** Stay on an island overnight and marvel at the star-studded sky.
Days 26–28: **Sacred Valley.** Tour the Inca heartland.
Days 29–32: **Cusco.** See one of the most beautiful cities in the Americas.
Days 33–35: **Lima.** End the tour in Peru's cultural and culinary capital.

BEFORE YOU LEAVE

Visas and entry requirements

Tourists from North America, Western Europe, Oceania, South Africa, and many Asian and South American countries can stay up to 183 days upon entry, requiring only a valid passport and a return ticket. If you wish to stay the maximum time, request this from the immigration official on arrival. Visitors wishing to extend their stay need to go to the office of the Dirección General de Migraciones at Prolongación Av. España, No. 734 Breña, in Lima. Overstaying carries a $1 daily fine that may not be payable at overland border crossings. Business travelers need to obtain a visa in advance at a Peruvian consular office.

Nationality	Visa Required
UK	✗
US	✗
Canada	✗
Australia	✗
New Zealand	✗
Ireland	✗
South Africa	✗

Embassies and consulates

Australia: 40 Brisbane Avenue, Barton, ACT 2600; tel: 612-6273-7351
Canada: 130 Albert Street, Suite 1901, Ottawa; tel: 613-238-1777
Ireland: Honorary Consulate, 67 Rocwood, Blackrock, Co. Dublin; tel: 1-288-9733
New Zealand: Honorary Consulate, Level 34, Vero Centre, 48 Shortland Street, Auckland 1140; tel: 09-377-0756/09-376-9400
South Africa: Brooklyn Gardens Building Block A, First Floor 235 Veale Street, 0181 Pretoria; tel: 271-2440-1030 and 1031
UK: 52 Sloane Street, London SW1X 9SP; tel: 020-7235-1917
US: 1700 Massachusetts Avenue NW, Washington DC 20036; tel: 202-833-9860 to 9869

Isla Taquile, Lake Titicaca

Vaccinations

No vaccinations are required to enter Peru. Immunization against hepatitis A and B and yellow fever are recommended, the latter at least 10 days before traveling. Malaria prophylaxis may be recommended if traveling to Amazon jungle areas. Buy travel insurance with adequate medical cover in advance of your journey.

Booking in advance

Book well in advance for the standard, wildly popular Inca Trail trip to Machu Picchu. Visits during the local holidays of Carnival and Easter Week (Semana Santa), and the activities during the July 28/29 independence holiday, should also be booked in advance. Some of the more adventurous rafting trips also need to be booked very early, as they only go ahead a few times a year.

Tourist information

Peru's official tourism authority is iPerú (tel: +511-574-8008, 24 hours; www.peru.travel), with 13 regional offices in the country but none overseas. The site has plenty of information including free, downloadable travel brochures that, in some cases, are poorly translated. In case of complaints, iPerú is also the place to go.

Maps

The Touring y Automóvil Club del Perú (TACP, Av. Trinidad Morán 698, Lince, Lima; tel: 01-614-9999; www.touringperu.com.pe (in Spanish), is the best source for maps and information. General maps are available from the South American Explorers' Club (www.saexplorer.org) and the Instituto Geográfico Nacional, Av. Aramburú 1190, Surquillo; tel: 01-475-3030; Mon–Fri 8am–6pm. Maps and street plans can also be bought at kiosks and bookshops. Offices of iPeru give out good maps of Peru, Lima, and other cities for free. Bookshops, particularly Ibero Librerías (Av. Larco 199, Miraflores), near Parque Kennedy in Lima, stock useful driving maps of Peru.

Books

Touching the Void, Joe Simpson. A tale of an ill-fated ascent of Siula Grande.
The Conquest of the Incas, John Hemming. The best modern account of the fall of the Inca Empire.
Peru: Society and Nationhood in the Andes, Peter Klarén. A balanced overview of Peruvian history from before the Inca to the return of democracy.
Captain Pantoja and the Special Service, Mario Vargas Llosa. A tongue-in-cheek story of a very special service to troops in the Peruvian Amazon.
The Peru Reader: History, Culture, Politics, Orin Starn. Essays portraying 20th-century Peruvian society.

Useful websites

www.andeantravelweb.com/peru – travel guide
www.theperuguide.com – Peru travel guide
www.saexplorer.org – the South American Explorers' Club's website
www.livinginperu.com – expat advice
www.iquitosnews.com – local guide
www.limaeasy.com – city guide
www.incas.homestead.com – local online guide
www.eventful.com/lima – events
www.mtc.gob.pe/estadisticas/index.html – official road maps
www.guiacalles.com – Automobile Club Peru road travel site.

Packing list

- Earplugs
- Batteries, memory cards, and adapters
- Quick-dry, long-sleeve clothing for tropical climates
- Windbreaker for cold Andean climates
- Sturdy shoes
- Unlocked GSM cellular phone
- Sunglasses and sun block
- Mosquito repellent

UNIQUE EXPERIENCES

Mountain highs

Rising abruptly from the Pacific coast, the world's longest mountain chain is Peru's backbone and heartland. From the remote north to Lake Titicaca and the Colca Canyon of the south, the Andes form myriad soaring peaks, icy and lush landscapes, home to archeological marvels and unique contemporary cultures.

Some 60 million years old, the Andes range continues to rise as a result of the violent clash between the Nazca and the South American tectonic plates. Their restless movement has made the Andes the tallest mountain range outside the Himalayas, and their geology has resulted not only in picturesque volcanoes and soothing hot springs but also deadly earthquakes.

Trekking the Andes is the nation's first and foremost adventure activity, the headline hike being the incomparable Inca Trail to Machu Picchu, but there are dozens of other popular routes scattered across the country, winding their way across the high passes and astounding scenery. Major areas for trekking are the Cusco region and the Cordillera Blanca, with Arequipa and the Colca Canyon, Chachapoyas, and mountain areas closer to Lima also growing in popularity.

Many of the ancient ruins are still being excavated and accessible only on foot or horseback, adding to the beauty of the treks. Economic growth and political stability have led to improvements in ground travel, with railways, roads, and airports being upgraded, as well as hotels, restaurants, and other tourism services. It can still get rough – roads outside the beaten track can be tricky, particularly during rainy periods.

Mist over Machu Picchu

Andean adventures aren't limited to trekking – mountain biking has mushroomed in popularity recently, especially around Cusco, while horseback riding and mountaineering each have their devotees and favorite areas.

Trails and treks

No skill is required for trekking, but some degree of fitness is recommended. Adventurers should be very aware of altitude as a potential cause of discomfort, disappointment, and occasionally serious problems. Andean trekking routes often cross high passes ranging from 4,000m to 5,000m (13,200 to 16,500ft). Take time to acclimatize and exercise gently at high-altitude locations like Cusco or Huaraz before trying strenuous activity. Narrow trails and high altitudes mean that people with a fear of heights should avoid the steepest hikes. Most essential trekking equipment *(see box below)* can be bought or rented in those cities, but not elsewhere. As a rule of thumb, if time is your constraint, sign up with an outfitter; if money, go independent, although this is impossible on the Inca Trail. If you go independent you'll also need a tent, multi-fuel or camping gas stove (wood fires are both impractical and unecological), and a first-aid kit.

Trekking food can be bought in the large towns and cities, but is not readily available on trails, so carry all you need for your trek. Packet soups, pasta, and noodles can be purchased in stores and markets, as can dried fruits and grains. Common spices are also available.

All drinking water should be sterilized with purification tablets, iodine solution, or a filtering pump. Powdered flavorings to disguise the nasty taste of treated water are available in stores.

The Sacred Valley

The Sacred Valley around **Cusco** and along the Urubamba River formed the heart of the Inca Empire. The area is studded with mountain peaks, Inca ruins, small valleys with patchworks of brightly colored fields, and levels off to the west around the steep, emerald-green forest surrounding Machu Picchu *(see pp.141–6)*.

You can trek to the ruins at Chavín de Huantar from Olleros

The magnificent **Inca Trail** to the fabled lost city is Peru's most famous trek. The four-day hike takes you from the trailhead 82km (51 miles) from Cusco to the ruins. The 'soft' route starting beyond Ollantaytambo is a good option for those with less time. Both are very popular, and advance booking – several months ahead of your trip if

Top 10 trekking equipment

- Hat
- Sunblock
- Sunglasses
- Raingear
- Flashlight
- Extra batteries
- Insect repellent
- Layers of both lightweight and warm clothing
- A good pair of walking shoes or boots
- A good sleeping bag

going in season *(see p.26)* – is mandatory to keep the number of trekkers to a maximum 500 per day. Five- to seven-day treks include the trek near 6,264m (20,551ft) **Salcantay**, Peru's second-highest mountain, before linking to the Inca Trail at Chaquicocha. Others like the **Ausangate Loop** take you through the Vilcanota Range for spectacular views of lakes, snowy peaks, and open Andean grasslands.

Cusco's surroundings offer numerous trails and options. Several ruins near the city are in walking distance, including the Sacsayhuaman fortress, Qenqo, Puca Pucara, and Tambo Machay. Less traveled, longer treks still inside the Cusco area include those to the village of Huayoccari and around the Lares Valley just north of Yucay. More remote, multi-day routes go to

A mountaineer tackles the Andes

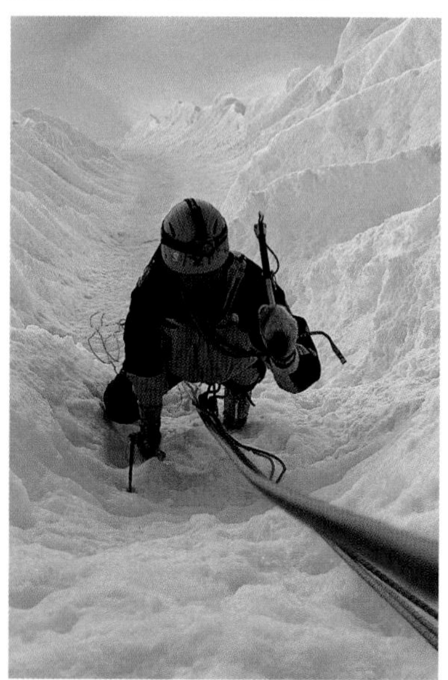

Choquequirao, a major Inca ruin still being excavated and restored, and to Espíritu Pampa and Vilcabamba, where the Inca made their last stand. There are many operators with attractive programs – don't let street touts snag you.

In Cusco, contact **Trekperu** (tel: 084-261-501; www.trekperu.com), **Peruvian Andean Treks** (tel: 084-600-500; www.andeantreks.com), or **Explorandes** (tel: 084-238-380; www.explorandes.com). Also, consider a $60 investment in the **South American Explorers'** club (www.saexplorers.org), which has up-to-the-minute information and club houses in Cusco (Atocsaycuchi 670; tel: 084-245-484;) and Lima (Piura 135, Miraflores; tel: 01-444-2150).

Cordillera Blanca

The mountains surrounding the Callejón de Huaylas are renowned among outdoors enthusiasts, particularly mountaineers eager to climb the glacier-studded **Cordillera Blanca**. Scenery and trails are world-class: the 5,947m (19,511ft) Alpamayo, once dubbed 'the most beautiful mountain in the world,' and 6,768m Huascarán (22,204ft), Peru's tallest peak.

Acclimatization hikes around **Huaraz**, the valley's tourism hub at 3,080m (10,105ft), allow visitors to adjust their lungs to the altitude. Among these, the ice-free **Cordillera Negra** to the west is less popular but has spectacular views over much of its sister range. The 7km (4-mile) hike to the small Wilkahuain ruin and hot pools of Monterrey also provides an introductory day trip. Stronger hikers might also attempt the separate treks to two beautiful

Taking in a view of the Cordillera Blanca

pe). For treks, try **Explorandes** (tel: 084-238-380; www.explorandes.com), **Huascarán Adventure Travel** (tel: 043-422-523; www.huascaran-peru.com), and **Peruvian Andes Adventures** (tel: 043-421-864; www.peruvianandes.com). In Caraz, contact **Pony's Expeditions** (tel: 043-391-642; www.ponyexpeditions.com).

Llamas are becoming popular as porters, and agencies in the major trekking destinations including, in Huaraz, **Peru Llama Trek** (tel: 43-425-661; www.perullamatrek.com), offer treks with these native animals.

lagoons, **Churup** and **Laguna 69**, after a day or two in the area.

Then, you're ready for the big treks. **Llanganuco to Santa Cruz**, the most popular, approaches 65km (40 miles) in length, depending on how many side trips you may want to take, such as taking in the view of the lake from the Alpamayo base camp. The trek to the ancient ruins at Chavín de Huantar from Olleros is easier and half the distance. It includes the hot springs at Quercos and landscapes studded with the *Puya raimondi*, a pot-bellied, 4m (13ft) bromeliad that looks like a cross between a pineapple and a missile.

The biggest adventure is the **Huayhuash Circuit**, which can range from a brief two-day hike to 12 days of wandering through difficult but spectacular terrain over some 6,000m (18,000ft) of vertical climbing.

For certified guides, check with the **Casa de Guías** in Huaraz (tel: 043-421-811; www.casadeguias.com.

Lake Titicaca

Still breathtakingly high but less challenging to hike is the region around the world's highest navigable lake, **Titicaca**. The most popular hikes are the visits to Taquile and Amantaní, easy jaunts around these mid-lake islands amid crystal-clear waters. Similar visits can be made on the Isla del Sol and near Copacabana on the Bolivian side,

Touching the void

In 1985 British climbers Simon Yates and Joe Simpson were descending from the summit of Huayhuash peak Siula Grande (6330m/20,800ft) when Simpson slipped and broke his leg. Yates's attempt to lower him to safety ended with a crippled Simpson dangling over an abyss. Unable to move, Yates finally cut the rope. Simpson survived the fall, and crawled out alone to their base camp. His book about the experience, *Touching the Void*, became an award-winning film.

Best times to go

Cordillera Blanca: The mountaineering season is from May to September. Treks can be made all year round, although it may rain in the afternoons from November to April

Sacred Valley: May to November. The Inca Trail is closed in February for clearing. June–September is the dry season, with July tending to have the least rain

Arequipa: The dry season is April–December

and all have views of Bolivia's snow-capped Cordillera Real.

In Puno, **All Ways Travel** (tel: 051-355-552) and **Pirámide Tours** (tel: 051-367-302; www.titikakalake.com) offer trips to the more remote islands of Suasi and Anapi. **Edgar Adventures** (tel: 051-353-444; www.edgaradventures.com) offer visits to the Uros Islands by reed boats.

It's also easier to climb 5,822m (19,101ft) Misti volcano by departing from Puno, on the lakeshore, than the closer Arequipa because Puno's altitude helps with the acclimatization. The trip is more of a trek than a climb.

Another active tour option is kayaking on the lake, run by **Explorandes** (tel: 051-13-36-7747; www.explorandes.com) from the village of Llachón.

Colca Canyon

The **Colca** and **Cotahuasi** canyons are the world's deepest, twice as deep as the Grand Canyon. Growing numbers of visitors are heading to the formerly remote area 100km (62 miles) from Arequipa. Attractions include colonial period chapels and pre-Hispanic terracing, along with hot springs and green oases deep in the arid gorges carved out by their eponymous rivers. Multi-day treks explore numerous valleys where you can crisscross canyons over narrow footbridges and relax sore muscles in hot springs. Altitudes vary considerably, from the Colca River's roughly 2,000m (6,560ft) to the 3,600m (11,800ft) of the famous **Cruz del Cóndor** outlook, where you may well spot the majestic giant vulture of the Andes soaring above. An additional trek is the five- to six-day hike from Andagua to the Colca Canyon, taking in high Andean landscape via the Valley of the Volcanoes and the Carani Pass.

Tours are best booked in Arequipa. Top agencies include **Lima Tours** (tel: 054-225-759; www.limatours.com.pe),

The Colca Canyon is the world's deepest

Men on their way from Urubamba to Cusco to sell horses

Colca Trek (tel: 054-206-217; www.colcatrek.com.pe), **Giardino Tours** (tel: 054-200-100; www.giardinotours.com), **Peru Adventure Tours** (tel: 054-221-658; www.peruadventurestours.com), **Condor Travel** (tel: 054-237-821; www.condortravel.com), and **Sky Viajes** (tel: 054-205-124; www.skyperu.com).

Climbing the Andes

The soaring peaks of the **Cordillera Blanca** make this area the mecca for mountain climbing in Peru. Dozens of peaks here rise above 5,000m (15,000ft), including Huascarán and Alpamayo, all within a small area. These and many other challenging peaks and mid-level climbs can be tried in season, while easy climbs are possible year-round as part of treks. Huaraz and Caraz offer services as bases for climbers.

Near Cusco, snow-capped **Salcantay** and **Ausangate** draw climbers from June to September. Arequipa, amid half a dozen peaks above 6,000m (18,000ft), offers excellent beginners' high-altitude climbs in Chachani and Misti, and the drier climate makes it an option for year-round ascents.

Unsurprisingly, **Colca** and **Cotahuasi** are also canyoneering areas. The sport combines walking, swimming, and rock climbing to traverse narrow canyons. Contact **Peru Adventure Tours** in Arequipa (tel: 054-221-658; www.peruadventurestours.com).

Mountain biking

To add adrenaline to your trips, hop on a mountain bike for downhill rushes through marvelous landscapes. Experts are best off bringing their own bike, with replacement inner tubes and brake blocks. In Peru you get what you pay for, so make sure any rental gear is in good shape and includes a helmet. Sacred Valley trips on asphalt roads and dirt trails take you through Andean villages and to Inca ruins, but tour operators including **Peru Adventure Tours** (tel: 084-984-201-239; www.peruadventurestours.com) also organize the extraordinary downhill trip from Cusco to the Manu jungle.

In Huaraz, contact **Chakinani Mountain Bike Adventures** (tel: 043-424-259; www.chakinaniperu.com) for trips around the Cordillera Blanca and Cordillera Negra.

Horseback riding

A more traditional mount is the horse. Tours are available around Cajamarca, Nazca, and Ica, as well as in Cusco, Arequipa, and the Callejón de Huaylas. Probably the best horse specialist in the country is Peruvian-Dutch outfitter **Perol Chico**, based on its ranch near Urubamba in the Sacred Valley (tel: 0974-798-890; www.perolchico.com). **Peru Adventure Tours** also offers horseback tours around the country.

Wildlife watching

The south-central Andes between Arequipa, Ayacucho, and Nazca are among the best spots in Peru to see Andean wildlife. December to August is the best time to see flamingos at the Salinas salt lake in the Salinas y Aguada Blanca nature reserve near Arequipa. Herbivores include the taruca, a vulnerable gray Andean deer, reddish-gray guanacos, the wild form of the llama, and the smaller vicuñas. Restocking has helped vicuñas recover from indiscriminate hunting, with the best place to see them the Pampa Galeras east of Nazca.

Commonly seen mammals include viscachas, which look much like relaxed, long-tailed hares, and the fox-like culpeo. Larger mammals include the spectacled bear – South America's only bear – pumas, and the rare mountain tapir in the far north near Ecuador. Birds are much more easily seen, from numerous hummingbird species to the great Andean condor, whose 3.2m (10½ft) wingspan is the largest of any land bird. Lima-based **Kolibri Expeditions** (tel: 01-273-7246; www.kolibriexpeditions.com) offer multi-day birding tours, some combined with mammal watching, throughout Peru.

Vicuñas in the Salinas y Aguada Blanca nature reserve

Visiting the locals

Many of the most picturesque hamlets are home to some of Peru's poorest communities, still struggling despite the country's recent economic growth. Visits to rural communities can help preserve and revive ancient traditions. The **Lake Titicaca** communities of Taquile, Amantaní, and Llachón, and on the Anapia archipelago, have blazed the trail: to visit the Taquile, contact **All Ways Travel** (tel: 051-35-3979; www.titicacaperu.com) or **Kolla Tours** (tel: 051-36-9863); try **Turperu** (tel: 051-35-2001; www.turperu.com.pe) or **Solmartour** (tel: 051-35-2586; www.solmarpuno.com) for the Amantaní. For Llachón, contact the **Federación de Turismo Rural de Llachón** (tel: 051-98-21392/96-36277/97-52227).

South of **Cusco**, stay near the Raqchi Inca ruins (contact the **Unidad de Coordinación del Proyecto**; tel: 084-35-1970; www.corredorpuno-cusco.org) or closer by the Inca capital at Chincheros, Chahuaytire, and Willoc-Patacancha, as well as near Pisac and Ollantaytambo. Try the **Asociación Hijos del Sol** (tel: 051-364-329).

A Peruvian lady making traditional crafts

East of Huaraz and the Cordillera Blanca are the Konchukos Tambo (contact via **Rainforest Expeditions**; tel: 01-421-8347; www.perunature.com), who run a trekking hotel, and Inka Naani (tel: 43-426-538; www.yachaquiwayi.org), along a well-preserved stretch of the Inca Road. Around the north Andean city of Cajamarca are the communities of Chaparrí, in dry forest near the coast, La Encañada, and Sulluscocha near Kuélap. Contact **Vivencial Tours** in Lima (tel: 01-224-3367; www.vivencialtours.com).

Responsible adventures

It's hard to know until after a trip how well a company treats its staff and the environment, but both will suffer if visitors haggle excessively. Make sure your company is packing up garbage and not dumping it en route, nor contaminating water supplies. Avoid plastic water bottles – boil or purify water instead. See that your outfitter treats its crew properly, giving them proper food, shelter, and medical care, and not overloading porters. When trekking independently with hired crew, remember those concerns are your responsibility.

Huaraz has two green information centers: **The Mountain Institute/Instituto de Montaña** (tel: 043-423-446) and the **Respons Sustainable Tourism Center** (tel: 043-427-949; www.respons.org). In Cusco contact the **Casa Bartolomé de las Casas** (tel: 084-233-466; www.cbc.org.pe).

Amazon adventures

Steamy and remote, Peru's share of the vast Amazon jungle is second only to Brazil's. This is the habitat of overwhelming numbers of animal and plant species, as well as indigenous tribes still clinging to their nomadic ways of life. While travel to fine lodges is easy nowadays, it doesn't get more exotic than this.

Peru's sparsely populated Amazon Basin covers some 60 percent of the country's territory. This includes the steep, forested Andes' eastern slopes, with spirited rapids and numerous endemic species – a paradise for both rafting enthusiasts and birdwatchers. Below 800m (2,625ft), the land flattens out into torrid forest crisscrossed by mighty rivers, the greatest of which is the Amazon. The extraordinary variety of plants and animals living here makes Peru one of the few mega-diverse countries on the globe.

The rubber boom of the late 19th century marked the first major outside encroachment on the Amazon. It brought miserable conditions for native tribes, but collapsed quickly once the British smuggled rubber plants to their Malaysian colony. The area and its original inhabitants are again under pressure, however, amid an influx of settlers seeking other resources, such as timber, oil, natural gas, and gold. Outside protected areas, almost the entire territory has been divided up for oil development. Even though major companies can produce oil much more cleanly than in the past, there are compelling reasons for worry.

Responsible tourism offers a real development alternative. With the help of outside visitors from Peru and beyond, native communities are being empowered to protect their homelands and wildlife, improving their lives through hard-earned money rather than via handouts from oil and mining companies. Reputable, high-quality operations are mushrooming.

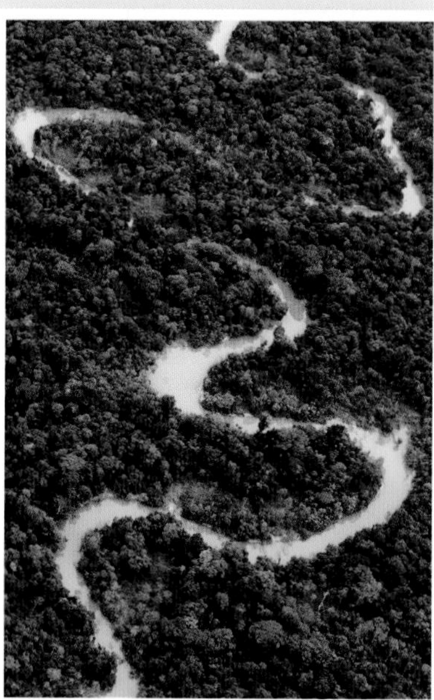

The Amazon is surrounded by rainforest

Peoples of the Amazon

Peru's Amazon Basin is home to dozens of indigenous groups, 15 of which are believed still to live in complete isolation from the outside world. Nomadic migrations throughout the Amazon and immigration from the Andes have led to a great mix of languages and other cultural practices. All groups, however, share a way of life based on hunting, fishing, and gathering, as well as the cultivation of minor plots – domestication of important plants such as cocoa and yucca began here. Today, many have exchanged their traditional clothing for Western dress, at least to go into town to buy supplies like batteries and diesel for motors.

Among the best-known peoples are the Amazon **Quechua**, who descended from the Andean highlands to live along the Huallaga, Napo, and Pastaza; the **Shuar**, infamous 'headhunter' warriors in the northern Amazon; and the **Asháninka** and the matriarchal **Shipibo**, both of whom have kept their cultures near-intact in the central Amazon and can be visited around Pucallpa, particularly near Lake Yarinacocha.

Many lodges work together with local communities and will arrange visits to jungle hamlets. Note that any restrictions on photography should be followed, and you will very likely be offered Amazon *chicha*: a milky-white, bitter drink made from fermented yucca pre-chewed by women. It's inexcusably rude not to accept at least a sip.

For an Amazon trip that mixes adventure with cultural immersion, **Pascana Amazon Services** in Iquitos (tel: 065-233-466; www.pascana.com) offers the experience of a lifetime: in the heart of the Pacaya-Samiria Reserve lies the village of San Martín de

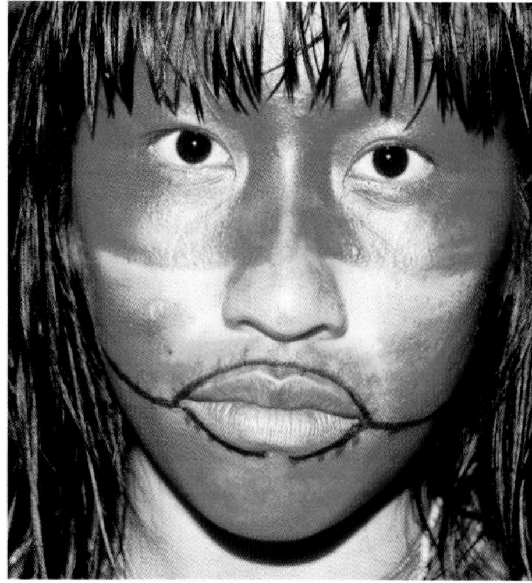

Indigenous Amazon woman

Tipishca, where the Cocama-Cocamilla people have built a house to accommodate small groups of visiting tourists. In the southeast, **Casa Matsiguenka** in Cusco (tel: 084-225-595) is linked to local communities inside the Manu National Park.

Jungle lodges

Other than providing an entry point by plane, bus, or boat, the towns of the Amazon generally cater much more to the demands of mining, oil, or logging interests than to travelers (although Iquitos, *see pp.231–4*, is an interesting melting pot of the contemporary Amazon, with modern hotels and restaurants). The beauty of the rainforest is best experienced at a distance from urban bustle.

As early as the 1960s, tour companies began to establish jungle lodges, most of them in the south in the **Manu National Park** and **Tambopata**

Top five rare species to spot

- **Jaguar** The largest cat in the Americas and an unforgettable sight if you are lucky enough to glimpse it in the jungle
- **Pink river dolphin** The largest river dolphin is less gregarious than its oceangoing relatives and prefers smaller rivers and lakes
- **Giant otter** One of the most endangered species in South America, this vocal, large semi-aquatic carnivore can still be seen in the Manu National Park
- **Harpy eagle** This large, slate-grey and white, crested eagle hunts monkeys in the forest canopies
- **Lowland tapir** Peru's biggest animal, an avid swimmer, can be seen at salt licks near several Amazon lodges

National Reserve and around Iquitos. The best have multilingual and native guides, and support the environment and their local communities. Unless you have ample time, however, you will likely have to choose between Iquitos on the mighty Amazon itself or a more easily accessible trip to the Madre de Dios jungle from Cusco.

Activities at lodges include day and nighttime hikes, walks in forest canopies, and short canoe trips to observe and learn about rainforest animals and plants, combined with evening lectures by guides or naturalists. Sports include swimming in lagoons and rivers as well as fishing, and tours also provide opportunities to visit local communities and buy crafts.

Around Iquitos, **Amazonia Expeditions** (Av. La Marina 100, Iquitos; tel: 065-242-792/233-080; www.perujungle.com) runs Tahuayo Lodge, comprised of 15 suitably rustic but comfortable cabins right on the River Tahuayo. Guides at this beautiful, remote lodge are top rate. **Explorama Lodges** (Av. La Marina 340, Iquitos; tel: 065-252-530) have been around for almost half a century. They now run four lodges, as well as the amazing Canopy Walkway that allows guests to walk above the tops of the rainforest trees. **Yarapa River Lodge** (Av. La Marina 124, Iquitos; tel: 065-993-172; www.yarapa.com) is a stunning, award-winning lodge on the river of the same name, with itineraries starting from three nights.

The vast Manu National Park and Tambopata National Reserve are relatively conveniently located a short

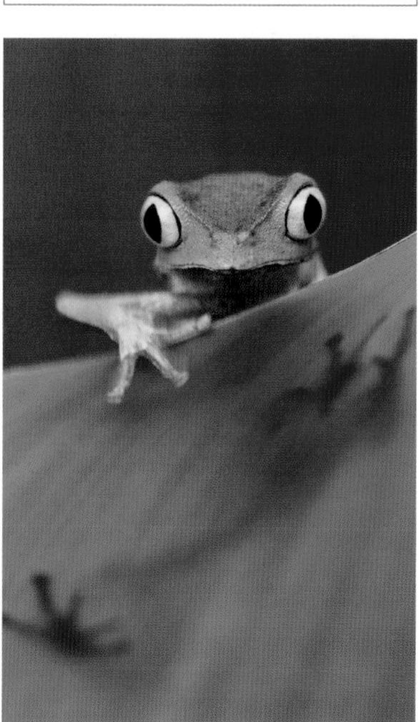

White-lined leaf frog in Manu National Park

Jungle lodges offer a comfortable base from which to explore the Amazon

plane ride from Cusco. **Manu Expeditions** (tel: 084-225-990; www.manuexpeditions.com) offers camping trips into the reserve, led by knowledgeable guides. **Manu Nature Tours** (tel: 084-252-721; www.manuperu.com) runs Manu Lodge, the only lodge inside the Manu National Park; Manu Cloud Forest Lodge is also available. They're at the upper end of prices for lodges, but suitably comfortable with excellent birdwatching opportunities.

Explorers' Inn (tel: 01-447-8888; www.peruviansafaris.com), about 60km (38 miles) from Puerto Maldonado on the Tambopata River, provides a good chance of observing wildlife, as does the **Libertador Tambopata Lodge** (tel: 082-571-726/084-245-695; www.tambopatalodge.com) four hours upriver from Puerto Maldonado.

Reserva Amazónica (tel: 01-610-0400; www.inkaterra.com) is a luxury lodge on the Río Madre de Dios, 15km (9 miles) from Puerto Maldonado. It includes trekking in the lodge's private reserve. The **Tambopata Research Center** (tel: 01-421-8347; www.perunature.com) is about six hours upriver from Puerto Maldonado on the Tambopata River. It has simple accommodations in low-impact native architecture, 15 minutes' walk from one of the world's largest macaw clay licks.

Amazon wildlife

As one of the world's most diverse natural habitats, the Amazon Basin is home to a staggering amount of birdlife. Almost 20 percent of all bird species live in Peru, and the eastern slopes of the Andes and the Amazon lowlands offer once-in-a-lifetime birding. Birdwatchers can enjoy brightly colored toucans and macaws, blue-faced hoatzins, and more than 130 species of hummingbirds, along with – if you're lucky – the red-black cock-of-the-rock and giant harpy eagle. Mammals include jaguars and ocelots – cats whose presence you most likely will see in footprints in the mud – tapirs, capybaras (the world's biggest rodents), multiple monkey species, giant otters and pink river dolphins.

Nighttime walks and canoe trips are great for viewing reptiles like the aquatic caimans and amphibians including miniscule arrow-poison frogs. The Amazon lodges mentioned above offer species lists and walks that will allow you to look for the animals, with expert guides to help you spot them in the heavy vegetation.

Amazon by riverboat

Iquitos has the most options for Amazon boat trips, with information at the local iPerú tourism office (Loreto 201; tel: 065-236-144). Tours of the waterborne district of Belén are cheap, while there are snazzy cruises from around $1,000 a night, including **Aqua Expeditions** (tel: 065-601-053; www.aquaexpeditions.com) and **Delfín Amazon Cruises** (tel: 065-262-721; www.delfinamazoncruises.com), on five-star floating luxury lodges.

Longer-distance travel is entirely different. Forget any lingering notion of punctuality. Most straightforward is the trip downstream toward the border with Brazil and Colombia near Santa Rosa, from where there are connections to Manaos. Four companies have fast boats that make the trip in 9–12 hours, departing at 6am, and have food and drink on board: **Brastour** (tel: 065-223-232), **Golfinho** (tel: 065-225-118), **Challenger** (tel: 065-225-556), and **Transtur** (tel: 065-221-356).

Further upstream, adventurous souls can travel from Pucallpa on the Ucayali River, reachable by road or air from Lima. Riverboats are the way most locals travel in the Amazon, giving you a real cultural immersion, but also will require a lot of patience and preparation. Mosquito nets, hammocks, and other supplies like water for the three-

Taking to the water in Manu National Park

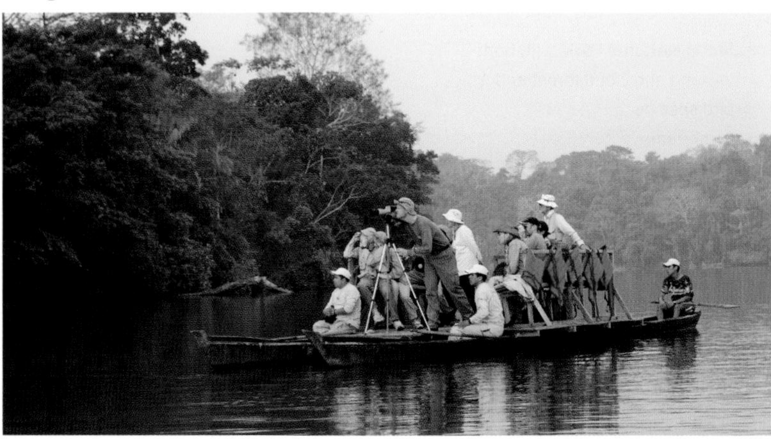

to-five day trip can be bought cheaply in town. Be prepared for delays, tight quarters on board, and hygiene that will likely not be for the squeamish.

Rafting

Hurtling down rapids on a raft or kayak is a world away from leisurely riverboats. Peru has some of the world's finest whitewater experiences in the Andes and the lush forests descending their eastern fringe. For sheer beauty, none tops the narrow, 3km (2-mile) **Pongo de Manique** (Manique Canyon) northwest of Machu Picchu that splits the Vilcabamba Range. It's still quite remote, however, and few tour operators run the multi-day trip. Contact Franco-Scottish-Peruvian **Eko Trek Peru** in Cusco (tel: 084-247-286; www.ecotrekperu.com). **River Explorers**, also in Cusco (tel: 084-779-619; www.riverexplorers.com), can take you rafting downstream from near Puno to Puerto Maldonado on a nine-day trip on the Tambopata River, with plenty of rapids but also the chance to see elusive wildlife. Cusco tour operators also run trips on the Urubamba and Apurímac rivers in the Andes.

Descending from Chachapoyas in the northern Andes, the city of Tarapoto is growing as a rafting hub. Try **Los Chancas Expeditions** (tel: 094-52-2616; http://chancas.tripod.com).

The Amazon jungle is ideal for fishing fans

Top five birdwatching areas

- **Manu National Park**, with both lowland and cloud forest and 1,000 bird species
- **Tambopata Nature Reserve**, featuring the Colpa Colorada parrot lick
- The **Manu Road** from Cusco to the Amazon: the world's greatest birding road
- **ExplorNapo Lodge** near Iquitos has one of the longest canopy walkways anywhere
- The **Oxapampa** and **Tingo María to Pucallpa** routes in the central Amazon

Fishing

Few culinary delights can rival the satisfaction of eating your own freshly caught fish in the jungle. Catfish and piranhas are delicious, the latter with a slightly smoky taste. Sport fishermen will enjoy tussles with some of the most exotic fish they are likely to encounter anywhere. The 6kg (12lb) peacock bass, called *tucunaré* locally, has a legendary fighting spirit. Other impressive fish are the pacu, weighing up to 25kg (50lbs), barracuda-faced giant wolf fish or payara, and the arahuana. **Dawn on the Amazon Tours and Cruises** in Iquitos (tel: 065-223-730: www.dawnontheamazon.com) offers top-notch fishing trips.

Riding the waves

Surfing may have been officially born in Hawaii, but Peruvians have been riding the waves of the Pacific for thousands of years. An immense 3,000km (1,900 miles) of oceanfront territory beckons visitors to explore one of the world's great surfing destinations, with ample room for novices and experts alike.

Thanks to the cold-water Humboldt Current, which carries frigid water from the Antarctic north almost as far as the Equator and keeps moisture from condensing, Peru's Pacific coast is a desert. With poor prospects for agriculture, humans had to turn to the sea for most of their food. Fish are abundant in the Humboldt Current, still one of the richest marine ecosystems on the planet. Instead of wood, people used bundles of tightly wound *totora* reeds to form their seagoing vessels from as early as 5000BC. Fishermen began to make lithe *totora* craft to pursue their catches at that time and still do today *(see picture p.40)*.

Board usage developed much more recently. Lima newspaper *El Comercio* reported that in 1909, some men used drawing boards to ride the waves. It took another generation for the modern surfboard to arrive, though. Peruvian globetrotter Carlos Dogny is credited with bringing the first surfboard to the beaches of Lima in 1942 from Hawaii. The Hawaiian influence was such that two beaches in Miraflores, Lima, drew their names, Makaha and Waikiki, from the US archipelago.

Hawaiian surfboards caught on fast. It took just 20 years for Peru to become a major force in the sport.

Máncora is a surfer's paradise – and a great spot for novices

In 1965 Felipe Pomar became the first-ever surfing world champion, winning the tournament in home waters at Punta Rocas south of Lima. Current top Peruvian surfers include Sofia Mulánovich from Lima, who in 2004 became the first South American woman to win a world surfing championship.

Of course, surfing isn't the only sport to be enjoyed on Peruvian beaches.

Besides boogie-boarding, kite surfing and the noisier variants of banana boats and jet skis, sea kayaking offers a fantastic, non-contaminating way to see sea-life. And thanks to the ample coastal desert, snowboard lovers can trek up some of the world's tallest dunes to ride down on sandboards.

Surfing swells and sand

Peruvian beaches have numerous surf schools for beginners and world-class waves for experts who might (almost) be forgiven for saying 'Machu-what?'

Check if surf instructors are registered with the National Surfing Federation (FENTA). Although Peru is a tropical country, the coolness of the water means wetsuits are recommended everywhere except the warmer north. Decent-quality Peruvian suits are available relatively cheaply. Peruvians excel at making surfboards, with reputable brands including Klimax, Swells, OX, and Wayo Whilar. Surfing is possible throughout the year, while swells are most common during the winter months of June to September.

Surfing advice

- Be respectful of locals – remember their ancestors have been riding the waves here for thousands of years – and never surf alone
- Remember to take enough water, sunscreen, and (in the center and south) a windbreaker for the afternoon wind
- Near Paracas and at some beaches in the north, ask locals about the presence of stingrays, which can inflict very painful injuries. Plastic wetshoes can offer protection
- Take a plastic bag along to take garbage with you. Animals can choke on litter

Brightly colored boards in Lima, which is close to many surfing hotspots

Máncora

Up north near the Ecuadorean border, over 1,160km (720 miles) from Lima, Máncora has become synonymous with surf and beach culture in Peru. Warm water and a laidback atmosphere make this the top spot for grommits (beginners) to learn to surf. Its eponymous point is south of the beach town. Máncora's waves are long, left-running, and swells form December through March. During the morning quiet, bottlenose dolphins often play in shallow waters along the long beach. The town has numerous schools and tour operators for surfing and kite surfing, including **Laguna**

Surf Club (tel: 073-671-727), **Máncora Kite Surf** (cell: 098-116-7745; www.mancorakitesurf.com), and **Octopus Surf Tours** (cell: 099-400-5518; www.octopussurftours.com), which also offers trips for advanced surfers.

For more good surfing, head to Los Órganos, with a left, tubular, 2m (7ft) wave, and El Ñuro further south – a good spot to escape the crowds, though there are some rocks and the access is more difficult. Máncora surf schools can take you here, as well as all the other spots along the northern coast.

Cabo Blanco

This fishing village south of Máncora is Peru's ultimate surfers' challenge, with South America's best left barrel, and excellent waves year-round. The aptly named Panic Point on its south side serves notice that this place is strictly for the pros. Waves crash down on sharp rocks and reefs after cresting at a height of up to 4m (13ft). Try **Máncora Kite Surf** and **Octopus Surf Tours** *(see above)*; tours here only operate in high season (November–March).

The waves aren't Cabo Blanco's sole claim to fame. The ocean here is a top spot for deep-sea fishing. Fishermen have caught world-record marlins in the area, and tuna is another favored catch. Locals like to claim the giant marlins here inspired Ernest Hemingway to write *The Old Man and the Sea*, though of course he wrote the novella in Cuba. While sharks eat the old fisherman's catch in the story, visitors can relax – shark attacks are unheard of in Peru.

Peru's beaches are as popular with sunbathers as they are with surfers

Chicama

Also known as Puerto Malabrigo, this village north of Trujillo boasts amazingly long waves. In fact, they may be the longest anywhere, allowing those who catch them rides of more than a kilometer, if their legs hold out that long. Less experienced surfers – or those not quite strong enough to paddle all the way out – can take the tow-dinghy to the point from the upscale **Chicama Surf Hotel** (tel: 44-576-206; www.chicamasurf.com). Local surfing outfits include **Malabrigo Left** (tel: 044-948-001-533; www.malabrigoleft.blogspot.com) and **Machapu Adventures** (tel: 086-277-7957; www.machapuadventures.com).

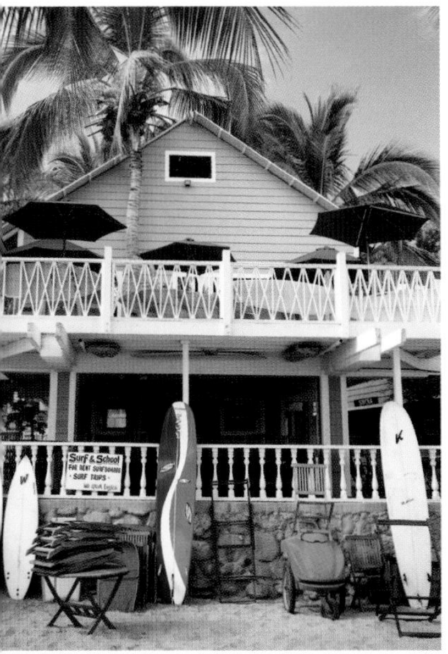

Surf clubs abound in Máncora

Peru's top five beaches

- **Punta Sal** A broad beach of white sands and deep azure water, fringed by green carob trees, with surfing waves on its north side and natural pools at low tide on its south side
- **Máncora** A long, white, palm-fringed beach and warm waters throughout the year make this Peru's surfing mecca
- **Colán** Spectacular sunsets bathe the wooden porches of elegant beachfront residences on this coconut-fringed beach of calm, warm waters near Paita
- **Paracas** Spectacular wildlife, landscape, and water sports make this the best beach in southern Peru
- **Puerto Inca** Ruins and remains of the Inca Road adorn this off-the-beaten-track beach, which has calm waters and charming bungalows

Lima's coast

Peru's vast capital has a surprising amount of excellent surfing beaches within easy distance, some even in central locations. The city's shore is known as the Costa Verde, or Green Coast, for the formerly vegetated cliff tops. Its beaches – La Pampilla, Makaha, Waikiki, and Redondo – are great for beginners, while La Herradura south of Barranco is for advanced surfers. Lima-based **Olas Perú** (tel: 01-243-4830; www.olasperu.com) offers trips and courses here, as well as along the rest of the Peruvian coast. Check for discounts at www.youxtreme.com.

South of Lima are the popular Señoritas, Punta Rocas, Puerto Viejo, and Pico Alto beaches – the latter's 10m (33ft) waves, the tallest in the country, are only for advanced surfers, however. Cerro Azul, 130km (81 miles) from the capital, is a beach town in its own right, with hotels and restaurants for a stay. **Rod'g Surf House** in San Bartolo (tel: 01-430-7300; www.rodgsurf.com) offers lessons and trips along the southern coast.

San Gallán

For Peru, frigid-water San Gallán is unique in two respects: this island inside the Paracas National Reserve, 5km (3 miles) from the mainland, has the major right-running wave in the country; and the water teems with hundreds of sea lions. Humboldt penguins are also among the local fauna. The spot is suitable only for experienced surfers; hire boat transport from the fishermen at El Chaco beach near the town of Paracas.

An ancient ride

Like a modern jet-setter on a sleek cigar boat, Tacaynamo, the mythical founder of the Chimú realm, arrived on Peru's north central coast astride an iconic *caballito de mar* around the year 900. The fishermen from Huanchaco to Pimentel still apply the age-old tradition that goes into these unique vessels. In just 30 minutes, two experienced fishermen can lash sun-dried bundles of *totora* reeds into the graceful, highly maneuverable craft that can carry a man, his nets, and the day's catch in a cavity near the stern. From tapered prow to squared-off stern, the boats measure 3–4m (10–13ft) in length and weigh close to 40kg (88lbs). Fishermen row out seated or kneeling on their 'sea horses' using paddles made of guadua bamboo.

Visitors to Huanchaco can approach fishermen on the beaches and join them for a ride in the surf for just a few soles. Alternatively, contact the **Muchika Surf School** (tel: 044-774-388; www.escueladetablamuchik.com/english.html).

Sea kayaking

Peru's Andean rapids are the country's best-known waters for kayaking. Sea or ocean kayaking has attracted much less attention, but it's one of the best ways to view the wildlife along the coast. **Nature Expeditions** in Miraflores, Lima (cell: 01-994-104-206; http://nature-expeditions-peru.com), which also has whale-watching

Caballitos de mar on the beach at Pimentel

Surf and sandboard events

- Surfing tournaments run January through October, with the national championship circuit February through July; many of them are held in and around Lima
- Check the websites of the **National Surfing Federation** (FENTA; www.surfingperu.com.pe) and **Olas Peru** (www.olasperu.com/calendario_nacional.htm) for up-to-date surfing events listings
- **Sand Board Peru** publishes a calendar of sandboarding events (www.sandboardperu.com/agenda.html)

Don't miss the opportunity to try sandboarding while in Peru

and other wildlife observation tours, offers trips ranging from half a day of paddling in Lima or Pucusana to five-day excursions south to Paracas. Independent travelers can rent sea kayaks in Paracas: contact **Nautiperú** (cell: 01-994-567-802).

In the Andes, kayaking tours offer an athletic way to experience the islands of Lake Titicaca, including Taquile, Amantaní, and the Islands of the Sun and Moon on the Bolivian side *(see p.166)*.

Sandboarding

South of Ica, top surfing beaches are few, but towering sand dunes offer adrenaline rushes of a different kind. From their summits, strap sandboards to your feet and coast down the dunes as if on snow.

Sandboarding offers exhilarating exercise. Independent trips are strenuous; it's tough climbing through the heat as, of course, there are no lifts. It's much easier to get the hang of it than on snowboards, however, and falls are softer, though you will get sand absolutely everywhere.

Many tours include comfortable buggy rides to the tops of the dunes. The tallest of them all, Cerro Blanco – the 'white peak' – soars to 2,068m (6,785ft), offering spectacular views of the Nazca desert from the top. Options beyond Cerro Blanco include the dunes near the Huacachina lagoon, a picture-perfect oasis, the remote Usaca dunes, and dunes near Arequipa.

Tours are available in Nazca from **Mystery Peru** (Simón Bolívar 221; tel: 056-522-379; www.mysteryperu.com), in Ica from **Huacachina Tours** (Av. La Angostura 355 – L47; tel: 056-256-582/257-095; www.huacachinatours.com), and from Arequipa-based **Peru Adventure Tours** (Jerusalén 210; tel: 054-221-658; www.peruadventurestours.com/en/sandboarding_tours.html).

Festivals and music

If you can't find a festival in Peru, you're not trying – there are more than 3,000 held every year, all over the country, from Lima to the smallest villages, from coast to Amazon. Peruvians take few things more seriously than official celebration, with parades, pomp, dance, and a cacophony of musical styles from traditional to modern.

Peru's earliest festivities emerged from the careful star- and sungazing of the ancients, who determined planting times by observing the changes in season visible even this close to the Equator. Conquest led to most of these festivals becoming blends of Catholic, Inca, and even earlier agricultural traditions. Many of the main events are linked to a town's or even a neighborhood's patron saint. In any Andean community at any time of the year, you may stumble on a village fiesta.

Others events emerged to commemorate survival and to ask for protection from natural disasters, particularly earthquakes. To celebrate, the faithful carry miraculous statues through the streets, sometimes on decorated litters weighing tons. More recent sources of inspiration for celebration are the events of Peru's independence battles and the two-day national holiday in July, which originated in the 19th century, and, most recently, festivals invented to honor Peruvian dance, food, and other traditions.

Celebrated with high spirits and a fitting sense of drama, these local events are colorful occasions, always accompanied by music, dance, vivid dress, and large quantities of food and – in the Andes – *chicha*, a beer-like drink made from fermented corn. Peru's

The Inti Raymi (Festival of the Sun) reenactments at Sacsayhuamán, Cusco

multicultural blend means that while many celebrations are similar to those in industrialized countries, including the main religious dates of Christmas and Easter, they have their own flavor here. Immigrant communities – above all, the descendants of Africans forcibly brought here – add their own spice along the coast and in Amazon towns.

The foot-stomping dances – the most

popular being the *huayno* and the *huaylas* in the Andes and the *marinera* on the coast – demonstrate the lively side of Peruvian life. More than 200 different dances have been recorded. Along with the pageantry of costumes donned in many celebrations, the music is their most distinguishing feature. Peruvian musicians still cherish numerous age-old genres, some of which indigenous chronicler Felipe Huamán Poma de Ayala described as early as the late 16th century. The music merges ancient drums and flutes with the harp, guitar, and violin that arrived from Spain.

The fusing of musical styles continues today. Artists are experimenting with music from other countries in the Andes, salsa from the Caribbean and rock from the US and UK, to create styles of their own.

Mixing traditions

Interest in pre-Hispanic culture, the political awakening of indigenous groups, and tourism have all helped reinvigorate the most important celebration that predates the Spanish arrival: **Inti Raymi**, the Festival of the Sun. Originally held at the start of the Southern Hemisphere's winter solstice, June 21, it marked the middle of the year with nine days of celebration. Catholic leaders realized it could not be stamped out and nudged it to June 24, the day of John the Baptist, on which it is still held today, with reenactments of the ceremony in many ruins. In the biggest pageant, in Cusco, the Inca Sapa (ruler of the kingdom) is carried on a throne from Qoricancha to the fortress of Sacsayhuamán, followed by priests, noblemen, and soldiers.

Celebrating La Virgen de la Candelaria

Most other indigenous festivities merge pre-Hispanic and Catholic traditions. Pilgrimages are common. One of the biggest is the May pilgrimage to **Qoyllur Riti**, a sacred glacier in the Cordillera Vilcanota not far from Cusco. Thousands of people, some of whom are dressed as bears, leave miniature models of things they desire in the hope that the Lord of the Snow Star will help them realize their dreams.

The first week of November is the **Jubilee Week**, the peak of Puno's many festivals. It celebrates the city's founding by the Spanish, followed by a reenactment of the emergence of the legendary founders of the Inca Empire, Manco Capac and Mama Ocllo, from the waters of Lake Titicaca.

Pre-Lenten **Carnival**, adopted from Spain, is widely celebrated, very noisily and with lots of water-hurling. **La Virgen de la Candelaria** (Candlemas) in February is another event mingling

Catholic and pre-Columbian rites, particularly in Puno, where the *diablada*, a devil dance involving grotesque masks, is the main event. Coastal festivals can also be lively, especially in Chincha, where the black population stages the **Fiesta Negra** in February with Afro-Peruvian music and dance. It's also linked to Candlemas.

Major festivals commemorating Peru's Independence, such as the **Fiestas Patrias** in late July, are celebrated nationwide, with regional variations. In Apurímac and Ayacucho, the **Yawar Fiesta** (Blood Festival) sees a condor tied to the back of a bull to symbolize indigenous resistance, a spectacle that fortunately is becoming less bloody.

Religious processions

On the Monday of Holy Week in Cusco, **Our Lord of the Earthquakes** (Nuestro Señor de los Temblores) celebrates the statue of Christ on the cross hanging in the cathedral, which is credited with saving the city from destruction during a major earthquake in 1650. The statue is carried through the streets on an ornate silver litter. Red flower petals, symbolizing the blood of Christ, are scattered in its path, and thousands of *cusqueños* join the procession, along with civic leaders, priests, nuns, and military personnel.

Lima's October celebration of **El Señor de los Milagros** (Lord of Miracles) sees thousands of people following processions headed by a black figure of Christ on the cross, one of the largest in South America. It is topped, however, by the gigantic, 10-day **Semana Santa** (Holy Week) celebrations in Ayacucho, for which hotels are booked out months in advance. The central Andean city hosts nightly processions by candlelight, and many other events including horse races. It culminates at dawn Easter Sunday when, amid fireworks, 200 bearers carry a figure of Christ on a gigantic, silvery-white litter through the Plaza de Armas, ending inside the cathedral.

Andean and Creole music

A love of melancholy seems to characterize the haunting melodies of Andean music: the deep tonality of the *quena* (flute) and *zampoña* (panpipes), and a single drum, are fused with instruments that arrived with or were adapted from the Spanish: 36-string harps; *charangos*, similar to mandolins; and guitars.

Corpus Christi procession, Cusco

Local girls joining in the fun on Arequipa Day

Calendar of festivals and holidays

January
January 18: Anniversary of the founding of Lima
End January: Festival de la Marinera, Trujillo

February
February 1–15: Cruz de Chalpon, Chiclayo
Early February: Virgen de la Candelaria, Puno
Mid-February: Carnival, especially in Puno, Cajamarca, Ayacucho, and Huaraz

March/April
Early March: Fiesta de la Vendimia, Ica
March/April: Semana Santa (Easter/Holy Week)

May
May 2: Cruz Velacuy, Cusco
May 2–4: Las Alasitas, Puno

June
Mid-June: Corpus Christi, Cusco
June 24: Inti Raymi (Festival of the Sun), Cusco
June 29: San Pedro y San Pablo (St Peter's and St Paul's Day; national holiday)

July
July 15–17: La Virgen del Carmen, Paucartambo
July 28–9: Peru's Independence celebrations (national holiday)

August
August 15: Arequipa Day
August 30: Santa Rosa de Lima (national holiday)

October
October 8: Commemoration of the Battle of Angamos (national holiday)
October 7–20: El Señor de Luren, Ica
October 18, 19, and 28: El Señor de los Milagros, Lima
October 19: Unu Urco Festival, Urcos and Calca (near Cusco)

November
November 1–7: Puno Jubilee Week

December
December 24: Festival of Santu Rantikuy, Cusco

The famous song *El Cóndor Pasa*, written in 1913 and popularized by Paul Simon and Art Garfunkel, and played ad nauseam in tourism hubs, is just a sliver of the music that conjures up the image of the steel-blue skies, Andean peaks, and men and women in typical, brightly colored wool clothing. Rhythms include the melancholy *yaraví* that goes back at least to the Inca and is popular in the southeast Andes. More upbeat is the *huayno*, which emerged in colonial times and may also be accompanied with saxophones, accordions, or trumpets, and is common in Ancash but also widely played elsewhere.

Música criolla (creole music) was born along the coast, merging Spanish and Andean influences with African music that was brought over by slavery. In the early 1900s, Lima experienced a burst of creativity soon threatened by the imported tango, but later revitalized as middle and upper classes sought to distance themselves from the Andean migrants arriving by the thousands in the capital. Its genres include the *vals peruano* (Peruvian Waltz), the *tondero*, popular in the northwest, and Afro-Peruvian dances like the *alcatraz* and *festejo*, well known via the dance group Perú Negro. The *marinera*, Peru's national dance, is celebrated in Trujillo in a festival every January.

Besides the festivals, the best places to experience these genres are the *peñas*, which range from small taverns to big beer-halls with large stages for shows. Lima's Miraflores and Barranco districts have many of them. Among the most famous are **Del Carajo** (San Ambrosio 328, Barranco; tel: 01-241-7977; www.delcarajo.com.pe) and **Sachún** (Av. del Ejército 657, Miraflores; tel: 01-441 0123; www.sachunperu.com). There are many *peñas* in central areas of Cusco,

Novalima are one of Peru's biggest bands

Chicha

Born in the 1960s, out of Colombian *cumbia* via Peruvian Amazonia, laced with infusions of melancholy Andean scales and lyrics, and named after a popular home-brewed beer, *chicha* is Peru's most popular modern musical style. It is twangy, wailing, intensely electronic, with a loping, danceable rhythm, and you will probably hear it on the radio during your first taxi ride in Peru. Chicha is strongly associated with the new urban migrant population, known as *cholos*. In its post-1990s incarnation, *tecnocumbia*, it retains its ties to both Andean and Amazonian Peru, and commands a mass following.

Traditional musicians on Lake Titicaca

Arequipa, Huaraz, and Ayacucho, well watered with beer and pisco sours.

Rock and jazz in Lima

The vibrant live rock scene in Lima is underground, classless, and fairly invisible in mainstream media. Off-label bands like Los Mojarras, Cementerio Club, Libido, the moody rebel Daniel F., and the Quechua-language hard rock and blues group Uchpa, are heard mainly in performance. **Galerías Brasil** (Av. Brasil 1275, Jesús María), a rather dingy but lively warren of music and CD stores between central Lima and San Ignacio, is the hub of the underground scene. More mainstream rock and pop is available at **Phantom** in the Larcomar shopping center in Miraflores, and www.perupoprock.com has an excellent overview of recent local releases and upcoming events. Live rock music venues center on Barranco and include the huge **La Noche** (Bolognesi 307; tel: 01-247-2186; www.lanoche.com.pe), **El Dragón** (Nicolás de Piérola 168; tel: 01-477-5420; www.eldragon.com.pe), and **Mochileros Bar** (135 Pedro de Osma; tel: 01-247-1225).

Chill-out music, with its strong influence from Brazil's bossa nova, was brought to Lima by locally born Jaime Cuadra, who fused it with *música criolla*, Andean music, and jazz. Peruvian band Novalima, who in 2006 won the Independent Music Award for best album in the world fusion category, emphasize their Afro-Peruvian musical heritage. Albums by both have begun to be distributed globally.

The top local jazz venues are **Jazz Zone** (La Paz 656, Miraflores; tel: 01-242-7090; www.jazzzoneperu.com), with jam sessions Monday through Wednesday, and the **Cocodrilo Verde** (Francisco de Paula Camino 226, Miraflores; tel: 01-242-7583; www.cocodriloverde.com).

Peruvian cuisine

Reflecting the country's amazingly diverse land, climate, and people, Peru's cuisine alone is enticing enough to attract people to visit. It offers an incredible variety of sweet, spicy, marinated, and cooked dishes, melding ancient indigenous traditions with those of immigrant communities.

Peruvians have celebrated their cuisine for centuries. The food appears not only on dining tables but is also immortalized in art form: in pre-Hispanic pottery, which sometimes takes surprisingly realistic forms of fruits and vegetables; in the centuries-old weavings found in many of the burial grounds that have been excavated; and in wall paintings.

Since the 1980s, chefs have helped rediscover ingredients and recipes from Peru's many microclimates and ethnic groups. Today, the cuisine is at the vanguard of Latin American gastronomy, with a culinary boom so great that an average of 20 new restaurants open in Peru every day. Fabled French culinary arts school Cordon Bleu has its only center in Latin America in Lima.

Except for cocoa, most typical foods from the Amazon have stayed off foreign plates, partly because they are hard to produce outside tropical areas. As a result, a trip to Peru offers the chance to try an array of mouth-watering dishes you have never sampled before.

The bountiful Humboldt Current has supplied coastal communities with seafood since time immemorial. Most typical in Peru are the cold, spicy marinated fish salads known as *ceviches* served only until mid-afternoon. New World meat dishes include *cuy* (guinea pig) and the lean alpaca.

The Andes and Amazon, meanwhile, provide an extraordinary variety of plants with which ancient Peruvians experimented on terraced

A traditional seafood dish is served with a gourmet twist in Máncora

mountain slopes and jungle plots. The crops they developed – including cocoa, tomatoes, and potatoes – helped shape global cuisine. There are more than 3,000, mostly uniquely Peruvian, varieties of potatoes, known locally as *papas*. Only a few dozen varieties, however, are regularly consumed, including the yellow *limeña*, the small purple potato, and the dried *chuño*, which is frozen in the harsh climate around Puno and Lake Titicaca. These potatoes can be stored for up to four years.

Corn or maize, an arrival from Central America centuries before the Spanish arrived, is grown in many varieties in Peru. Chili peppers, known locally as *ají*, or *morrón* for the non-burning types – have also been cultivated for many centuries and are so much in demand that Peruvian chefs are worried that they could become scarce.

Other plants, including the purple-flowered *kiwicha* and the golden quinoa – both kinds of amaranth – were banned on supposedly religious grounds, and disappeared from the Peruvian diet for several centuries. They are now being rediscovered as healthier variants to the potato, and used once more in breads, cookies, soups, and salads, as well as coming under intense scientific scrutiny.

In the Amazon, bananas replace potatoes as the staple, with many different kinds for frying, boiling, or eating fresh. The other staple is yucca (also called manioc or cassava), which accompanies most meals, and is also fermented to make a strong alcoholic drink called *masato*.

Making traditional ham sandwiches in Lima

Novoandina cuisine

The experimental and evolving trend of *novoandina* cuisine has fueled Peru's current gastronomy boom. Highland ingredients once disdained as 'Indian food' have been discovered by the Lima elite, and upscale restaurants now serve the high-altitude quinoa grain, along with delicious highland potatoes, *aguaymanto*, an acid wild Andean fruit, and alpaca meat, esteemed for its low fat and cholesterol content. A controversial ingredient for some is the native coca leaf with which some chefs have experimented.

The *novoandina* culinary movement started back in the mid-1980s with Bernardo Roca Rey, but one chef has come to epitomize the new Peruvian cuisine: Gastón Acurio, who enjoys near rock-star status, and who, after studying at Le Cordon Bleu in Paris, went on to launch the **Astrid y Gastón** restaurant in Miraflores (Cantuarias 175; tel: 01-242-5387; www.astridygaston.com; *see p.88*) with his German wife Astrid Gutsche. Now arguably the most famous restaurant in Peru, if not Latin America, it has a menu that changes every few months. An excellent option for those getting to know Peruvian food is the restaurant's *menú degustación*, a three-hour, 12-course menu with dishes from around the country.

Other exponents of Peru's haute cuisine are Daniel Manrique's seafood restaurant **Segundo Muelle** (Av. Rivera Navarrete 530, San Isidro; 01-221-1499; www.segundomuelle.com; *see p.90*), which has also started to expand internationally; Lima oceanfront *cevichería* **Punta Sal** (Malecón Cisneros Cuadra 3, Miraflores; tel: 01-242-4524; www.puntasal.com), founded by north Peruvian Adolfo Perret; and **Brujas de Cachiche** (Bolognesi 472, Miraflores; tel:

Menu reader

- **Aguadito** Thick rice and fish soup served early in the day
- **Ají** Chili
- **Arroz Chaufa** Sautéed rice with chopped meats and vegetables
- **Causa** Cold entrée made from mashed *papa amarilla*, served with tuna or chicken in mayonnaise
- **Ceviche** Marinated raw white fish or seafood, served early in the day
- **Chicharrón** Fried entrée of fish, seafood, chicken, or pork
- **Chupe** Hot soup with vegetables, milk, chili, and cheese, mostly served with shrimp
- **Cuy** Guinea pig
- **Seco** Chicken or mutton first fried, then cooked in a pan
- **Sudado** Steamed fish or seafood

Cuy (guinea pig) is a typically Peruvian delicacy

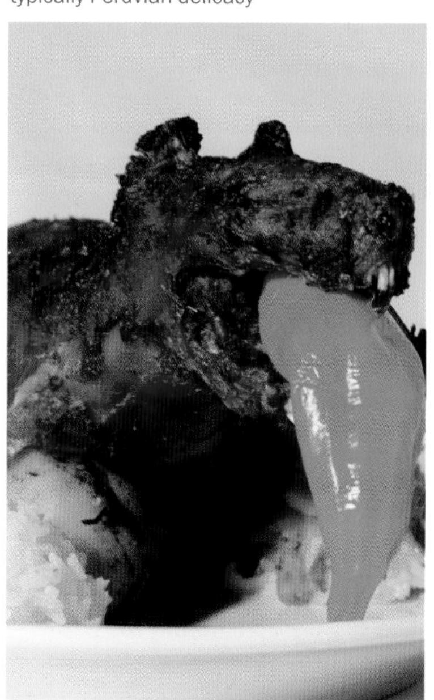

Tasty *chupe de camarones* (shrimp stew), served up with a fried egg

01-447-1133; www.brujosdecachiche.com.pe; *see p.89*), named for a village near Ica famous for its sorcerers and specializing in classic *criollo* dishes and shrimp.

Regional specialties

Many previously regional dishes are nowadays available in restaurants around the country, including *causas*, *(see box, left)*, *ceviches*, and desserts like *suspiros limeños (see p.287)*. Yet there are some that are probably best enjoyed in their original setting, such as spectacular fresh seafood in coastal towns from Tumbes to Tacna.

Celebrations in the **central Andes** feature the *pachamanca*, composed of the Quecha words for 'earth' and 'pot,' which goes back at least to the time of the Inca. While stones are heated on a fire, a hole is dug deep enough to hold the meal for the entire party. Different types of meat like beef, mutton, pork, guinea pig, alpaca, and chicken are seasoned and then all cooked together on the hot stones with potatoes, sweet potatoes, plantains, lima beans, yucca, and corn for approximately two hours, the whole thing wrapped in banana leaves.

Another ancient meat dish is the *pepián* guinea pig from **Cusco**, served with boiled rice and potatoes. It comprises a sweetcorn stew and guinea pig meat seasoned with onions, garlic, and golden and red peppers.

Arequipa is another center for Peruvian cuisine. A typical dish is the *ocopa*: boiled potatoes or shrimp served with a sauce similar to the more common *huancaína*. The sauce is made with seared dry sunflower seeds (another plant domesticated in the Americas), onions, garlic, vanilla, peanuts, a sprig of marigold, salt, and vegetable oil. All these ingredients are ground or liquefied to obtain a slightly pasty consistency and a characteristic, greenish-ochre color. The final dish is adorned with a hard-boiled egg and an olive.

A dish originally from the tropical **Amazon** is the *juane*, whose name has a somewhat macabre background. It's most often eaten during the feast of St John the Baptist, as the finished round product – fully wrapped in a ball of *bijao* leaves – was a reminder of the prophet's tragic end, on a plate for Salomé. The food itself is much less bloody than the story might imply. It's made from rice, chicken, olives, eggs, and spices. Yucca, rice, *tacacho* or plantains are other options, boiled in the *bijao* leaves for close to 90 minutes.

Markets and street food

For rock-bottom prices and local atmosphere, the markets in towns of any size are impossible to beat. Use common sense in picking a clean stall, unless your stomach can take anything. When shopping for food, remember to bargain when buying multiple items and ask for *la yapa* – a little something extra. Popular street food includes *anticuchos* – beef hearts on a stick – and *tamales* and *huitas* made from corn dough and filled with chicken, pork, or cheese and wrapped in banana leaves.

In **Lima**, the big Surquillo no. 1 market (in the Surquillo district adjacent to Miraflores, at Paseo de la República expressway and Narciso de Colina) is where the chefs go to buy their ingredients. In 2010, a

A lively Sunday market in Pisac, Sacred Valley

special restaurant section opened. Parque Reducto in Miraflores has a Bio-Feria of organically produced food Saturdays 8am–3.30pm. **Cusco's** Santa Ana market is close to the train station. **Arequipa** has a large covered market at San Camilo, and that of **Trujillo** is on Gamarra on the fringe of the center. **Iquitos** has two noteworthy markets, Sargento Lores and Belén, with innumerable juices made from local fruit, and typical Amazon dishes. Beware, however, that there's no control over food made from rare animals, so don't buy or consume anything called *lagarto* (caiman, like a small crocodile), *tortuga*, *taricaya*, or *motelo* (all names for turtles).

Culinary Tours (tel: 01-243-6074; www.culinarytours.com.pe) offers tours of Lima markets. **Lima Tours** (Jr. de la Unión 1040, Lima; tel: 01-619-6900; www.limatours.com.pe/perugourmet) takes you on six-day gastro-tours through Lima, Cusco, and Arequipa to sample the *novoandino* cuisine where it's being developed. If Pisco sampling is more to your taste, they also offer three-day trips to the center of the Peruvian spirit *(see p.96)*.

In 2009 in a public-private partnership, Peru's gastronomic organization, Apega, and the government launched **Mistura** (www.mistura.pe) as a great showcase food fair. President Alán García, who launched the fair and whose girth indicates a love of his country's food, says that Mistura will be bigger than Munich's Oktoberfest. While this is not necessarily true or desirable, a visit to the annual event, held in September in Lima's Parque Exposición, is an

If you're visiting Pisco, be sure to sample its namesake cocktail

opportunity to discover popular food, sweets, and fruit juices from around Peru.

Cooking classes

There are relatively few opportunities for non-professionals to learn to cook Peruvian cuisine. Most cooking schools are higher-education culinary institutes, of which there are about 120 for budding chefs. Fortunately, the **Gastrotur Perú** institute in Lima (Santa Luisa 265, San Isidro; tel: 01-422-9565; www.gastronomiadeperu.com), offers one-off evening courses for Spanish-speakers that it advertises in advance on its website. **Lima Tours** *(see above)* also runs evening cooking classes. In Huancayo in the central Andes, **Incas del Perú** (Av. Giraldez 652; tel: 064-223-303; www.incasdelperu.org) holds classes, including shopping for ingredients at the local market.

Shopping for crafts

Drawing from thousands of years of tradition, crafts in Peru are still very much alive, and shopping for them in an indigenous market is an essential Peruvian experience. For traditional through modern tastes, Peru's textiles, ceramics, and painstakingly fashioned folk art will offer something for everyone.

Long before the Inca, Peru was a land of craftspeople. Fine weaving found in the funeral bundles at Paracas, gold pieces worked by the Chimú people in northern Peru, and startlingly realistic Moche ceramics pay testimony to a people for whom work done with the hands was always important. In the Inca Empire, specially chosen women dedicated their lives to such tasks as weaving delicate capes from the feathers of exotic birds. Metallurgy was also a high-status occupation long before the Spaniards arrived in the New World.

Fortunately, these artistic traditions were not obliterated by the European conquest, and today there are few places in Peru where handicrafts – some little changed from those of centuries ago, others modified for the tourist market – cannot be found.

Handicrafts played multiple roles in indigenous cultures, none of which had a written language. Moche ceremonial cups were not simply for drinking: they told stories – depicting everything from festivities to daily events – which archeologists have analyzed to unravel mysteries of their way of life.

Likewise, patterns on clothes woven in the highlands have revealed some of the secrets of how the Aymara people lived. The designs used in some clothes depicted the status of the wearer; other garments were used only for special fiestas, and still others had woven into them motifs that were important to the community.

Colorful embroidered bands on display in Máncora

After the Spanish conquest, handicrafts began to fuse the old and new ways, as Indian woodcarvers whittled statues of the Virgin Mary dressed like a *campesina* (peasant), or angels with Indian faces.

Some handicrafts are found all over the country, but in different colors and designs, such as the popular wall hangings displayed in outdoor markets. Other items come from only one community or region. The decorative gilt-edged mirrors sold in Peru generally originate in Cajamarca; authentic ceramic Pucara bulls are crafted in Pupuja, near Puno; real Yagua jewelry comes only from the jungle area near Iquitos; but artisanal items from all over the country can be picked up in Lima. Some of the goods on sale, such as the Christmas tree ornaments and *arpilleras* – embroidered and appliquéd scenes – are produced by women's cooperatives in Lima's shantytowns.

Textiles

Peruvians have woven textiles since at least around 1000BC; they are still essential for survival in the cold of the high Andes. The domestication of llamas and alpacas supplied wool, but the creativity of the artisans produced beautiful garments, some of which the desert has helped to preserve for centuries. Different styles identify the wearers, indicating their places of origin and social and marital status.

Some of the best and most authentic places to look for textiles, including wall hangings, belts, sweaters, hats, gloves, ponchos, llama rugs, *chuspas* (small woolen bags that are used to carry coca for chewing), and

Traditionally dressed stallholders in the Colca valley

blankets, are the regular markets held throughout the Andes. The most famous in the Sacred Valley is held Sundays in **Pisac**, but there are others in **Chinchero** and **Huilloc** near Ollantaytambo.

Knitted items are available from many shops in **Cusco**, and some of the best bargains (although the quality is hit-and-miss) come from the women selling their wares in the bazaars in the streets off the Plaza de Armas. Be wary of assurances as to whether the item is made of wool from sheep, llama, or alpaca (usually, they say it is baby alpaca, which local guides cynically refer to as 'maybe alpaca'). Stop at some of the upmarket shops like **Alpaca 111** (www.alpaca111.com), with retailers in many major cities in Peru, and feel the difference between wools from the three animals before starting your shopping.

Puno also has an important market near the train station, and other major towns have crafts markets; **Lima's** is in Miraflores *(see p.78)*. Depending on the size and vitality of the town, the markets may last only from pre-dawn to mid-morning once a week, or they may go on for days.

Woolen cloth which is purported to be antique usually is not, as the damp highland climate does not allow wool to last indefinitely. Many weavers now use dark colors and ancient designs to give the impression that the textile has been around for centuries, but such cloth is no more antique than are the rustic-looking dolls that some unscrupulous sellers claim have come from ancient graves.

The **Titicaca** island weavers of Taquile are particularly well regarded, and their work is sold by the local cooperative there. In central Peru, **Huancayo**'s Sunday market is the most visited, while **Arequipa** is the center of products made with the pinnacle of quality: wool sheared from the delicate and wild vicuña, the smallest relative of the llama *(see box, right)*.

Weavers of woolen goods officially honored as master craftsmen by the Peruvian government are **Alfonso Sulca** (Plaza Santa Ana, stand No. 83, Ayacucho; tel: 066-312-990) and **Leoncio Tinoco** (Jr. Florida 280, Huancayo; tel: 064-213-028).

Jewelry made from shells and stones

Forbidden goods

Beware of unscrupulous merchants selling antiques from grave sites, as these are almost certainly fakes; in any case it is illegal to buy or take pre-Columbian antiques out of the country. Much the same goes for most goods made from vicuña. If the item really does contain vicuña fibers, which is unlikely, it may have been made illegally. Make sure it is from a legitimate source such as Tambo Cañahuas (a village in the Reserva Nacional Salinas y Aguada Blanca whose residents are allowed to shear vicuñas once a year). Don't even consider buying souvenirs made from the feathers, skins, or shells of rainforest creatures.

Inca-inspired pottery

Ceramics

After textiles, ceramics are the most remarkable feature of Peruvian arts and crafts, and also have a history going back at least 3,000 years. Many are still produced with clay from the same centuries-old quarries, and ancient designs from the Pacific Coast, Andes, and Amazon continue to be repeated. In Nazca and Trujillo, artisans have retained the traditional motifs of their Nazca and Chimú ancestors. Rural villages have specialized in different forms of ceramics, including the miniature bulls – *toritos* – from Pucará, near Juliaca, and Quinua. Traditional earthenware comes from Simbilá near Piura, Santo Domingo de los Olleros near Lima, Taricá in the Ancash department, and from Aco and Mankalluta in Junín.

Ceramics from Chulucanas and La Encantada near Piura are also rooted in centuries of tradition, but artisans there have taken a different angle and become extremely successful. Apart from small sculptures and polychrome figurines, they have developed elegant and modern vases, plates, and other decorative ceramics with geometric and abstract forms derived from basic black and white. Notable Peruvian masters of the ceramic art include **Edilberto Mérida** (Carmen Alto 133, San Blas, Cusco; tel: 082-221-714; and Sinchi Roca 2447, Lince, Lima; tel: 01-472-5774) and **Gerásimo Sosa** (Jr. Ayacucho 1152, Chulucanas).

Jewelry and metalworking

The stunning gold and silver objects produced by the Inca and other cultures astounded the Spanish conquerors, but also ignited their greed. What remains in museums is but a fraction of the treasure that once existed. Today, gold and silver items, ranging from silver-rimmed crystal glasses to fruit bowls and candelabras, are available from a large number of boutiques in Lima. The conquistadors also found skilled craftsmen working gold and silver into finely turned jewelry and adornments. This tradition has not been lost, as evidenced by the intricate gold filigree produced in Catacaos outside Piura in the northern desert. These complicated pieces, which try an artist's patience and imagination, dangle from the ears of the townswomen, who claim that gold shines even brighter under the desert sun. These are the big, drooping earrings that women dancing the *marinera* wear. In San Jerónimo, near Huancayo in the central highlands, silver filigree is tooled into peacocks, fighting cocks, and doves.

Among the best-known current silversmiths are **Gregorio Cachi** (Urbanización T U-4, Pasaje Navidad Wanchaq, Cusco; tel: 084-224-052) and **Víctor Flores** (Jr. Garcilaso de la Vega 496, Ayacucho; tel: 066-313-880). Peru's best-quality hand-painted ceramic jewelry, meanwhile, is designed by the **Association of Artisans of Virgen del Carmen** in Pisac.

Religious scenes

A very different kind of handicraft are the colorful *retablos*, originally made in Ayacucho, which derive from the small portable shrines brought to Peru by the conquistadors. Usually smaller nowadays, and tucked into decorated wooden boxes or the hollow of a reed, these depict busy scenes that may be solemn or comical in mood, depending on the artist's inclination. The subject matter used always to be religious, and often still is – Nativity scenes are the most common – but even the scenes showing religious processions may be turned into rollicking fiestas, overflowing with figures made of wood, plaster, papier mâché, or clay.

Superb *retablos* fashioned from hollow gourds are still a specialty in Ayacucho, as well as the traditional wooden ones, some tiny, some as much as 1m (3ft) high. Wooden *retablos* may be found in most outdoor

Top five best buys

- Alpaca sweaters
- Chulucanas ceramics
- Replicas of pre-Hispanic pottery
- Gourds with miniature religious scenes
- Replicas of Baroque Spanish sculpture and mirrors

Souvenirs on sale at the Huaca de la Luna (Temple of the Moon), Trujillo

Crafts from the Uros islands

markets, but the most delicate ones – carved from the white and gray Huamanga stone some call Peru's marble – are found only in boutiques and cooperatives in the Santa Ana neighborhood. Actually a type of soapstone, Huamanga is carved into anything from matchbook-sized Nativity scenes to oversized chess sets – with figures of Inca and llamas replacing kings and knights. Top *retablo* sculptors in Ayacucho include **Julio Gálvez** (Plazoleta Santa Ana; tel: 066-314-278) and **Sergio Pillaca** (Jr. Libertad 961; tel: 066-313-070). In the same city, one of the largest selections is at the Wari crafts gallery (Jr. Mariscal Cáceres 302, Santa Ana; tel: 066-312-529).

Other crafts

Peru produces great quantities of other handmade crafts. Finely etched gourds – some hollowed out to include wooden figures – are among the most distinctive. Sculptors and carvers work in wood to make figurines, Baroque-style picture frames and gold-colored mirrors; in Cusco and Puno they also use the common volcanic stone called andesite. Inlays are another form of decorating frames, while painters depict religious and rural scenes. Hat makers work their crafts in straw along the coast, and leather and, above all, felt in the cold Andes.

Stores in Lima, while far more expensive than bargain handicrafts from the Andean markets, offer the best quality. Among them are **Figuras Peruanas** (Copérnico 179; tel: 01-459 2175), **Silver Llama** (Av. Velasco Astete 1360 Dp. 103; tel: 01-372-4726), **Artesanías Urin Huanca** (Ricardo Palma 205; tel: 01-241-9780), and **Kuntur Wasi** (Ocharán 182; tel: 01-447-7173/444-0557).

PLACES

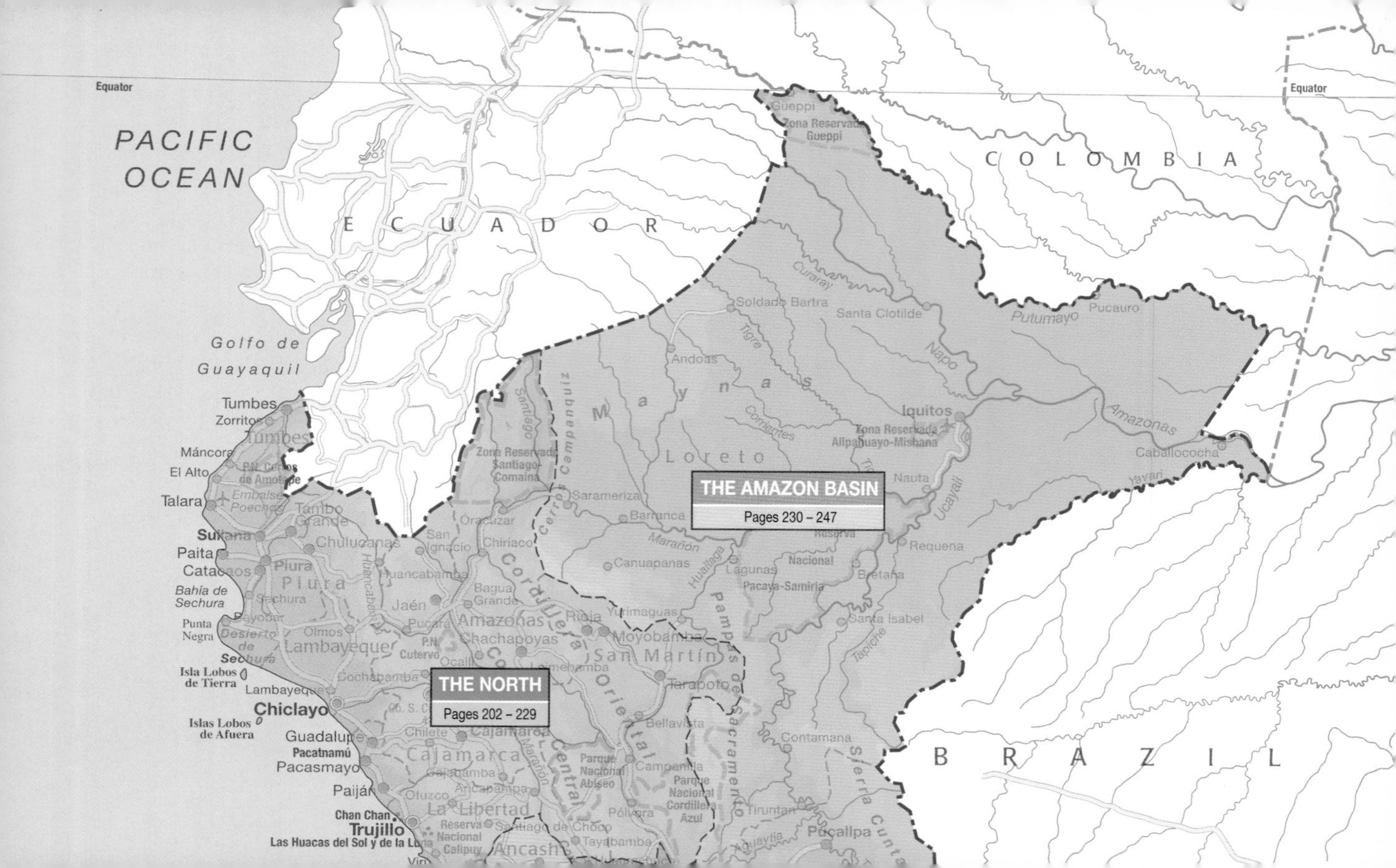

THE AMAZON BASIN
Pages 230 – 247
THE NORTH
Pages 202 – 229
PACIFIC OCEAN
ECUADOR
COLOMBIA
BRAZIL
Equator
Golfo de Guayaquil
Tumbes
Zorritos
Máncora
El Alto
Talara
Sullana
Paita
Catacaos
Bahía de Sechura
Sechura
Punta Negra
Bayóvar
Desierto de Sechura
Isla Lobos de Tierra
Islas Lobos de Afuera
Lambayeque
Chiclayo
Guadalupe
Pacatnamú
Pacasmayo
Paiján
Chan Chan
Trujillo
Las Huacas del Sol y de la Luna
Tambo Grande
Chulucanas
Piura
Olmos
Huancabamba
Jaén
Pucará
P.N. Cutervo
Cochabamba
Chilete
Cajamarca
Cajabamba
Otuzco
La Libertad
Reserva Nacional Calipuy
Ancash
San Ignacio
Chiriaco
Oracuzar
Bagua Grande
Amazonas
Chachapoyas
Rioja
Moyobamba
San Martín
Tarapoto
Bellavista
Yurimaguas
Lagunas
Pacaya-Samiria
Reserva Nacional
Saramerizа
Barranca
Canuapanas
Marañón
Huallaga
Santiago
Zona Reservada Santiago-Comaina
Cerros Campanquiz
Cordillera Central
Cordillera Oriental
Parque Nacional Abiseo
Parque Nacional Cordillera Azul
Campanilla
Pólvora
Tayabamba
Santiago de Chuco
Pampas de Sacramento
Contamana
Tiruntan
Pucallpa
Aguaytía
Sierra Cuntamana
Santa Isabel
Tapiche
Bretaña
Requena
Ucayali
Nauta
Iquitos
Zona Reservada Allpahuayo-Mishana
Loreto
Maynas
Andoas
Soldado Bartra
Tigre
Corrientes
Curaray
Santa Clotilde
Napo
Putumayo
Pucauro
Amazonas
Caballococha
Yavarí
Güeppí
Zona Reservada Güeppí
P.N. Cerros de Amotape
Embalse Poechos

Getting your bearings

Three very distinct regions form Peru. A narrow desert plain stretches along the Pacific coast, bordered by the Andes, which rise steeply to more than 6,000m (18,000ft). To the east, the torrid Amazon Basin is still sparsely populated. This is just the broadest division, however: Peru's challenging geography has historically led to major difficulties in communication and numerous different sub-regions which still exist today.

The coast includes Lima, the capital, in which about a quarter of Peruvians live. To the south are grape-growing valleys in the desert and Peru's second city, Arequipa. In the Andes lies the heart of the Inca area, the Sacred Valley, with the former Inca capital, Cusco, the great Lake Titicaca, and the Callejón de Huaylas, Peru's fabled mountaineering district. The North, with beaches, archeology, and jungle, forms a chapter on its own, as does the vast Amazon Basin. For easy reference when using this guide, each region has a dedicated chapter and is color-coded for quick navigation. Detailed regional maps are included within each chapter.

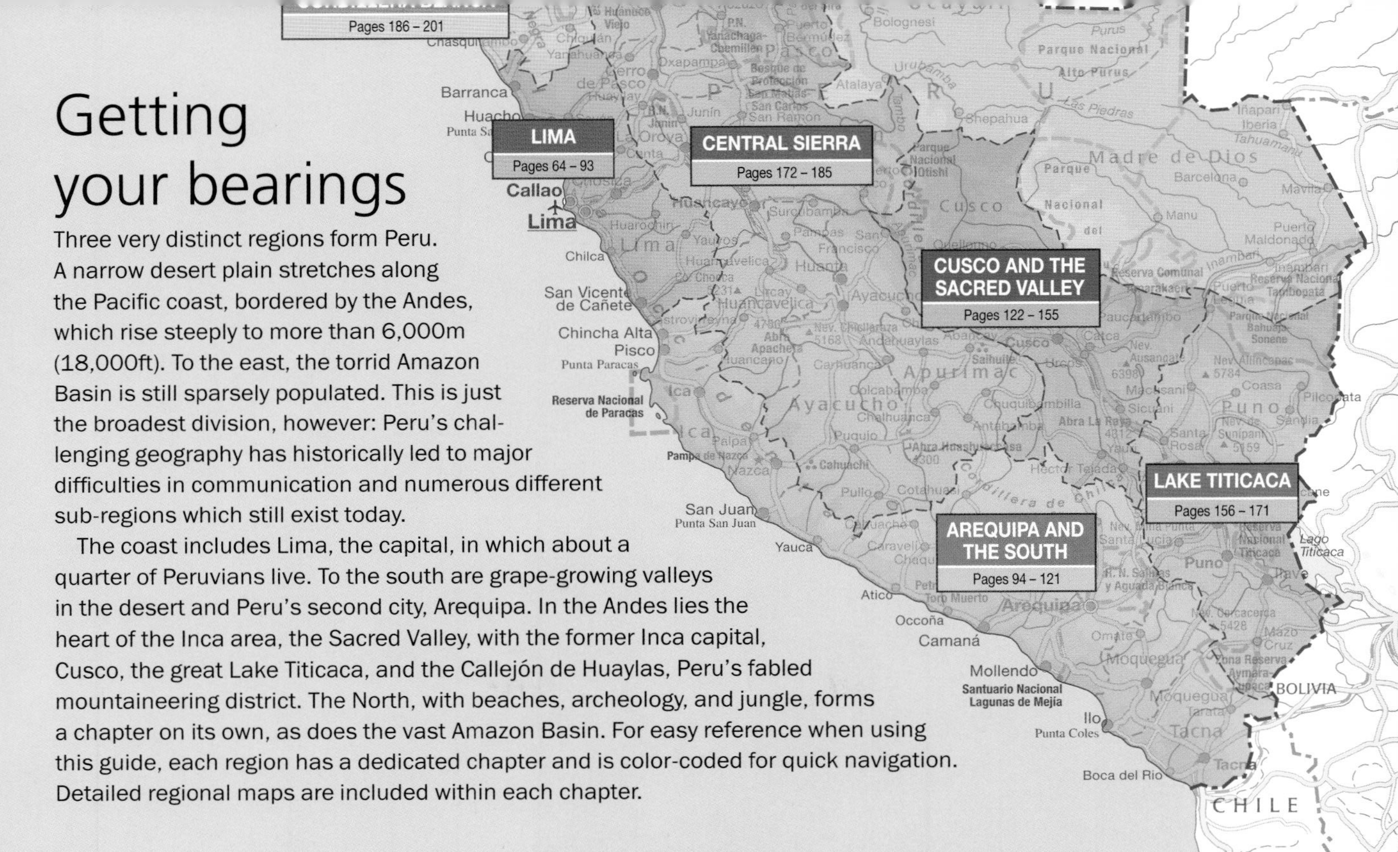

Lima

Most travelers to Peru begin their journey in Lima, a city of rare fascination and unexpected pleasures. It has both decaying colonial splendor and the teeming vitality of an oriental bazaar. Gritty, noisy and chaotic it may be, but the hidden treasures of the Peruvian capital are worth seeking out – from the old colonial heart, cloaked in history, to modern Miraflores.

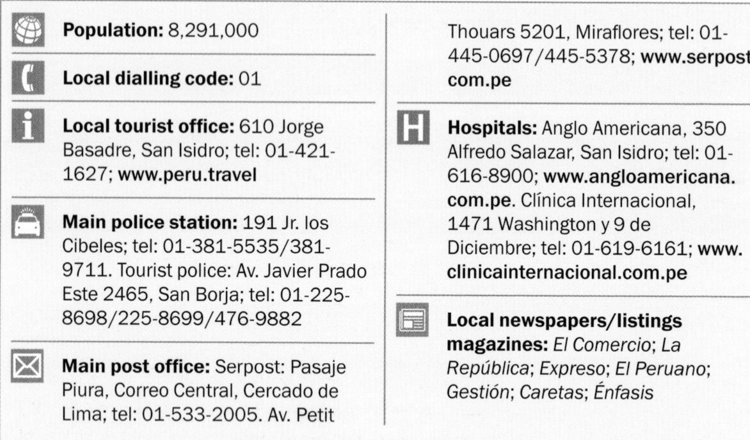

Population: 8,291,000

Local dialling code: 01

Local tourist office: 610 Jorge Basadre, San Isidro; tel: 01-421-1627; **www.peru.travel**

Main police station: 191 Jr. los Cibeles; tel: 01-381-5535/381-9711. Tourist police: Av. Javier Prado Este 2465, San Borja; tel: 01-225-8698/225-8699/476-9882

Main post office: Serpost: Pasaje Piura, Correo Central, Cercado de Lima; tel: 01-533-2005. Av. Petit Thouars 5201, Miraflores; tel: 01-445-0697/445-5378; **www.serpost.com.pe**

Hospitals: Anglo Americana, 350 Alfredo Salazar, San Isidro; tel: 01-616-8900; **www.angloamericana.com.pe**. Clínica Internacional, 1471 Washington y 9 de Diciembre; tel: 01-619-6161; **www.clinicainternacional.com.pe**

Local newspapers/listings magazines: *El Comercio*; *La República*; *Expreso*; *El Peruano*; *Gestión*; *Caretas*; *Énfasis*

Peru's vast capital is a city with many different faces. Its appeal may not be instant, and the impoverished urban sprawl is hard to ignore, but visitors who judge the city on first impressions and move swiftly on risk missing out on a fascinating place. As the former center of Spanish South America, it retains some fine colonial architecture, and treasures from all over the country can be found in its impressive museums.

Lima ❶ was founded in 1535 by the Spanish conquistador Francisco Pizarro, who named it Ciudad de los Reyes – City of Kings. For two centuries after its foundation, Lima was the political, commercial, and ecclesiastical capital of Spanish South America, and the seat of the Inquisition as well as of the viceroys. A powerful earthquake in 1746 destroyed much of the city, and the palaces, churches, mansions, and monasteries we see today were subsequently rebuilt and expanded.

It was only in the early 20th century, following the building of the first railways, that the city burst its 17th-century Spanish limits and embarked on a process of change and growth that has lasted to the present day. Infill development created an area of middle-class suburbs between the city center, Callao, and Chorrillos. Outside this triangle, Andean migrants made their homes in sprawling, self-built shantytowns stretching north, south, and northeast, occupying the vacant desert sands in the shadow of the Andean foothills *(see box p.77)*. The shantytowns now contain half the city's estimated population of over 8 million.

Historic Lima

A major program of urban renewal is in progress in the historic center of the city. Under the auspices of Unesco it has been declared part of the 'Cultural Heritage of Mankind,' and there have been spectacular changes in both architectural restoration and street cleanliness and security.

The interior of the Catedral San Juan Evangelista

Plaza Mayor

Plaza Mayor

The usual starting point for exploring Lima is the **Plaza Mayor** Ⓐ (formerly Plaza de Armas), which has benefited greatly from recent renovation. Stand in the middle of this handsome square, by the 17th-century bronze fountain, and you are at the city's historic heart. The *Angel of Fame* on the fountain is a copy of the original that, according to legend, flew away in 1900. Most of the buildings are 18th-century reconstructions, but the spirit of the conquistadors permeates the square.

The eastern side of the square is dominated by the **Catedral San Juan Evangelista** (Mon–Sat 9am–4.30pm; charge), on a site chosen by Francisco Pizarro but reconstructed several times after earthquakes. The present building was begun in the 18th century, after the almost complete devastation of the previous one in the 1746 earthquake. Much of the exterior has been painted in

Lima

0 1 km
0 1 mile

N

Aeropuerto Internacional Jorge Chávez
Rimac
Av. del Emsor
Av. Elmer J. Faucett
Av. Pe
Av. 12 de Octubre
Av. Morales Duarez
Av. Morales D
Av. Maq
Terminal Marítima
Pl. Fanning
Av. República Argentina
CALLAO
Rimac
Supe
Av. 2 de Mayo
Zepita
Lazareto
Fuerte Real Felipe Museo Militar
Playa Chucuito
Montezuma
Av. Saenz Peña
Guardia Chalaca
Av. Benavides
Av. Elmer J. Faucett
Gamarra
Paz Soldan
Av. Buenos Aires
Loreto
Virgil
Guisse
Bolognesi
Alfonso Ugarte
Colina
Ovalo Saloom
Av. República de Venezuela
Playa Cantolao
LA PUNTA
Av. Bolognesi
Av. Grau
Playa Carpayo
LA PERLA
Av. Costanera
Jose Galvez
Canuide
Av. Santa Rosa
Av. de la Marina
Av. de los Precursores
PARQUE DE LA LEYENDA
Playa Malecón
Av. la Paz
Av. Libertad
Av. de los Patriotas
Manco II
SAN MIGUEL
Av. Libertad
Feria Internacional del Pacifico
MAGDALENA

PACIFIC

OCEAN

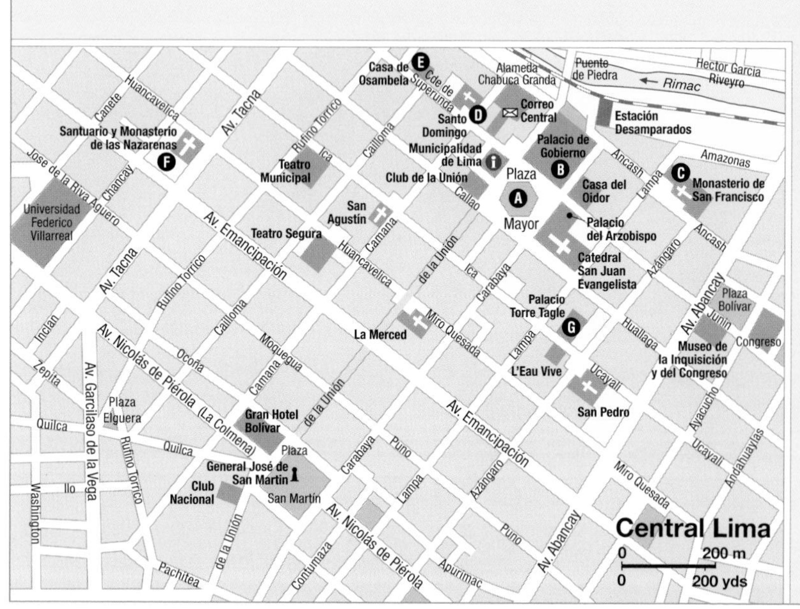

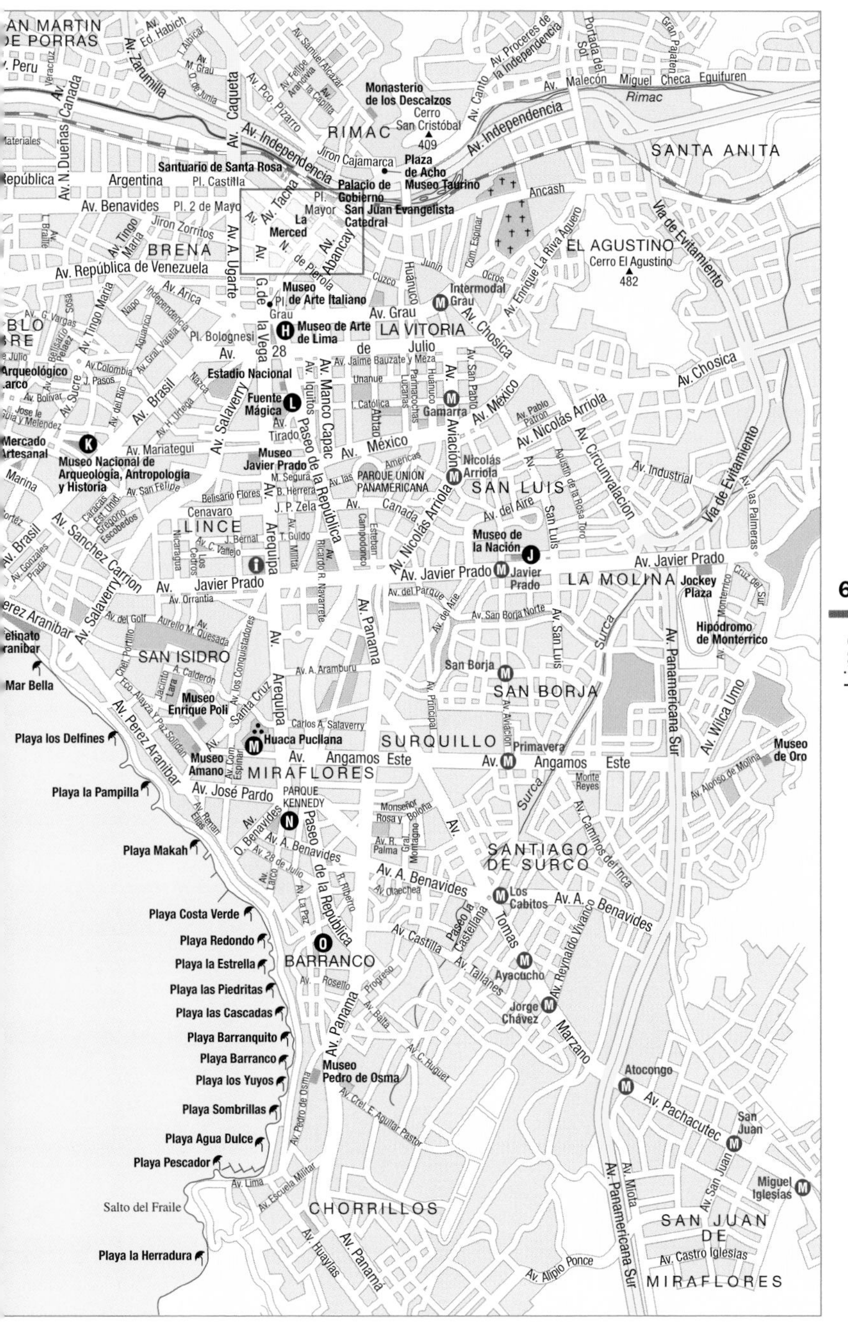
RIMAC
SANTA ANITA
BREÑA
EL AGUSTINO
LA VITORIA
SAN LUIS
LINCE
LA MOLINA
SAN ISIDRO
SAN BORJA
SURQUILLO
MIRAFLORES
SANTIAGO DE SURCO
BARRANCO
CHORRILLOS
SAN JUAN DE MIRAFLORES
Monasterio de los Descalzos
Cerro San Cristóbal 409
Santuario de Santa Rosa
Plaza de Acho
Museo Taurino
Palacio de Gobierno
San Juan Evangelista
Catedral
La Merced
Cerro El Agustino 482
Museo de Arte Italiano
Museo de Arte de Lima
Estadio Nacional
Fuente Mágica
Museo Javier Prado
Museo Nacional de Arqueología, Antropología y Historia
Mercado Artesanal
PARQUE UNIÓN PANAMERICANA
Museo de la Nación
Jockey Plaza
Hipódromo de Monterrico
Museo Enrique Poli
Huaca Pucllana
Museo Amano
Museo de Oro
PARQUE KENNEDY
Museo Pedro de Osma
Mar Bella
Playa los Delfines
Playa la Pampilla
Playa Makah
Playa Costa Verde
Playa Redondo
Playa la Estrella
Playa las Piedritas
Playa las Cascadas
Playa Barranquito
Playa Barranco
Playa los Yuyos
Playa Sombrillas
Playa Agua Dulce
Playa Pescador
Salto del Fraile
Playa la Herradura
Intermodal Grau
Gamarra
Nicolás Arriola
Javier Prado
San Borja
Primavera
Los Cabitos
Ayacucho
Jorge Chávez
Atocongo
San Juan
Miguel Iglesias
Av. Independencia
Av. Abancay
Av. Tacna
Av. Grau
Av. Javier Prado
Av. Arequipa
Av. Panamericana Sur
Av. Angamos Este
Av. José Pardo
Av. A. Benavides
Av. Pachacutec
Av. Pérez Aranibar
Av. Salaverry
Av. Brasil
Av. Sánchez Carrion
Av. Manco Capac
Paseo de la República
Av. Aviación
Av. México
Av. Nicolás Arriola
Av. Circunvalación
Vía de Evitamiento
Av. Chosica
Av. República de Venezuela
Av. Mariategui
Av. Panamá
Av. Reynaldo Vivanco
Av. Wilca Umo

Lima transport

Airports: Jorge Chávez International Airport (LIM), **www.lap.com.pe**, is 16km (10 miles) northeast of downtown in Callao. Public buses are available on Av. Elmer Faucett but not recommended for passengers with luggage. Transfer services are available 24 hours a day from Super Shuttle (Av. Jose Pardo 610; tel: 01-517-2558; **www.supershuttleairport.com**) from US$15 per person.
Taxis on the street are unmetered. Authorized taxi companies available at international and domestic arrivals are CMV (tel: 01-517-1892/422-4838/517-1891; email: **cmv@exalmar.com.pe**), Mitsui (tel: 01-517-1893/349-7722; email: **remisse@mitsuiautomotriz.com**), and Taxi Green (tel: 01-484-4001/99957-5781; email: **taxigreen@peru.com**). Journey times to San Isidro and Miraflores are 35–45 minutes. For domestic flights there is an airport tax of US$6 (approximately) at all airports

Public bus: El Metropolitano operates a route system through Lima. Express buses don't stop at all stations, and the system runs 6am–9.50pm. Route maps are available online at **www.metropolitano.com.pe.** Payment is on electronic toll cards. The Metropolitano system links with the Terminal Terrestre de Plaza Norte national inter-urban bus terminal at the Tomás Valle station north of the city center. Always check the departure point for the journey you are making when buying tickets. Reliable bus companies have their own terminals, including: Civa (cnr Av. 28 de Julio and Paseo de la República, La Vitoria; tel: 01-418-1111; **www.civa.com.pe**), Cruz del Sur (Av. Javier Prado Este 1109, San Isidro; call center: 01-311-5050; **www.cruzdelsur.com.pe**), Ormeño (Paseo de la República 801, La Vitoria; tel: 01-427-5679; **www.grupo-ormeno.com.pe**), Tepsa (Av. Paseo de la República 151-A, La Vitoria; call center: 01-202-3535; **www.tepsa.com.pe**)
Combis: minibuses that squeeze up to 10 people on urban routes. They are cheap and attempt to hurtle through the city at breakneck speeds but not particularly safe. Fares are S./1–S./2

Local rail: The Tren Eléctrico (tel: 01-224-2444; **www.aate.gob.pe**) is scheduled to begin operating in 2012 between Grau in the center of Lima and Villa El Salvador in the southeast. Trains run at 6-minute intervals from 6am–10pm. Payment of S./1.50 is via electronic ticket

Taxis: Unmetered taxis are plentiful and cheap, but the fare must be negoatiated in advance. Taxi companies (radio taxis) are slightly more expensive but safer. Taxi services in Lima include: airport taxi companies *(see above)*, Taxi Móvil (tel: 01-422-3322), Taxi Prime (tel: 01-247-7070), Taxi Real (tel: 01-215-1414), Taxi Seguro (tel: 01-241-9292)

yellow ochre, as part of a successful policy to brighten up dusty facades with colors used in the colonial period. Inside, the cathedral is large and unusually austere for a Baroque church, following extensive late 19th-century restorations. Notable are the 17th-century wooden choir stalls. To the right of the entrance is a small side-chapel dedicated to Pizarro, where his skeleton lies in a sealed wooden coffin.

Next door to the cathedral is the **Palacio del Arzobispo** (Archbishop's

Changing of the guard at the Palacio de Gobierno

Palace), rebuilt in the 1920s with an impressive wooden balcony. Opposite stands the **Municipalidad de Lima** (City Hall), built in the 1940s after fire destroyed its predecessor. The pleasant interior includes a fine library. Next to it on the square is the headquarters of the **Club de la Unión**, a lunchtime haunt of politicians and professionals. Between them at the mouth of Pasaje Santa Rosa is a monument, in the form of a large chunk of rough-hewn stone, to Taulichusco El Viejo, the last *cacique* (chief) of pre-conquest Lima, which was unveiled in 1985 as a belated antidote to the ghost of Pizarro.

On the north side of the plaza is the **Palacio de Gobierno** **B** (Government Palace; Mon–Fri 8.30am–1pm, 2–5pm; free; or a free two-hour guided tour – take a copy of your passport at least one day before), built on the site of Pizarro's palace, where he was assassinated in 1541 – the first Latin American coup d'état. The present building was completed in 1938, and suffers from the taste for grandiose French Baroque which afflicted dictatorial leaders of the time. Much of the ground plan at the rear of the building remains the same as in Pizarro's day. At 11.45am, every day except Sunday, you can catch the Changing of the Guard, performed in the front courtyard by goose-stepping troops from the Húsares de Junín regiment, dressed in the red-and-blue ceremonial uniforms and ornamental helmets of the independence period.

Bohemian breather

Every major city needs its bohemian bar full of decaying grandeur. In Lima's old town, the place is **Cordano**, on Jirón Ancash across from the **Desamparados**, an old train station turned cultural center. Opened in 1905, it is the place for a sentimental step back in time in Lima's historic center, with high ceilings, old photographs, and a vast wooden bar unchanged through the decades. Stop by for a pisco sour and a *butifarra* (pork sausage) or traditional Peruvian cuisine after visiting the catacombs of the nearby San Francisco monastery, or for a break from the bustle of the Plaza Mayor, also only a block a away.

To arrange a guided tour of the palace, go to the office of Relaciones Públicas in the same building to make an appointment, or tel: 01-311-3908.

On a charming street corner (the intersection of Jirón Carabaya and Jirón Junín) you will find the oldest building in the square, the **Casa del Oidor**. Dating from the early 18th century, it has the wooden balconies in the form of enclosed galleries projecting from the first floor that were colonial Lima's most graceful feature.

With the removal of the street vendors, a new promenade, the **Paseo Chabuca Granda**, has been created behind the Presidential Palace on the southern bank of the Río Rimac. Many *limeños* (the people of Lima) like to stroll here at the weekends, and the municipality organizes concerts and theater performances in specially constructed arenas.

Bustling Jirón de la Unión

Monasterio de San Francisco

The **Monasterio de San Francisco** Ⓒ (Plaza de San Francisco, Jirón Alcash; Mon–Sun 9.30am–5.30pm; guided tours; charge) is the jewel of colonial Lima. The church faces a small paved square, full of pigeons and portrait photographers. The outside is attractively painted in colonial yellow, but it is the interior that is fascinating; much of it is decorated in the geometrical Mudéjar (Andalusian Moorish) style. Its outstanding features include the 17th-century library, with 25,000 leather-bound volumes and 6,000 parchments dating from the 15th to the 18th century. The cupola has a superb Mudéjar carved wooden ceiling of Panamanian cedar, dating from 1625. In a gallery above the nave of the church are 130 choir stalls and 71 panels with carvings of Franciscan saints, made of the same wood. Restoration work has exposed (under eight layers of paint) 17th-century murals in the cloister and adjacent chambers. The monastery's collection of religious art includes paintings from the workshops of Rubens and Zurbarán.

San Francisco has probably survived more recent earthquakes because of the solid base provided by its catacombs, which were used as Lima's cemetery until 1810. A network of underground chambers, which are open to the public, contains hundreds of skulls and bones, stored in racks according to type.

One of the catacombs in the Monasterio de San Francisco

Colonial churches

There are many other colonial churches in the center. The **Iglesia de Santo Domingo** D (cnr Camaná and Conde de Superunda; Mon–Sat 9am–12.30pm, 3–6pm, Sun 9am–1pm; charge), which has a pleasant cloister with tiling from Seville, contains the tomb of San Martín de Porres, a black saint who lived and died in Lima and is venerated throughout Latin America. There is also an urn here which holds the ashes of Santa Rosa de Lima, the patron saint of the New World and the Philippines as well as the city of Lima. Continue along Conde de Superunda and turn right on Avenida Tacna to reach the **Santuario de Santa Rosa** (daily 9am–1pm, 3–6pm; free). The sanctuary, a modest hut built in the 16th century on the site of the saint's birthplace and now set in a pleasant garden, contains relics of Santa Rosa.

The Conde de Superunda is one of several streets in the center with fine colonial balconies. The **Casa de Osambela** E (Jirón Conde de Superunda 298; tel: 01-427-7989; Mon–Fri 9am–5pm; free), right by Santo Domingo, is open to the public and well worth visiting. A late 18th-century mansion with an ornamental cupola, beautifully restored in the 1980s, it houses a small art gallery and the offices of various cultural institutions.

Another important church in the historic center is the Baroque **Santuario y Monasterio de las**

Nazarenas F (cnr Avenida Tacna and Jirón Huancavelica; Mon–Sat 7am–noon, 4–8.30pm; free) which houses the image of El Señor de los Milagros (The Lord of Miracles), the black Christ painted by a freed African slave that has become the most important focus of popular religious feeling in Lima. The miracle was that the wall on which the painting appeared was the only part of a 17th-century shantytown to survive an earthquake. In October the image is borne around the city center for several days (October 18, 19, and 28) by teams of men wearing the purple robes of the brotherhood of El Señor de los Milagros. Hundreds of thousands of people turn out to accompany the image in what is one of the largest public gatherings in South America. The church can be visited, but the convent is a closed Order.

Four blocks east of Las Nazarenas stands the **Iglesia de la Merced** (Jirón de la Unión; daily 8am–noon, 4–8pm; free), built on the site of the first Catholic Mass celebrated in the city, in 1534. Like most churches in Lima, it suffered severe earthquake damage and was rebuilt in the late 18th century. Nearby, the **Iglesia de San Pedro** (Jirón Azángaro; daily 9.30–11.45am, 2–5pm; free) is another Baroque church with Mudéjar influences, which was consecrated in 1638.

Palacio Torre Tagle

The city center contains several fine examples of secular colonial architecture. Outstanding is one on Jirón Ucayali, close to San Pedro: the **Palacio Torre Tagle** G (Jirón Ucayali 323; tel: 01-311-2400; Mon–Fri 9am–

A young bullfighter at the Plaza de Acho

The finely carved wooden balconies of the Palacio Torre Tagle

4.30pm by appointment only; free) was completed in 1735 and gives a good idea of the opulence of Lima in its colonial prime. It now houses the Foreign Ministry, but visits are allowed to the courtyard, from where you can see the finely carved wooden balconies.

Rimac

Behind the Palacio de Gobierno, the little **Puente de Piedra** (Stone Bridge), built over four round arches in 1610 (its mortar reputedly bound with thousands of egg whites for strength), leads over the river to **Rimac**, once the playground of the aristocracy and now a lively working-class district. Here you'll find the **Plaza de Acho**, the oldest bullring in the Americas. The **Museo Taurino** (Mon–Fri 9am–6pm, Sat–Sun by appointment only; tel: 01-481-1467) has a collection of bullfighting memorabilia and, notably, some Goya engravings. There is a panoramic view of the city from Cerro San Cristóbal. Organized tours visit the Rimac district and this hill several times a day. Buses leave from the main plaza, and the tour includes a visit to the bullfighting museum.

At the foot of the hill is the **Alameda de los Descalzos**, laid out in 1610 as a pleasure garden with statues and wrought-iron railings, but now rather run-down. It leads to the restored **Monasterio de los Descalzos** (Monastery of the Barefoot Friars; Tue–Sun 10am–6pm; charge), worth a visit for its collection of colonial paintings. To the right is the **Paseo de Aguas**, another pleasure garden created in the 18th century by Viceroy Amat for his famous mistress, La Perrichola, but also sadly in need of repair.

Plaza San Martín

South of the Plaza Mayor, the largest square and hub of Lima's first expansion is the **Plaza San Martín**. It's best approached via the pedestrianized **Jirón de la Unión**, once Lima's most elegant shopping street, now a teeming mass of shoppers and fast-food joints. The colonnaded Plaza San Martín, restored and repainted and brightly lit, is an important

Quirky climate

Lima may be a tropical capital, but its climate would hardly give that away. For over half the year – April through November – the city is draped in a damp blanket of low cloud called *garúa*. Cool temperatures with highs around 18°C (64°F) accompany the dreary weather, created by condensation above the cold Humboldt Current off the coast. Rainfall hardly amounts to more than a few nights of drizzle, however. November through April, the summer months, are pleasant, with highs rarely topping 27°C (81°F).

gathering place for political meetings. In the center is an equestrian statue of General José de San Martín, Peru's Argentinian independence hero. On its west side is the **Gran Hotel Bolívar**. Built in the 1920s, it retains much of its former atmosphere. A Palm Court trio serenades people drinking afternoon tea in the domed lobby, and its giant pisco sours (called *catedrales*) remain justly famous. Even if you are not staying here, the Bolívar is the perfect place to stop and rest during a city tour; the decor and ambience make the high price of the drinks worthwhile.

Next to the Bolívar is **Jirón Ocoña**, the center of Lima's street foreign exchange market, where money-changers buy or sell dollars round the clock. The market is sophisticated, and in times of high inflation rates change constantly. Across La Colmena from the Bolívar is the **Club Nacional**. Though it is no longer the watering-hole of Peru's once all-powerful

Gran Hotel Bolívar

oligarchy, it has recently taken on a new lease of life, with the revamping of the city center. The clients now are a blend of old-money families and prominent members of the business community.

Museums

Lima has a wealth of museums, but the larger ones are scattered in the vast area between the center and the Miraflores and San Isidro districts where most visitors stay. Fruit of individual and government-sponsored collecting, they display some of the best of the pre-Columbian treasures unearthed from sites around the country.

Just south of Plaza San Martín, the **Museo de Arte de Lima** **H** (MALI; Paseo Colón 125; www.museodearte.org.pe; daily except Wed 10am–5pm; free on Mon) contains an extensive collection of Peruvian art of all forms from 900BC to the present and is undergoing a modernization. It has a photography exhibition and two auditoriums where concerts are given, and is surrounded by a very pleasant public park.

The **Museo Arqueológico Rafael Larco** **I** (Avenida Bolívar 1515; www.museolarco.org; daily 9am–6pm; charge), in an 18th-century mansion, has a vast, 45,000-piece collection of pre-Columbian ceramics, gold and silver objects, and some interesting textiles. A small annex holds a fascinating collection of erotic pottery from the Moche period.

The large, modern **Museo de la Nación** **J** (National Museum; Av. Javier Prado Este 2465; Tue–Sun 9am–5pm; charge), in the San Luis district, has a wonderful collection of artifacts from the Chavín culture, including an ingenious replica of a Chavín stela, woven articles found at Paracas, and ceramics from Nazca, among 12,000 total objects, making it one of the best museums in the city.

Last but not least, the **Museo Nacional de Arqueología, Antropología y Historia** **K** (National Museum of Archeology, Anthropology, and History; Plaza Bolívar; http://museonacional.perucultural.org.pe; Tue–Sat 9am–5pm, Sun until 4pm; charge), in the suburb of Pueblo Libre, is one of the most interesting museums in the country, with a superb collection of pottery and textiles from all the main cultures of ancient Peru as well as colonial art.

Moche headdress at the Museo Arqueológico Rafael Larco

It is well laid out, in chronological order, and the curators have resisted the temptation to swamp visitors with too many exhibits.

In 1998 it was discovered that a large proportion of the exhibits at the aging **Museo de Oro** (Gold Museum; Av. Alonso de Molina 1100, Surco; daily 11.30am–7pm; charge) were modern replicas, and the museum hasn't properly addressed the problem.

Fuente Mágica

One of Lima's favorite recent attractions is the **Circuito Mágico del Agua** (Wed–Sun 4–10pm; charge) in the Parque de La Reserva. Thirteen spectacular fountains make an incredible display of music, water, and light. Visit at dusk and you'll see them come to life in a kaleidoscope of spotlit colors. There's a tunnel of water which you can walk through (and stay relatively dry) and a fountain in which you can attempt to dodge the timed water spouts (and end up soaking wet). The **Fuente Mágica** Ⓛ spouts 80m (260ft) into the air, reaching its climax with an orchestral crescendo which you can watch from a classical folly nearby. The fountains reportedly cost US$13 million to build, which provoked rumblings of discontent over 'frivolous' spending, but they have proved a hit with *limeños* and visitors alike. The delight on the faces of fellow visitors is almost as wonderful as the fountains themselves. The fountains are located on the corner of Av. Petit Thouars and Jr. Madre de Dios, to the south of the Estadio Nacional.

Modern Lima

Lima's explosive 20th-century growth included a move by the upper and middle classes south to the spacious,

The spectacular fountains of the Circuito Mágico del Agua

Dusk at the Larcomar complex in upscale Miraflores

villa-dotted Miraflores and the new district of San Isidro, laid out as a leafy garden suburb. Peppered with smart boutiques, cafés, and big new shopping centers, they're in easy reach of the surfing beaches and the bohemian barrio of Barranco.

San Isidro

Two main arteries, the Avenida Arequipa and the Paseo de la República expressway, link the city center with the business district of **San Isidro**, where you might take a look at another museum: a very special private collection called the **Enrico Poli** (Lord Cochrane 466; daily, tel: 01-422-2437 for an appointment, call one or two days before; charge). It's well worth a stop to see the School of Cusco paintings and silver and gold work from colonial and pre-Columbian times.

Miraflores

The adjacent area, modern, affluent **Miraflores**, is the main area for restaurants, cafés, nightlife, and shopping *(see tour, pp.78–9)*. It is really a place for the here and now, but there is one museum worth a look, a few blocks from the Enrico Poli museum: the **Museo Amano** (Retiro 160, 11th block of Av. Angamos; tours Mon–Fri at 3, 4, and 5pm; tel: 01-222-5827, call two or three days before for an appointment; free, donations welcome), which displays a beautiful collection of textiles, mostly from the Chancay culture.

Pueblos jóvenes

Many Andean communities suffered greatly during the 20th century, and between the 1960s and 1980s Lima seemed like a promised land to the rural poor. Thousands of migrants gradually filled the city with a huge Andean population. Urban authorities were unable to satisfy the basic needs of these migrants, and thus the *pueblos jóvenes*, or shantytowns, surrounding Lima came into being. They started as squatter settlements of rush-matting huts, but decades of hard work have turned some into pleasant districts. Many others remain desperately poor, lacking electricity, piped water, or paved streets.

TOUR OF MIRAFLORES

Miraflores has broad avenues, leafy side streets, and trendy restaurants all the way to Larcomar, one of the best lookouts over the Pacific Ocean – perfect for a leisurely day to get over jet lag.

Start off at the **Huaca Pucllana** *(see p.80)*, a 23m (75ft) adobe pre-Inca pyramid with six remaining platforms and a ceremonial center dating from AD200 to 700, as well as a site museum. The stark, sandy expanse comes as a surprise in the middle of the vast city, and is the best place in Lima to imagine what the area was like before the Spanish arrived. If you arrive late in the morning, consider lunch at the elegant restaurant of the same name adjacent to the site *(see p.89)*.

Huaca Pucllana, a massive pre-Inca adobe pyramid site

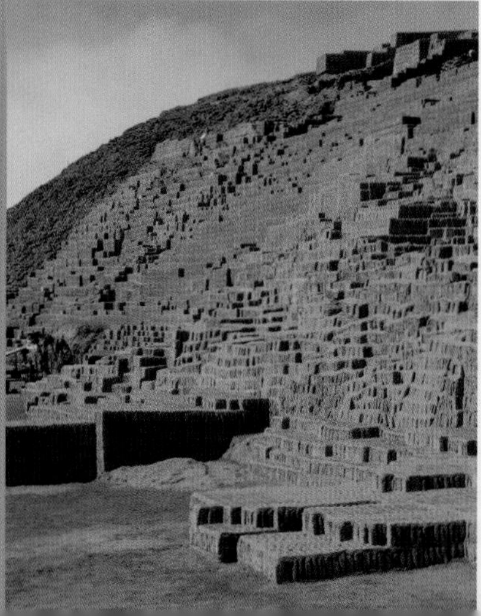

From the pyramid, head down Borgoña and left on Avenida Angamos. Turn right on Avenida Petit Thouars. There, between Vidal and Avenida González Prada, vast markets with hundreds of stalls overflow with traditional handicrafts from all over the country, from jewelry and ceramics to alpaca wool and wood sculpture. Some relaxed haggling is customary, and recommended considering the markets have excellent selections, but higher prices than elsewhere in Peru.

After scouring the markets, head right on General Pershing, which cuts diagonally to Avenida Arequipa and the center of Miraflores, the Óvalo. For lunch, numerous restaurants and cafés surround the adjacent **Parque Central/Parque Kennedy**, including the pedestrian Boulevard San Ramón, more colloquially called the Calle de las Pizzas. There are several more formal establishments. Most famously, Astrid y Gastón *(see p.88)*, one of the foremost examples of the surging Peruvian culinary scene, is on Cantuarias, which meets the park at the front of the

Tips

- Distance: 1.8km (1 mile) from Huaca Pucllana to the museums; 2.9km (2 miles) from Huaca Pucllana to Larcomar
- Time: A half- to full day
- Break for lunch around Parque Kennedy
- Consider timing the end of the tour to enjoy the sunset at Larcomar or Rosa Náutica

1939 neo-Baroque church Iglesia de la Virgen Milagrosa. People-watching par excellence can be done at traditional Café Haití *(see p.89)* on Diagonal and the slightly more upmarket Café Vivaldi a block away (Av. Ricardo Palma 268).

The park itself is green, well-kept, and home to plenty of activity, with live music tempting couples to take part in open-air salsa dancing in the small amphitheatre. Local painters offer their works on Paseo de los Pintores, a road bisecting the park.

Afternoons, both of the most important museums in the area are open. To reach **Museo Enrique Poli** *(see p.77)*, notable for Poli's personal collection of pre-Columbian and Spanish colonial art, take a short taxi ride from Parque Kennedy. The nearby **Museo Amano** *(see pp.77–80)* houses Lima's best collection of pre-Hispanic ceramics and high-quality textiles. It's only open by appointment, however. To reach it from the Poli museum, walk three blocks east on Sucre and head right on Chamberi. The museum is a half-block past Angamos.

Alternatively, from Parque Kennedy, walk down Diagonal (officially Mariscal Oscar Benavides) to visit the cliffside parks overlooking the Pacific Coast beaches. Brave souls can even paraglide in tandem – most gliders take off from Parque Raimondi. A walkway leads down to the Costa Verde beach, where the expensive Rosa Náutica (Espigón 4 Circuito de Playas) offers seafood on a pier directly over the water.

More easily reachable is the Larcomar shopping center that juts over the

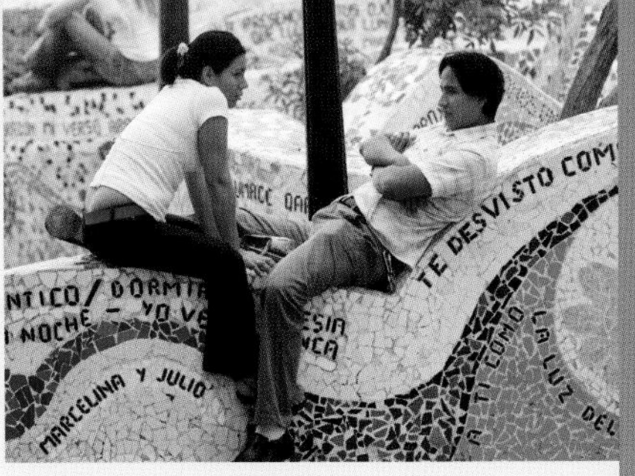

Relaxing in Parque del Amor, one of Miraflores's cliffside parks

cliff at Parque Salazar a few blocks south. It can get noisy, particularly when thronged with crowds on weekends, but has bars in which to unwind and watch the sun set over the ocean. Besides the run-of-the mill stores, it has high-quality crafts for those short on time, along with movie theaters, a gallery, and a theater for entertainment.

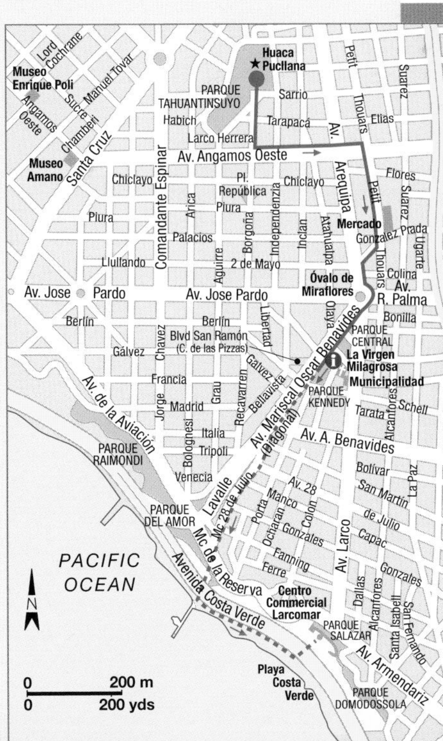

Huaca Pucllana

Close to Avenida Arequipa is the massive pre-Inca adobe pyramid site called the **Huaca Pucllana** Ⓜ (Tue–Sun 9am–5pm; charge; frequent guided tours). When the renovation crews moved in, some neighbors were at first disappointed it wasn't destroyed altogether, as the dust can soil laundry left hanging to dry. But the wide, dry expanse in the middle of modern Lima has been rescued from abandon. Visitors will find evidence of the Lima, Huari, and Inca cultures explained in an on-site museum, illuminated at night and visible from the smart adjacent restaurant of the same name.

At the top end of Avenida Larco is the **Parque Kennedy** Ⓝ, where artists sell paintings at the weekend. From here, a cobbled road leads down a gully to the sweep of beaches known as the **Costa Verde**. *Limeños* flock here in their thousands to bathe on summer Sundays, but the sea is polluted (the resorts to the south of the city are better for swimming).

Callao

Now joined to the capital, the port of **Callao** was originally a settlement apart, some 15km (9 miles) west of the city. Though Callao is poor and run-down, it has several points of interest. The **La Punta** area is one of them. There the Club Universitario restaurant, the Rana Verde (Green Frog; Plaza Gálvez; tel: 01-429-8453), is open to visitors at lunchtime. Permission is required to enter the docks, but from the neighboring wharf launches take passengers for trips round the bay. Nearby is the 18th-century **Fuerte Real Felipe**, the last royalist redoubt in Peru, captured by Bolívar's forces in 1826 after a year-long siege. The fort now contains a military museum – the **Museo Militar** (daily 9am–4pm; charge).

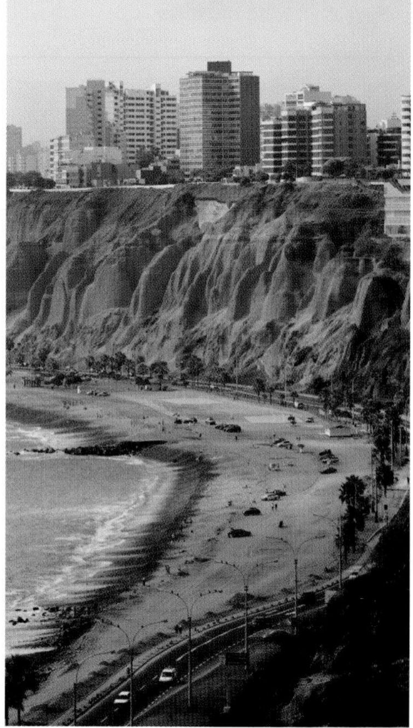

A Barranco beach with a view of Miraflores

Barranco

South of Miraflores, **Barranco** Ⓞ is a beautiful district of colonial and 19th-century housing, much of which has been recently restored. This romantic neighborhood is the home of many bohemians, writers, and artists. It has become the center of the city's nightlife, with a score or more of *peñas* (folk clubs) and bars where music of all kinds is played. The bar La Noche

(Av. Bolognesi 307) is a popular place for a beer, and it's recommended for a night out in Barranco *(see p.91)*. For a more traditional evening, go to Juanito's (Av. Grau 274), an old family-run bar on the plaza and a popular haunt of generations of *barranquiños*.

Opposite the attractive main square is the wooden **Puente de Los Suspiros** or Bridge of Sighs, a traditional meeting place for lovers, set among gardens overlooking the Pacific. Cross the bridge, follow the path by the church, and you'll find several small bars where *anticuchos* (cured and marinated beef-heart kebabs) are served. From the bars right at the end you have a good view of the Costa Verde.

South of Lima

With rapid growth has come investment in infrastructure and new services, particularly along the Pan American highway south of Lima. Beach resorts have seen improvements, as have small towns inland – above all pretty Lunahuaná. Pachacamac is the most accessible large ruin from Lima, while Caral to the north has gained fame as the oldest city of the Americas.

Pachacámac

Some 32km (20 miles) south of Lima, **Pachacámac** ❷ is normally visited on a day trip from the city. Although the more recent Inca culture has overshadowed much of the earlier development of this site, the artisan work left by the pre-Inca civilizations proves that they were more sophisticated in terms of both ceramics and textiles. The ruins of the original settlement occupy a vast site on a low sand hill overlooking

Shoeshine in the sunshine

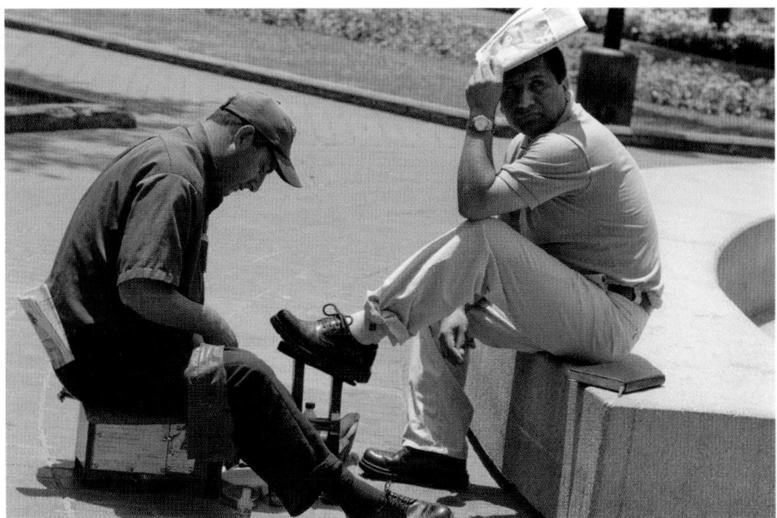

★ VILLA EL SALVADOR

Villa El Salvador is more than just another shantytown formed by aspiring migrants. Tucked behind sand dunes not far from the Inca shrine of Pachacámac, about 30km (20 miles) south of Lima, it was founded in 1971 by an initial wave of 10,000 migrants who had fled from the mountain areas around Huaraz in the wake of the devastating earthquake. Today it is home to around 350,000 people, and is a prototype of self-determination by Peru's marginalized majority.

The settlement's success has brought international recognition. It has been nominated for the Nobel Peace Prize, won Spain's Prince of Asturias award for social achievement, and been designated by the United Nations as a Messenger of Peace. Its key factor is the Andean tradition of community organization centered on the family unit.

Each block of houses, or *manzana*, comprises 24 families; 16 blocks make up a residential group, and 22 of these form a sector. Health centers, communal kitchens, and sports grounds bond the groups together. Education is prioritized, and illiteracy in Villa El Salvador is minimal, unlike in other similar shantytowns. Most of the houses are built of adobe bricks or concrete, and have drainage, mains water, and electricity.

The community is crisscrossed by

Villa El Salvador

roads and dotted generously with shady poplar, eucalyptus, pomegranate, and banana trees. Clever irrigation, worthy of the residents' Inca forebears, has converted hundreds of hectares of sandy desert into arable land, using the community's own treated sewage. Fruit and cotton are cultivated in the fields, as are corn and fodder crops for the thousands of privately and communally owned cattle whose milk and cheese are sold locally.

Villa El Salvador's first martyr was Edilberto Ramos, who was killed resisting police attempts to expel the original settlers. It was his death that forced the government to hand over the land, but the locals' sense of survival was also tested by subversion attempts from Sendero Luminoso guerrillas during the early 1990s.

The town's libraries and written bulletins demonstrate the determination to communicate, and the belief that education genuinely brings self-advancement and change. The industrial park, created in 1987, provides much-needed local employment and exports products to many parts of the world.

Villa El Salvador continues to flourish despite enormous problems of malnutrition and continuing underemployment. It is an oasis that has tapped a spring of hope from beneath the desert floor.

While there are no official tours to Villa El Salvador, it's often possible to arrange a visit through your hotel. If you do go, be respectful (and careful) with your camera.

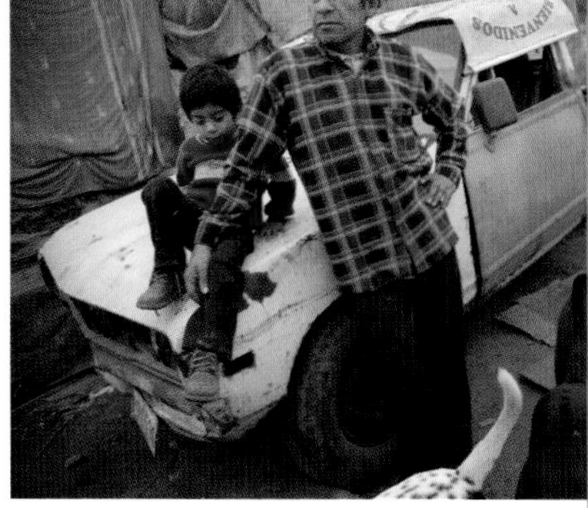

Man and his child with a truck outside their home

Walking through the settlement

the ocean. There is also a reconstruction of the Inca Templo de las Vírgenes (House of the Chosen Women), also known as *mamaconas*.

Pucusana

Another 35km (22 miles) further south lies the coastal resort town of **Pucusana** ❸, very popular with *limeños*. It is also a charming fishing village with panoramic views from its cliffs and good seafood in several of its restaurants. During the Peruvian summer, from January to April, the beaches at Pucusana, La Isla, Las Ninfas, and Naplo can get crowded on weekends. If you want peace and quiet, go on a weekday, when Pucusana reverts to being a fishing town and vacationers are fewer. Also, local fishermen ferry passengers around the island in the bay, and to other beaches, so you may be able to negotiate a ride to one of the more isolated stretches of sand, such as Naplo, first arranging to be picked up later in the day. You may want to take a trip past the **Boquerón del Diablo**, literally the Devil's Big Mouth, which is a tunnel carved in the rock. If you decide to tempt fate by entering the tunnel either on foot or in a boat, do not be surprised if the astonishing din, described as 'the groans of a thousand devils,' makes you wonder if you will ever come out alive.

Lunahuaná

Some 75km (47 miles) down the coast a road from San Vicente de Cañete leads inland to **Lunahuaná** ❹, a pretty village that has begun to attract *limeños* and foreign visitors.

The monumental Caral complex

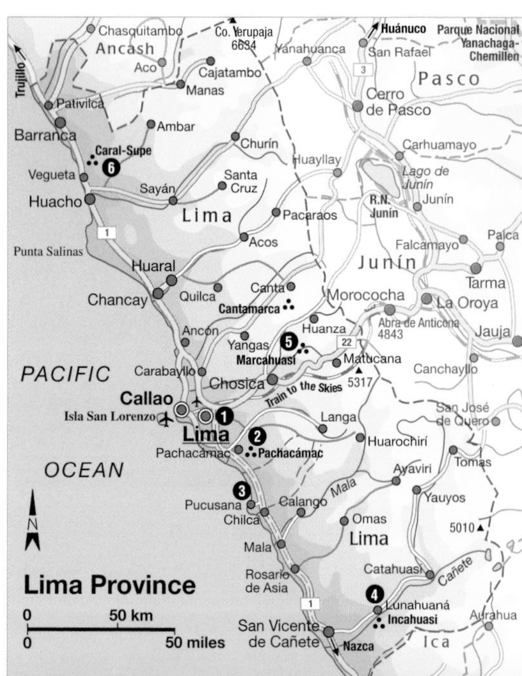

Delightful Pucusana is a favorite getaway for Lima residents

The village is set in a wine-growing valley; there are a couple of wineries that can be visited, and a wine festival – the Fiesta de la Vendimia – in March. The Incahuasi (Incawasi) ruins lie just outside the village, and river-rafting trips on the Río Cañete during the rainy season have become popular.

Marcahuasi

Some 50km (30 miles) east of Lima, near the road to Huanuco, are the amazing, colossal rock formations of **Marcahuasi ❺**. These are a magnet for rock climbers. The copper-rich stones are reported to have protective properties, and are said to shield visitors from negative energy. A large flat plain in the middle of the formations is the scene each year (July 28–30) of a local festival bringing together music and dance groups from all the surrounding villages.

Caral

At the same time as the great civilizations of Mesopotamia, Egypt, India, and China began, the monumental **Caral-Supe ❻** site rose around 2,600BC to become what's now considered the oldest civilization in the Americas. Three thousand people lived on the now arid, isolated 66-hectare (163-acre) site, 185km (115 miles) due north of the capital, that was then irrigated from the Supe River and close to the ocean. Six pyramids amid a series of other buildings, including a notable circular amphitheatre, have been dug up so far. Archeologists have found that the ancient civilization of fishermen and shell collectors built large buildings by carrying the construction material in woven, reed *shicra* sacks, piling them on to build walls like modern-day sandbags used to stop flooding. The sacks were flexible enough to allow the structures to withstand earthquakes.

ACCOMMODATIONS

Lima hotel options are vast and varied, but most travelers will head to the southern districts – Barranco, San Isidro, Miraflores – for proximity to evening venues, or stick to the improving historic center and its convenience for the main sights. International luxury chains, elegant new boutique hotels, and boisterous backpackers' hostels are all present. Many offer free airport pickups.

Accommodations price categories

Prices are for one night's accommodation in a standard double room (unless otherwise specified)

$ = below US$20
$$ = US$20–40
$$$ = US$40–60
$$$$ = US$60–100
$$$$$ = over US$100

Historic Lima

Gran Hotel Bolívar
Jr. de la Unión 958, Plaza San Martín
Tel: 01-619-7171
Opulent like a grand hotel should be, with old-style comfort and fancy original early 20th-century decor, including chandeliers and a stained-glass cupola. Very centrally located, facing Plaza San Martín and in easy walking distance of historic sites, but not a safe area at night. **$$$$**

La Posada del Parque
Parque Hernán Velarde 60
Tel: 01-433 2412
www.incacountry.com
Old mansion in quiet cul-de-sac, with antiques and artworks; big rooms with private bathroom. **$$**

Modern Lima

B&B Tradiciones
Av. Ricardo Palma 955
Tel: 01-445-6742
Email: bbtradiciones@hotmail.com
This small, family-run guesthouse in Miraflores is a real find. The owners speak numerous languages and are an endless

The stunningly located rooftop pool at the Miraflores Park Hotel

source of kindness and information. You'll feel less like a tourist and more like a guest in a Peruvian home. Free WiFi access. **$$$**

Miraflores Park Hotel
Av. Malecón de la Reserva 1035
Tel: 01-610-4000
www.mira-park.com
The most luxurious hotel in Miraflores – part of the Orient Express chain – has a modern style tinged with neo-classic elements, with spectacular ocean views from the 11th-floor outdoor pool and terrace. It has special offers for advance booking. **$$$$$**

One Hostel
Av. Miguel Grau 717
Tel: 01-277-7989
www.operu.com
A family-owned, quiet and friendly place to relax near the ocean in Barranco. Great value with a traditional-style, tiled patio, wireless internet access, and simple, clean rooms. **$$**

The Point
Malecón Junín 300
Tel: 01-628-7952/247-7709
www.thepointhostels.com
A perfect backpackers' place, this fun hostel has dorms and some private rooms with en suite bathrooms. A lively place, right by the ocean and part of a hostel chain that has also expanded to Arequipa, Cusco, Máncora, and Puno. It has space to park motorcycles. **$$**

Hotel San Isidro
Av. Juan Pezet 1765
Tel: 01-264-2019/3363
www.sanisidroinn.com.pe
A quiet, traditional hotel in a large, Spanish mansion-type building in the San Isidro neighborhood. Conservative styling with a solarium, outdoor terrace, and patio with a fountain. WiFi is available in communal areas. **$$$$**

Second Home Peru
Calle Domeyer 366
Tel: 01-247-5522
www.secondhomeperu.com
This gorgeous guesthouse in English Tudor

Comfort and style at Second Home Peru

Revival style, once an artist's mansion, has five modern rooms, some with wide Pacific views. A peaceful haven with a splendid pool overlooking the ocean in Barranco. **$$$$$**

Hostal Señorial
José González 567
Tel: 01-241-2173
www.senorial.com
Colonial-style house in a quiet street in Miraflores three blocks from Larcomar, with garden, patio, a Jacuzzi, and rooftop outdoor terrace. Comfortable rooms with wireless internet, and a friendly atmosphere. **$$$$**

Youth Hostel Malka
Los Lirios 165 (Javier Prado Este)
Tel: 01-442-0162
www.youthhostelperu.com
Excellent location in the middle of Miraflores, open 24 hours. Shared and private rooms a good step above the average youth hostel comfort, with or without bathroom. Malka also has a garden, WiFi access, and a ping-pong table. **$$**

Chic tableware at Astrid y Gastón

RESTAURANTS

Lima is the center of Peru's world-class cuisine, most famously serving up innovative *novoandina* food and *chifa* (Chinese-Peruvian). But as one of South America's biggest cities, with a booming economy and numerous immigrant communities, there's food from around the globe to taste.

Restaurant price categories

Prices are for a three-course menu including juice but no wine or coffee

$ = below US$2
$$ = US$2–5
$$$ = US$6–10
$$$$ = over US$10

Historic Lima

L'Eau Vive
Ucayali 370
Tel: 01-427-5612
Fine provincial dishes prepared and served by nuns. The sky-lit inner courtyard is one of Lima's most pleasant settings for lunch (the nuns – and customers – sing *Ave Maria* daily at 3pm and 9pm). **$$**

Modern Lima

Astrid y Gastón
Calle Cantuarias 175, Miraflores
Tel: 01-242-5387
Still the epitome of Peru's exquisite *novoandino* cuisine culture. International fame doesn't mean that Astrid and Gastón are resting on their laurels: they change the menu every few months. **$$$$**

Bohemia
Santa Cruz 805, Ovalo Gutiérrez, Miraflores
Tel: 01-445-0889/446-5240
A stalwart of non-pretentious food in Miraflores, Bohemia has great salads and sandwiches for quick meals, and international dishes – as well as delightful desserts – if you've got more time. **$$$$**

El Bolivariano
Pasaje Santa Rosa 291, Pueblo Libre
Tel: 01-261-9565
If you want to eat traditional Peruvian fare, this is one of the best places in Lima. Big,

and furnished in a 19th-century hacienda style, it serves fish, seafood, meats, and poultry in large helpings, and a big Sunday brunch buffet. **$$$$**

Brujas de Cachiche
Bolognesi 472, Miraflores
Tel: 01-447-1883
This fashionable and elegant restaurant offers both traditional Peruvian and *chifa* dishes as well as seafood, including lobster. Buffet lunches are available in this Miraflores mansion that also has a reservation-only wine cellar. **$$$$**

Café Haiti
Diagnal 160, Miraflores
Tel: 01-445-0539
Unavoidable as it is enjoyable, this is probably the best people-watching experience in Lima, if not the whole of Peru. A haunt for young and old near Parque Kennedy, it's Lima's classic sidewalk café, with typical dishes and great pisco sours – or, of course, coffee. **$$$**

Cebichería Lobo de Mar Otani
Colón 587, Miraflores
Tel: 01-242 1871
A real institution among Miraflores *cevicherías*, this small place is unknown to most visitors. Located halfway between Parque Kennedy and the Larcomar mall, it also serves numerous seafood dishes. **$$**

Chifa LungFung
Av. República de Panamá 3165, San Isidro
Tel: 01-441-8817
One of the city's best Chinese restaurants, in business since 1966, specializing in traditional Cantonese food but also serving dishes developed by chef Michael Mai Chen. **$$$$**

La Costa Verde
Playa Barranquito, Barranco
Tel: 01-477-0090
One of the best oceanfront views in Lima comes with a price, but also with a mind-boggling buffet so big that La Costa Verde claims it's recognized as the world's most varied in the *Guinness Book of World Records*. **$$$$**

La Gloria
Calle Atahualpa 201–205, Esq. 2 de Mayo, Miraflores
Tel: 01-445-5705
Delicious Mediterranean, especially Italian, food – the quality of its original dishes and pisco sours is commensurate with the price of an elegant restaurant in a mansion rated among the best in Peru. **$$$$**

Huaca Pucllana
Gral. Borgoño Cdra. 8 s/n
Tel: 01-445-4042
This good restaurant overlooks the ancient adobe pyramid of the same name, beautifully floodlit at night. The menu features new twists on classic *criollo* cooking, with a price and crowd that match the special location. The best views are from the outdoor terrace. **$$$$**

Juanito's
Av. Grau 274, Barranco
Tel: 01-9949-6176
On Barranco's square, Juanito's has served Lima's writers, poets, and wannabes with legendary pork sandwiches since the 1930s.

Seafood fans won't be disappointed in Lima

Myriad bottles of wine and spirits adorn the walls of this friendly Bohemian favorite. **$**

Panchita
Av. Dos de Mayo 298, Miraflores
Tel: 01- 242-5957
Star chef Gastón Acurio's latest venture serves generous portions of upmarket *criollo* food. It's the most elegant spot to sample the breadth and depth of Peruvian market food without the risks of curbside dining. Reservations recommended. **$$$**

Punto Azul
Calle San Martin 595, Esq. Alcanfores, Miraflores
Tel: 01-445-8070
Seafood-themed Punto Azul serves up some of Lima's best *ceviche* and is branching out in several places in the city. Lunch only as befits a *cevichería*; go around noon to avoid the wait. Excellent portions for the price. **$$$$**

Segundo Muelle
Av. Conquistadores 490, San Isidro
Tel: 01-222-5097
Cheaper in its four Lima locations than at its foreign restaurants but still oozing modern elegance, this chain specializes in seafood – succulent *sudados* (spicy onion stews) – and a touch of *chifa* and *criolla* food. **$$$$**

El Señorío de Sulco
Malecón Cisneros 1470, Miraflores
Tel: 01-441-0183
Exquisite cuisine in an elegant quayside setting. Most tables have ocean views. Large lunch buffets Thursdays through Sundays and five-course degustation menus provide a sybaritic introduction to Peruvian food. **$$$$**

Las Tejas
Diez Canesco 340, Miraflores
Tel: 01-444-4360
Outdoor tables, waiters who don't mind if you order in English, and generous portions make this a great mid-range place in Miraflores. Excellent Peruvian food include *anticuchos*, *cuy* (guinea pig), and vegetarian platters. Plus, they have live *criollo* music (Thur–Sat). **$$$$**

Valentino
Manuel Bañón 215, San Isidro
Tel: 01-441-6174
Excellent Italian cusine – easily one of Lima's best Italian restaurants – in a relaxed, calm atmosphere, with authentic *antipasti* served at the bar as if you were in Milan. **$$$$**

Dining out at the Larcomar center

NIGHTLIFE

Lima offers some of the best music from all over Peru. Not only are there good groups performing Andean folk music, but there are Afro-Peruvian bands, salsa, *tecnocumbia* dance music, and some jazz bands. The *peñas* which put on Andean folk music get very crowded at the weekends, as do the *salsódromos* where young Peruvians love to dance the night away. Most venues are located in Barranco, Lima's bohemian suburb of cafés, bars, and live music.

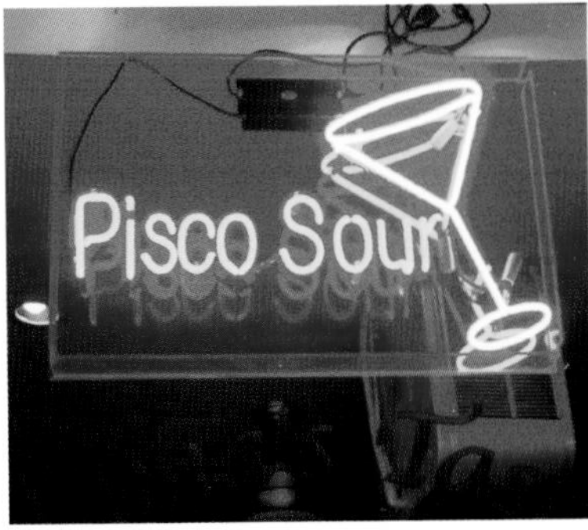

A pisco sour is the perfect accompaniment to a night out in Lima

Live music

Brisas del Titicaca
Jr. Wakulski 168
Tel: 01-332-1901/1881
www.brisasdeltiticaca.com (in Spanish)
One of the best-known *peñas* in Lima, with spectacular folkloric nights Tue–Sat showcasing the dance and food of Puno and other regions. Specialties from the Altiplano served.

La Candelaria
Av. Bolognesi 292, Barranco
Tel: 01-247-1314/2941
In the heart of Barranco, La Candelaria has live music and a folklore floorshow every weekend from 10pm and serves cocktails and snacks.

La Estación de Barranco
Pedro de Osma 112, Barranco
Tel: 01-247-0344/447-5030
www.laestaciondebarranco.com (in Spanish)
A quarter century of bohemian revelry Tue–Sat, shows at 10pm ranging from stand-up comedy to folk and rock from Lima's underground scene.

Manos Morenas
Av. Pedro de Osma 409, Barranco
Tel: 01-467-0421
Set in a beautiful early 20th-century house in the most happening part of Barranco. Folk music from about 10pm until late every day except Sunday and Monday, as well as excellent *criollo* cuisine.

Restaurant Turístico Hatuchay
Mariscal Miller 883, Jesús María
Tel: 01-431-0506/332-8860
The best night out for budget-conscious travelers and anyone else who is willing to get into the informal spirit. Shows on Friday and Saturday at 9pm.

Sachún
Av. del Ejército 657, Miraflores
Tel: 01-441 0123/441 4465
http://sachunperu.com
Tue–Sat traditional Andean and Afro-Peruvian dances.

Bars and nightclubs

La Noche
Av. Bolognesi 307, Barranco
Tel: 01-247-1012
La Noche has the reputation for being the best spot for live music in Lima. It occupies a large multilevel house and does mainly jazz, indie rock, and electronic gigs. The jam sessions on Monday nights are a Lima classic.

Discoteca Gótica
Centro Comercial Larcomar, Miraflores
www.gotica.com.pe (in Spanish)
One of Lima's best nightclubs.

ENTERTAINMENT

Lima has dominated Peru's cultural life for centuries. Correspondingly, it has numerous venues, many founded by immigrant groups and foreign cultural institutes in Miraflores and San Isidro, which also have most of the capital's art galleries. The economic boom has helped the arts scene grow, most visibly in the restored Teatro Municipal.

Paragliding from Lima's clifftop parks is a popular pastime

Cultural centers

Centro Cultural de la Pontificia Universidad Católica del Perú
Av. Camino Real 1075, San Isidro
Tel: 01-616-1616
http://cultural.pucp.edu.pe
Beyond its art gallery and theatre presentations, the university's cultural center is Lima's number one place for independent film; it has even hosted international film festivals.

Instituto Cultural Peruano Norteamericano
Av. Angamos Oeste 160, Miraflores
Tel: 01-706-7000
www.icpna.edu.pe
The US-Peruvian cultural institute has one of the most varied cultural programs in the capital, including temporary art exhibitions, music, and dance.

Theater

Teatro Municipal
Ica 377, Lima
Tel: 01-428-2303/462-7576
Reopened after a fire devasted the neoclassic 1920 venue, in 2011 Lima's main theater started its first season of opera and symphony music in a dozen years.

SPORTS AND ACTIVITIES

It may be gray for much of the year, but rain is rare in Lima and the weather is rarely hot, making it a great place for outdoor sports. The beaches are full of surfers all year long. Surfing schools help newbies get their feet wet; new shops open regularly, with competitions happening as well. The spectacular cliffs above the beaches draw visitors for an airborne paragliding trip.

Paragliding

Perufly
Cell: 9-9308-6795
www.perufly.com
Enzo and Andy leap into the void from the oceanfront Parque del Amor in Miraflores from 11am–6pm. Best to call in advance to check weather conditions. They also have other flying sites all over Peru.

Surfing

Academia de Tabla Edgardo del Pino
Malecón Cisneros 214 Oficina 1102, Miraflores
Tel. 01-445-404
One of many surf schools in Lima. Edgardo del Pino offers eight classes for $100, a dozen for $120, as well as individual classes.

TOURS

Tours to sights all over the country can be arranged through agencies in Lima. Relatively few, however, offer top tours of the capital itself.

Lima Tours
Jr. de la Unión 1040
Tel: 01-619-6900
www.limatours.com.pe
One of the largest tour organizers in Peru, with branches in every major destination. Lima Tours has exclusive rights on visits to some colonial houses in Lima, including evening dinners in 17th-century mansions, and culinary tours.

FESTIVALS AND EVENTS

For all its new cosmopolitan influences, Lima has its share of old religious festivities to celebrate every year. It's also the center of the two-day Independence commemorations.

January

Anniversary of the founding of Lima
Celebration of the anniversary of the founding of Lima by the Spanish conquistador Francisco Pizarro on January 18, 1535.

April

National contest of *Caballos de Paso*
In the third week of April, this exhibition and contest in Mamacona, 30km (18 miles) south of Lima, involves horse breeders from the most important regions of Peru.

July

Independence festivities *(Fiestas Patrias)*
On July 28–9, the celebrations include civilian and military parades – and fireworks on the Plaza de Armas on the evening of the 28th.

August

Santa Rosa de Lima
Every August 30 *limeños* celebrate the patron saint of Lima with a procession in Santa Rosa de Quives, where Santa Rosa lived.

October

El Señor de los Milagros
A massive procession in honor of Lima's patron saint, on October 18.

Parades are an important part of the *Fiestas Patrias*

Arequipa and the south

South of Lima, there lies a long stretch of coastal desert with sandy beaches set against a backdrop of dunes and cactus-covered cliffs. People venture here to see the Nazca lines, watch the wildlife in the Paracas National Park, and sandboard in Ica. Inland, Arequipa has some of the most beautiful colonial architecture in the country.

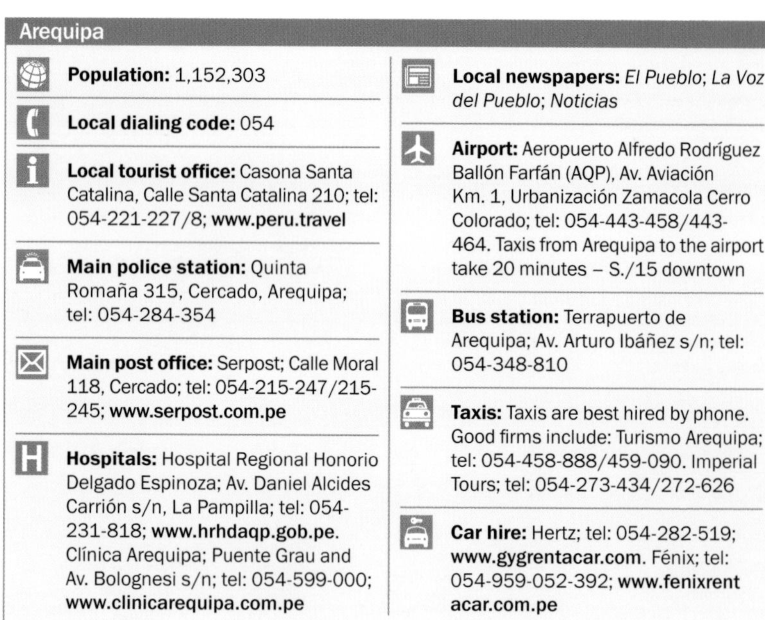

Arequipa

Population: 1,152,303

Local dialing code: 054

Local tourist office: Casona Santa Catalina, Calle Santa Catalina 210; tel: 054-221-227/8; **www.peru.travel**

Main police station: Quinta Romaña 315, Cercado, Arequipa; tel: 054-284-354

Main post office: Serpost; Calle Moral 118, Cercado; tel: 054-215-247/215-245; **www.serpost.com.pe**

Hospitals: Hospital Regional Honorio Delgado Espinoza; Av. Daniel Alcides Carrión s/n, La Pampilla; tel: 054-231-818; **www.hrhdaqp.gob.pe.** Clínica Arequipa; Puente Grau and Av. Bolognesi s/n; tel: 054-599-000; **www.clinicarequipa.com.pe**

Local newspapers: *El Pueblo*; *La Voz del Pueblo*; *Noticias*

Airport: Aeropuerto Alfredo Rodríguez Ballón Farfán (AQP), Av. Aviación Km. 1, Urbanización Zamacola Cerro Colorado; tel: 054-443-458/443-464. Taxis from Arequipa to the airport take 20 minutes – S./15 downtown

Bus station: Terrapuerto de Arequipa; Av. Arturo Ibáñez s/n; tel: 054-348-810

Taxis: Taxis are best hired by phone. Good firms include: Turismo Arequipa; tel: 054-458-888/459-090. Imperial Tours; tel: 054-273-434/272-626

Car hire: Hertz; tel: 054-282-519; **www.gygrentacar.com.** Fénix; tel: 054-959-052-392; **www.fenixrentacar.com.pe**

Peru's southern desert coast, although inhospitable at first glance, is a historical and geographical encyclopedia of a handful of highly developed pre-Inca cultures known for their masterful pottery, fine weaving, medical advances, and for the enormous and mysterious drawings they left on the desert plain at Nazca. When conquistador Francisco Pizarro arrived in 1532 the coast was less desolate. The native people had developed sophisticated irrigation systems, and fields of vegetables and grains were grown in the desert. Today, agricultural settlements still flourish around the oases formed by rivers running down from the Andean slopes, creating fertile valleys in the otherwise bare terrain. The south, in fact, has become one of Peru's agricultural heartlands and, a production of colonial times, spawned its national spirit, immortalized in the *Pisco Sour*. Beyond the Nazca lines, the sea and birdlife of Paracas attract visitors, as do the giant dunes down which they can coast.

Ica region

Ica's vast surroundings hold an amazing variety of agriculture, and it is teeming with wildlife along its gorgeous rocky coast, oases, and Andean foothills behind some of the word's tallest sand dunes. The area's highlights are the pre-Inca geometric lines and animal likenesses drawn into the desert itself near Nazca, so huge that they are best appreciated from the air.

The Ica region has some of the world's largest sand dunes

Chincha Alta

About 200km (125 miles) south of Lima lies the coastal town of Chincha Alta, known for producing wine, fine-quality cotton, and excellent athletes. Grape and cotton flourish here, thanks to an elaborate system of irrigation and the re-routing of the Cochas River. The city's fairly modern coliseum pays tribute to the longstanding sporting tradition here. Chincha has turned out a number of

Visitors head to Ica to take part in adventure sports

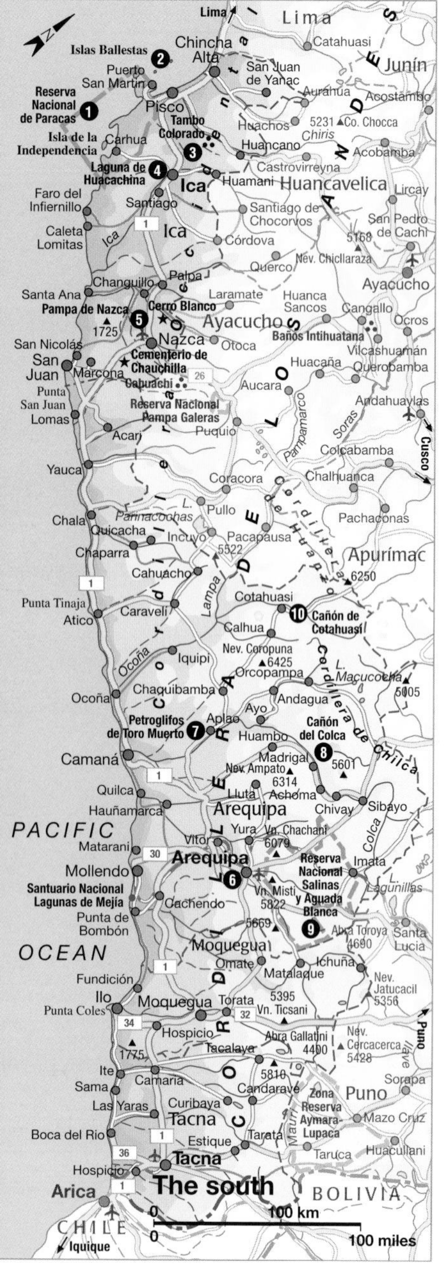

the country's sports stars, principally in the fields of soccer (football) and boxing. The great Peruvian boxer Mauro Mina came from Chincha, as does the distinguished athlete Fernando Acevedo, 'the Harpoon of Chincha', who has held Peru's 100-, 200-, and 400-meter sprint records since the 1970s. This town, and nearby El Carmen, are home to much of Peru's Afro-Peruvian population, descendants of slaves brought here to work on coastal plantations. As such, it is the center for Afro-Peruvian dances and festivals *(see p.121)*.

Close to Chincha is the Casa Hacienda San José (Mon–Sat 9am–3pm; charge), a large country estate built in 1688. The estate was a rich sugar- and cotton-growing operation, and at its height owned 1,000 slaves. A fascinating but sinister feature of the hacienda is the labyrinth of catacombs under the house, once used for storing and punishing slaves. Tunnels are said to lead all the way to the port of Pisco, where slave ships unloaded their human cargo. The hacienda features a gorgeous Baroque chapel and a main building surrounded by colonnaded courtyards and cool terracotta floors, and is set in green gardens full of trees. The earthquake in 2007 forced its hotel to be closed for restorations, though the restaurant is open periodically.

Pisco

Continuing south on the Panamericana you come to **Pisco**, a port city that gave its name to the clear white-grape alcohol that is Peru's national

Pisco is Peru's national drink, and the basis for the famous pisco sour cocktail

drink, and is used to make the famous pisco sour *(see p.98)* cocktail. The invention of pisco is believed to have been a mistake made by the Spaniards when they were introducing grapes and wine production into the dry coastal area of the New World. But it seems that once they tried this smooth yet potent version of brandy they decided it had merit of its own – and many Peruvians (and their southern neighbors) have gone on thinking so ever since.

The city of Pisco (pop. 90,000) joined the bandwagon when revolutionary fever overtook the continent in the early 1800s. In Pisco's **Plaza de Armas** there is a statue of General José de San Martín, the hero of the War of Independence against the Spanish.

Construction of the opulent Baroque **Catedral** started after the 1687 earthquake, and was completed in 1723, only for it to be destroyed again in 2007 when the city was rocked by another devastating earthquake *(see box below)*. Flooding caused additional damage in March 2011.

Post-earthquake, several of the hotels are operating as normal, and Pisco continues to be a good base for visits to the Paracas Peninsula National Reserve *(see p.100)* and the Islas Ballestas *(see p.101)*. The offices of all the city's tour agencies were centered around the Plaza de Armas and were consequently destroyed in the earthquake. Tours are operating, however, and your hotel will be able to put you in touch with guides. Nonetheless, the town is still very much under reconstruction.

Pisco earthquake

On August 15, 2007, southern Peru was struck by one of the strongest earthquakes in the country's history. Measuring 7.8 on the Richter scale, the epicenter was very close to the city of Pisco, and nearby Ica and Chincha also suffered extensive damage. In Pisco, the damage was most severe around the Plaza de Armas, where many beautiful colonial churches and buildings were brought down or damaged beyond repair. Over 500 people were killed and 80 percent of the city's homes were destroyed.

PISCO

Most of southern Peru's grape harvests are used to make the country's signature brandy, pisco. Pisco is the key ingredient in the wildly popular pisco sour, mixed with lime juice, ice, sugar, and egg whites as well as a few drops of bitters, topped off with a sprinkling of cinnamon. Sweet, light, and delightfully refreshing, pisco sour is as ubiquitous a drink in Peru as beer, and makes the perfect companion to Peru's exquisite cuisine.

Almost as popular as soft drinks, pisco sour's potency should not be underestimated. Pisco is a clear brandy, 76° to 96° proof and distilled from grape juice and must. It is similar to Italy's grappa.

According to *iqueños* (people from Ica, probably the greatest pisco experts), the *puro*, or pure, is the best type from which to make pisco sour. It is made from one of three grape varieties (but without blending): *quebranta*, most commonly used; *mollar*; or *negra corriente*. The *quebranta*, in particular, has a complex flavor, yet a soft aroma that won't distract from the taste. In Peru, it's aged in massive clay pots.

Grapes arrived in South America under colonial rule. They were originally used to make wine for the masses, but the Spanish bureaucracy had other

Pisco sour is both popular and potent

ideas, and in the 17th century tried to impose a monopoly over wine for their home country. Resourceful *criollos* (locally born people of Spanish ancestry) made the best of things, and they developed a brandy similar to grappa around Pisco.

A long-running dispute over the origin of pisco has had nationalists in Chile and Peru going head to head for many decades. Peruvians claim that only the brandy made in Pisco and a few valleys around it should be allowed to carry the pisco name. For its part, Chile renamed the town of La Unión in the grape-growing Elqui Valley as Pisco Elqui in 1936, allegedly to head off a move by Peru to have pisco internationally recognized as a denomination of origin specific to that country.

The origin of pisco sour, too, is disputed: it was apparently developed by an English bar owner, Elliott Stubb, in Iquique after 1872, when that city was still part of Peru; it's now part of Chile.

Nationalist sour grapes continue to make the name a sticking point between the two countries, but Chile is one of the biggest buyers of Peruvian pisco. Since 2003, Peru has celebrated a national Pisco Sour Day on the first weekend of February. Bolivia seems to have avoided any such controversy by giving its own very similar brandy a different name: *singani*.

Probably of greater concern to pisco enthusiasts is the fact that upstream pollution from mining is posing a threat to Peru's grape industry in general.

A bartender making Pisco's legendary drink

Pisco is distilled from grapes grown in the region

Paracas

Some 15km (9 miles) down the coast from Pisco lie the bay and peninsula of Paracas which, together with the Islas Ballestas, comprise the **Reserva Nacional de Paracas** ❶. The area, named after the Paracas winds – the blustery sandstorms that sweep the coast – has a wide variety of sea mammals and exotic birds, among them the red and white flamingos that allegedly inspired General San Martín to design the red and white independence flag for the newly liberated country. A monument marks the spot where San Martín, coming via Chile, after liberating it and Argentina, set foot in Peru on September 8, 1820.

The beach here is lovely, although craggy for swimming and there are also jellyfish – some of them enormous and with a very unpleasant sting. There are a number of good jellyfish-free beaches around the isthmus: La Mina, Mendieta, La Catedral, and Atenas, the last very popular for windsurfing.

At the famous **Candelabro** there is a candelabra-shaped drawing, scratched onto the highest point of a cliffside overlooking the bay, which can be seen from the beach, although it is best viewed from a boat. Some scientists link the drawing to the Southern Cross constellation; others say it is actually a stylized drawing of a cactus – a symbol of power from the Chavín culture, which flourished farther north but whose influence has been found at great distances from its seat of power. The magic associated with the cactus is related to both its hallucinogenic powers and its use by high priests in ancient indigenous cultures.

A variety of sealife can be seen at Reserva Nacional de Paracas

Punta Arquillo

Most Islas Ballestas tours also take in **Punta Pejerrey**, which is almost at the northernmost point of the isthmus and the best onshore spot for seeing the Candelabro.

On the exact opposite side of the isthmus is **Punta Arquillo** and the Mirador de Los Lobos, or sea-lion lookout point. This rough and rocky place can be reached by an hour's trek on foot, but take care, because the sun is very strong. It is far better to go by car, and if you are with a tour group transport should be provided. Looking down on the sea-lion refuge you will find yourself almost face to face with a congregation of noisy sea mammals.

On lucky days, a look skyward is rewarded by the sight of a pair of condors soaring above. These majestic birds sweep down on sea-lion carcasses, then use the intense coastal winds to wing themselves up to the high altitudes they normally frequent.

Extensive exploration of the peninsula is best done with the help of a guide, as paths are not clearly marked and it is easy to become lost. In June and August, Paracas is foggy – a reaction to the heat and extremely sparse precipitation combined with the water-laden ocean winds that caress the coast.

Islas Ballestas

A visit to the **Islas Ballestas** ❷ is highly recommended and should be organized in Paracas or Pisco as you usually have to go with a tour group. Ask your hotel to arrange this. Most of the trips start off quite early in the morning. For conservation reasons. visitors are not allowed to land on the island, but boats will take you close enough to get a good view of the wildlife. Here sea lions, seals, penguins, guano-producing birds, and turtles rarely found at this latitude converge before photo-taking tourists. Dozens of bird species thrive here, among them albatrosses, pelicans, boobies, cormorants, and seagulls.

Desert burial grounds

Paracas is the name not only of the area but also of the ancient civilization founded here over 3,000 years ago, a pre-Columbian (and pre-Inca) culture that was uncovered in 1925 when Peruvian archeologist Julio C. Tello

The Tambo Colorado adobe settlement

unearthed hundreds of so-called 'funeral fards' – or burial cocoons. The sand and the extreme dryness of the desert protected the textiles around and inside the funeral bundles. The fine weavings in both cotton and wool, with intricate and detailed embroidered designs and brilliant colors, still astound modern-day textile experts. The **Museo Julio C. Tello** (opening times vary – check with tour agencies; charge), near the necropolis on the isthmus joining the Paracas peninsula to the mainland, has exhibits of artifacts discovered during the archeological dig, and although much of the collection was lost in a robbery, it is well worth a visit.

Heading some 48km (30 miles) inland from Pisco you will come to remains dating from another culture: the Inca **Tambo Colorado** ❸. This adobe settlement, called *colorado* (colored) because of the red paint on many of the walls, is among the best Inca ruins on Peru's southern coast; the complex includes a palace, temple, keep, barracks, and warehouses.

Ica

About 80km (50 miles) south of the ruins is **Ica**, a bustling oasis amid one of the continent's driest deserts, and Peru's richest wine-growing region. Ica was hit quite badly by the El Niño flooding in 1998, but thanks to rapid clean-up and reconstruction work life got back to normal fairly fast. Ica suffered again, however, in the 2007 earthquake *(see p.97)* and many buildings were damaged beyond repair. Rebuilding is underway, but it will be some years before the town returns to normal. Early in 2011, less than 40 percent of reconstruction was completed.

Local vineyards and wineries can be explored all year round, but there is most to see during the grape harvest, from February to early April. The **Bodega El Carmelo** pisco distillery, open to the public, has an ancient grape press made from a tree trunk. Tours (in Spanish) can be taken at the **Vista Alegre** wine and pisco distillery in Ica, where there is a good shop. Peruvian wines are very sweet, although the best ones, Ocucaje and Tacama, and Tabernero, are finer and drier.

Every March, the city goes all out with its annual wine festival, featuring grape-treading beauty queens and a flow of homemade wine. The week-long event, called the Fiesta Internacional de la Vendimia, is punctuated by sports contests, cock fights, music, drinking, religious ceremonies, dancing, and general merrymaking. Although the festival is the best time to experience the area's wine heritage, hotels fill up fast at fiesta time, and the rates rise steeply as well. The same problem arises during the week-long celebration of the town's foundation in mid-June, and at the festival of El Señor de Luren, on Maundy Thursday, when an image of the crucified Christ is paraded around the city in processions that go on through the night.

In 1963, floods seriously damaged much of the town, which explains why most of its colonial buildings have been replaced by more modern structures. Still, the city center retains its square-block layout, based on a chessboard design.

Although Ica was founded by the Spanish in 1536, European attempts to control the city were constantly fraught with problems. Local residents resisted the Spanish presence, and Ica was never granted a coat of arms, owing to its repudiation of attempts to make it a colonial center. Its current citizens remain proud of that rebellious image. Today, just a 20-minute walk or a short bus ride from Ica's center, this region's revolutionary role is traced in a room at the **Museo Regional** (Av. Ayabaca block 8; Mon–Fri 8am–7pm, Sat–Sun 9am–6pm; charge), one of Peru's most interesting small regional museums. Even more interesting are exhibits of mummies (including a fascinating

Ceramic urns used for making pisco

rehydrated mummy hand), ceramics, and skulls from the Paracas, Nazca, and Inca cultures. On display are a number of *quipus*, the mysterious knotted strings believed to have been used to keep calculations, records, and historical notes for the Inca, who had no system of writing. The museum also has an excellent collection of Paracas textiles and feather weavings.

Around Ica

Outside Ica is the Las Dunas luxury resort. Las Dunas was in the forefront of the sandboarding frenzy that recently overtook this dune-covered coastal area. Principally attracting European sports fans, especially from Italy and France, the hotel has sponsored competitive sandboarding events on Cerro Blanco – a massive dune some 14km (8 miles) north of the town of Nazca, purportedly the world's biggest sand dune *(see p.41)*.

Also on the outskirts of Ica is **Laguna de Huacachina** ❹, a green lagoon of sulfur waters that Peruvians claim has medicinal value. Since Angela Perotti, an Italian living in Ica, began extolling the curative properties of the waters in the 1930s, this spot has become a favorite pilgrimage center for people suffering from rheumatism and skin problems. This peaceful setting, just 5km (3 miles) outside Ica, also draws those just looking for sun, solitude, and sandboarding beside the palm trees and dunes that ring the lagoon.

Nazca

Thanks to irrigation, cotton fields and ribbons of orange trees mark the landscape on the voyage farther south, following the line of the coast, to **Nazca**, the home of the mysterious lined drawings that have prompted theories ranging from the fanciful to the scientific.

The Nazca lines are an intriguing part of the landscape

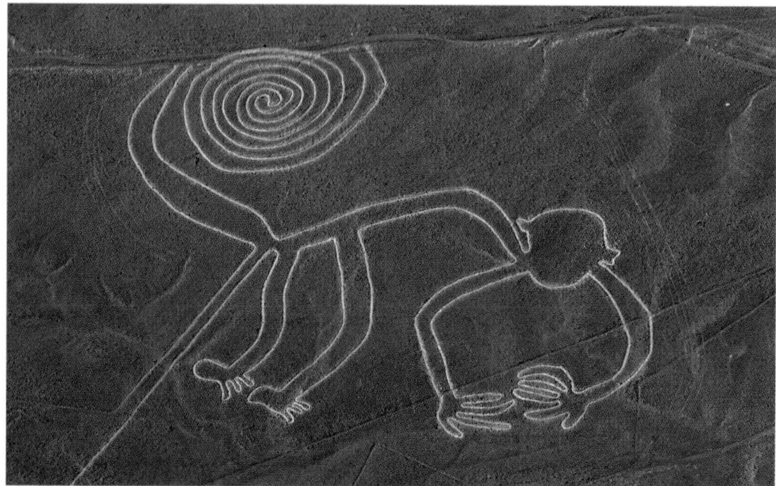

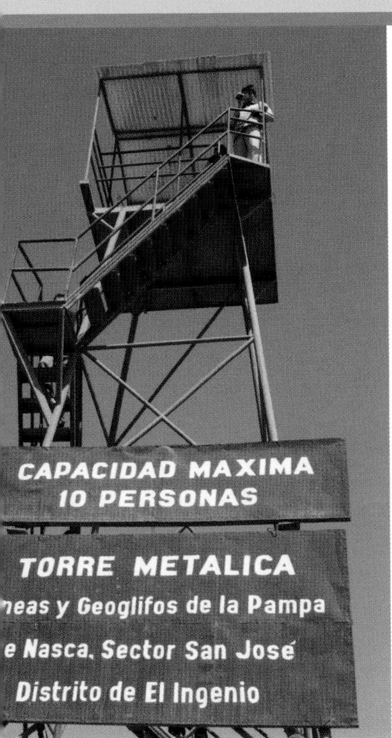

Viewing platforms allow you to see the Nazca lines from above

Sixty years ago Nazca was like any other small Peruvian town with no special claim to fame, except that it was necessary to cross one of the world's driest deserts to reach it from Lima. But it is that desert that has since drawn thousands to this sun-bleached colonial town and made the *pampa*, or plain, north of the city one of the greatest scientific mysteries in the New World.

The **Pampa de Nazca** ❺ (Nazca lines) are a series of drawings of animals, geometrical figures, and birds ranging up to 300m (1,000ft) in length, scratched onto the arid crust of the desert and preserved for about 2,000 years (it is estimated) owing to a complete lack of rain, and winds that cleaned – but did not erase – the surface of the *pampa*. The drawings were made by removing surface stones and piling them beside the lighter soil that was revealed beneath.

It wasn't until 1939 that Paul Kosok, a US anthropologist flying over the dry coast in a small plane, noticed the lines, then believed to be part of a pre-Inca irrigation system. A young German mathematician, Maria Reiche, spent the best part of fifty years studying the lines, and concluded that the sketches corresponded to the constellations, and thought they were part of an astronomical calendar made by the people of the Nazca culture, designed to send messages to the gods. Other theorists say that the lines marked tracks for running competitions; that they were walkways linking ancient sites; that they were enlarged designs used in weaving and textiles; or that they are actually an enormous map of the Tiahuanaco civilization that once flourished near Lake Titicaca. It has even been argued that the *pampa* was part of an extraterrestrial landing strip. But the idea that the drawings were some kind of message to the gods, appealing to them to send rain, is one that has recently been given backing by new scientific research, and in this barren landscape it is certainly a believable theory.

Today, it is illegal to walk or drive on the *pampa*. Some 20km (12 miles) north of Nazca, just off the Panamericana, there is a *mirador* (observation tower), although the only lines that can

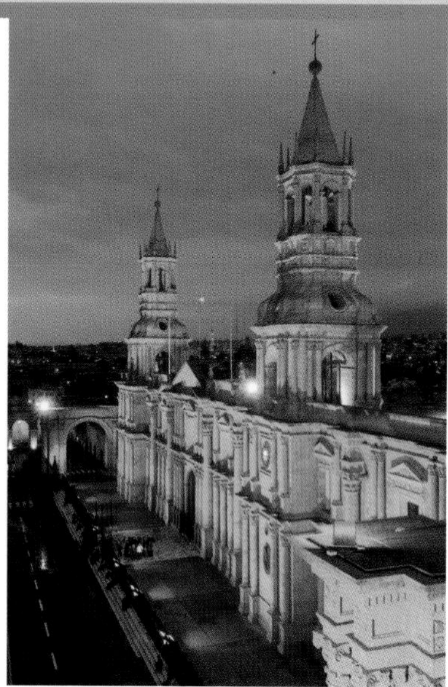

The magnificent facade of the cathedral in the Plaza de Armas

be seen clearly from here are the *arbol* (tree) and the *manos* (hands). The best way to capture the impact of the lines is to fly over them in small propeller planes. Aero Cóndor offers flights from Lima, Ica, and the small airport in Nazca. Lunch and a stop in the archeological museum in downtown Nazca are included in the day-long Lima package, but it is the most expensive of those on offer. The Nazca flight, the cheapest of the options, takes about 30 minutes, and the best time to go is mid-morning. Earlier in the day there is sometimes a haze over the *pampa*; later on, the winds that buffet the plane leave observers more concerned about their stomachs than about the spectacle spread out beneath them.

Unless visitors take the Aero Cóndor flight from Lima, the only way to reach Nazca from the capital is by bus. The trip can take six to seven hours down the Panamericana, but it's quite an impressive trip through the vast coastal desert. If you are approaching Nazca from the south, there are also regular buses from Arequipa and Cusco.

Arequipa

Far from Lima, isolated in a fertile Andean valley tucked between desert and mountains and crowned by turquoise skies, **Arequipa** ❻ was a key stop on the cargo route linking the abundant silver mines of Bolivia to the coast. Built from the white sillar rock that spewed out from **Volcán Misti**, one of a trio of imposing volcanoes looming behind it, this is Peru's second-largest urban area and one of the country's most prosperous. In colonial days it had the largest Spanish population and

Mario Vargas Llosa

The world's most famous *arequipeño* is writer Mario Vargas Llosa. Born in 1936, his works span a 50-year career writing dramatic, comic, and detective novels and short stories, among others, portraying both Peruvian society and those of other countries such as Brazil and the Dominican Republic. While often controversial, his works have been successful with both critics and the public, starting with his first novel, *The Time of the Hero* (originally called *La ciudad y los perros*), published in 1962. He lost to Alberto Fujimori in the 1990 election campaign. In 2010 he won the Nobel Prize for Literature.

the strongest European traditions; cattle and farming industries dating from that period remain principal sources of income for the region. Arequipa has grown into a magnificent city and the intellectual capital of modern Peru.

There are many ways of getting here: frequent flights from Lima, Cusco, Juliaca, and Tacna (on the Chilean border), and buses from Lima, Nazca, Cusco, and Puno. How you travel will depend on your budget, time scale, the degree of comfort you require, and how much of the country you want to see.

Plaza de Armas

Arequipa's **Plaza de Armas** Ⓐ is one of the most beautiful in Peru. Wander around it before you start your tour of the city, taking in the facade of the cathedral and the two-story arcades that grace the other three sides of the plaza, with its palm trees, old gas lamps, and a white stone fountain nestling in an English-style garden. The plaza's thick stone buildings with busily carved portals, their Moorish touches evident, breathe 460 years of history. An earthquake in 2002 caused considerable damage, but most of the main historical buildings have now been restored.

On the southeast corner of the plaza is **La Compañía** Ⓑ (9am–noon, 3–6pm; charge). The frontispiece of this two-story Jesuit church is a compilation of columns, zigzags, spirals, laurel crowns, flowers, birds, and grapevines, into which is embroidered in rock abbreviations of the Good Friday masses, the city's coat of arms, and the

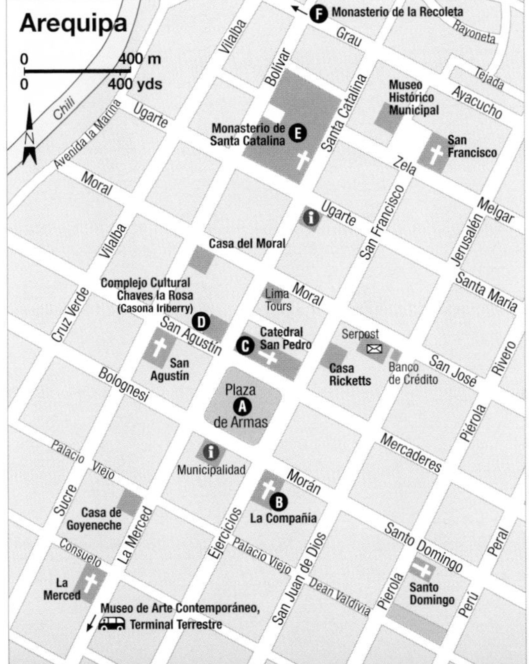

Military parade on the Plaza de Armas

date the massive work was completed (1698). What lies inside La Compañía is equally impressive. The gilded main altar is the apogee of Peruvian Baroque, and the sacristy's ceiling is covered with miniature paintings and carvings of crimson and gold. The view from the steeple is fabulous, especially at sunset when the late light casts a pink, then mauve, glow on the city's gracious white buildings.

Across the square stands the massive twin-towered **Catedral San Pedro** Ⓒ (daily 7.30–11.30am, 4.30–7.30pm; free), rebuilt (at least partially) a dozen times since 1583 after it was damaged by fire, a volcanic eruption, and earthquakes – which La Compañía escaped. The cathedral's ornate exterior is probably a bit misleading because the interior is unusually bare and simple, except for a chandelier and elaborately carved wooden pulpit.

Colonial mansions

Arequipa is full of dignified patrician homes built in the 18th century, which have somehow withstood the tremors that regularly shake the city. The single-story structures are replete with massive carved wooden doors, French windows with ornate grilles, and high-ceilinged rooms clustered around spacious central patios. Opposite the cathedral on Calle San Francisco is **Casa Ricketts** (9am–1pm, 4–6pm). Built as a seminary in 1738, it is now the Banco Continental, but there is a small museum and art gallery inside. In the street round the back of the cathedral the **Casona Iriberry** Ⓓ, built in the late 18th century, houses the **Complejo Cultural Chaves la Rosa**, a cultural center offering a regular program of films, art exhibitions, and concerts. Nearby, on the corner of Moral and Bolívar, is the **Casa del Moral** (9am–5pm;

Casa Ricketts was built in 1738 and once functioned as a seminary

The Casona Iriberry, which houses the Complejo Cultural Chaves la Rosa

charge), which is also a bank – the Banco Sur. The carvings above the door depict pumas with snakes slithering out of their mouths – the same designs found on the ceramics and fabrics of the Nazca people.

Convents and churches

One block north of Casa del Moral is the 16th-century **Monasterio de Santa Catalina** Ⓔ (8am–5pm; charge), the most astonishing site in Arequipa, which was opened to the public in 1970 after almost 400 years as a cloister. Despite the closed doors, little heed was paid to the vows of poverty and silence, at least in the early days. During its heyday this convent's sleeping cells were luxurious, with English carpets, silk curtains, cambric and delicate lace sheets, and tapestry-covered stools. As for silence, French feminist Flora Tristan, visiting the convent in 1832, said that the nuns – daughters of aristocrats – were nearly as good at talking as they were at spending huge sums of money. Each had her own servants, and dined off porcelain plates, with damask tablecloths and silver cutlery.

Entering the cloister you can see the spacious patios, the kitchen and slave quarters, and stone washtubs. The narrow streets, arches, and gardens of the convent bear their original names: Calle Córdoba, its whitewashed walls stark against the pots of bright red geraniums; Plaza Zocodober with a granite fountain; Calle Sevilla with archways and steps. About 30 nuns still live in the convent, which once housed up to 500.

Picanterías

To unwind in Arequipa in the evening, do what the locals do: head to a *picantería* for a cold *arequipeña* beer and some spicy food – stuffed peppers, pressed rabbit, or marinated pork. If you opt for the peppers *(rocoto relleno)*, take care – they are scorchingly hot. Tourist reactions to this spicy dish are a source of amusement for other diners and concern for restaurant owners. The beer will be accompanied by a dish of *cancha* or salty fried corn which, like potato crisps, makes you even thirstier.

Close to Santa Catalina is the **Museo Histórico Municipal** (Mon–Sat 9am–5pm; charge), which is interesting for an overview of the city's history. From here it is only a few yards to the **Iglesia de San Francisco** (daily 9am–noon, 4–5.30pm), the focus of attention every December 8 during the Feast of the Immaculate Conception. A fairytale coach topped with the image of the Virgin Mary surrounded by angels and saints, is paraded through the streets in a colorful procession of pilgrims carrying flowers and candles.

To reach the most interesting museum in the city, the **Monasterio de la Recoleta** **F** (9am–noon, 3–5pm), cross the Río Chili, by either the Puente Grau or the Puente Bolognesi. The monastery has a vast library of 20,000 books, and a collection of religious art. There is also the **Museo de Arte Contemporáneo** (Tacna y Aríca 201; Mon–Fri 10am–4.45pm, Sat–Sun until 1.45pm; charge), showing 20th century art and housed in the old railway manager's house opposite the station.

Museo Santuarios Andinos

Arequipa's 'Juanita,' the Ice Maiden, was found in 1995 near the summit of the Ampato volcano after an eruption melted her icy, centuries-old grave. She was an adolescent chosen for sacrifice by the Inca, and her remains are the main exhibit of the Museo Santuarios Andinos (Museum of Andean Sanctuaries) at the Catholic University of Santa Maria (USCM; La Merced 110; Mon–Sat 9am–6pm, Sun 9am–3pm; charge.)

Looking out over the breathtaking Cañón del Colca

Around Arequipa

There are some interesting trips to be made outside Arequipa. One is to **Sabandía**, about 7km (4 miles) from the city, near the pleasant suburb of Paucarpata. Here stands a flour mill, made of volcanic rock, which was built in the 17th century and restored, stone by stone, in 1973 by architect Luis Felipe Calle. The mill, which is open to the public, is set in some of the area's most beautiful countryside.

Two hours from the city, on the road to Lima, are the **Petroglifos de Toro Muerto** **7** (Toro Muerto petroglyphs), hundreds of volcanic rocks believed to have been engraved

Andean condor

One of the world's deepest canyons is the best place to view the biggest land bird by wingspan, the Andean condor *(Vultur gryphus)*, in the wild. Just a little shorter normally than its North American cousin, the California condor *(Gymnogyps californianus)*, it is nevertheless heavier at 11 to 15kg (24 to 33lb) for males, and its wings measure 2.74 to 3.1m (8.99 to 10.2ft). Being on the coat of arms of many South American nations hasn't protected it from indiscriminate hunting, although as a carrion eater it is harmless.

and painted more than 1,000 years ago by Wari (Huari) people living in the region. The petroglyphs show realistic depictions of llamas, condors, pumas, guanacos, dancers, and warriors.

Canón del Colca

Four hours away from Arequipa, and drawing almost as much tourist attention these days, is the **Cañón del Colca** ❽, one of the world's deepest gorges, cut 3,182m (10,607ft) into the earth's crust, and now one of the most popular tourist attractions in southeastern Peru *(see p.26)*. Far deeper than the Grand Canyon, the Colca is shadowed by snow-topped peaks – many of them volcanoes – and sliced by the silvery Río Colca. The base of this canyon is cold and windy, and draws daredevil kayaking enthusiasts and researchers. Above, at the brink of the chasm, Quechua-speaking farmers irrigate narrow terraces of rich volcanic earth in much the same way as their ancestors did centuries ago.

The most popular section of the canyon is the **Cruz del Cóndor** (Condor Cross), where visitors scan

A town in the Colca Valley

the skies for a glimpse of the majestic birds soaring above in pairs. They use the thermal air currents produced in the early morning or the early evening, and few who visit at those times in the hope of spotting them are disappointed.

The Cruz del Cóndor is included in a variety of one- and two-day trips, which can be organized in Arequipa. En route, many of the tours take in the **Reserva Nacional Salinas y Aguada Blanca** ❾ (at 3,900m/12,800ft you will notice how thin the air is), where groups of shy vicuñas can often be seen.

Even more remote than Colca, the **Cañón de Cotahuasi** ❿ has only recently been exposed to tourism. Now believed by many to exceed Colca in depth, making it the world's deepest canyon, it is a pristine area of great natural beauty ideal for adventurers and nature lovers *(see p.26)*. Accommodations can be found in the small town of Cotahuasi.

Southernmost Peru

Off the beaten track, except for those traveling to and from Chile, this desert corner of the country has beaches popular with *arequipeños* and a popular birding sanctuary near Mollendo. If you are not in a hurry, the dusty old rail link from Tacna to Arica in Chile is an interesting, albeit somewhat rickety, alternative to the standard border crossing via bus.

Following the Panamericana

The Panamericana continues down the coast from Nazca to Camaná (about 220km/135 miles), which has some good beaches and is a popular

The entrance to the railway terminal in Tacna

Local musicians taking a break from their endeavors

summer resort for Arequipa residents. Buses from the town center head to La Punta (about 5km/3 miles) and the fine, although undeveloped, beach area. Camaná was, in colonial times, the unloading point for cargo headed to Arequipa and then on to the silver mines in Potosí in Bolivia.

From Camaná the highway goes inland, and after about 130km (80 miles) it divides, going farther inland to Arequipa, toward Moquegua, Tacna, and the Chilean border, or back to the coast to **Mollendo**. Mollendo and its sister resort, Mejía, 15km (10 miles) farther south, are popular with upper-class *arequipeños*. Mollendo was a principal port before being replaced by **Matarani**, 14km (8 miles) to the north. Now its attractions are three sandy beaches and its closeness to the **Santuario Nacional Lagunas de Mejía**, a nature reserve that is home to a variety of coastal birds and a stopping place for many migratory species. You can get a bus from the town to the reserve and to the agricultural lands of the Río Tambo Valley, where an ambitious irrigation project means that rice and sugar can be grown. Mejía used to be a fishing village, and a few old fishermen's cottages still remain. There are no hotels, but *arequipeños* spend part of the summer in their holiday homes here.

Moquegua

The road from the valley rejoins the Panamericana, which continues south to Moquegua, a parched and dusty town on the banks of the Río Moquegua, at the spot where the Peruvian coastal desert reaches its driest point. Buildings here – even the cathedral – are roofed with sugar cane stalks daubed with mud. Its streets are cobblestones, and its residents' topiary skills are evident on the Plaza de Armas, where most of the bushes are trimmed into the form of llamas. Wine and avocados are shipped out of this city, and both are worth sampling.

Tacna

Peru's southernmost city is **Tacna**, separated from Chile by a still-mined stretch of desert that marks the border between the two nations. Unlike other border cities on the continent, Tacna is fairly well developed and has some of Peru's best schools and medical facilities – perhaps owing to its importance as a military base. The downtown area has been refurbished, and its main boulevard is cut by an attractive flower- and tree-studded promenade. A pedestrian mall passes by the shops, and here ice cream, or cold drinks such as *horchata*, the popular icy cinnamon-laced soy-milk beverage, help offset the intense heat during the Tacna summer. The tree-shaded **Plaza de Armas** is a welcome relief from the unrelenting sun. The centerpiece of the plaza is the huge arch that was built as a monument to the heroes of the War of the Pacific.

The **Museo Ferroviario** (Railway Museum; Mon–Fri 9am–5.30pm; charge) at the railway station has train engines from the turn of the 20th century when the British began constructing the complicated and, in some cases, rather reckless railway system in Peru.

War of the Pacific

Chile conquered mineral-rich provinces of Bolivia and Peru in the 1879–83 War of the Pacific, one of the few major wars in South American history. Having won control over the sea-lanes, Chile took hold of the coastline by landing surprise troops and winning pitched battles from Arica to Lima. Lacking an exit strategy, guerrilla warfare tied down Chilean troops until 1883. Chile returned Tacna to Peru after a referendum; Bolivia continues to demand restoration of sovereign access to the coast.

Detail of Tacna's Plaza de Armas

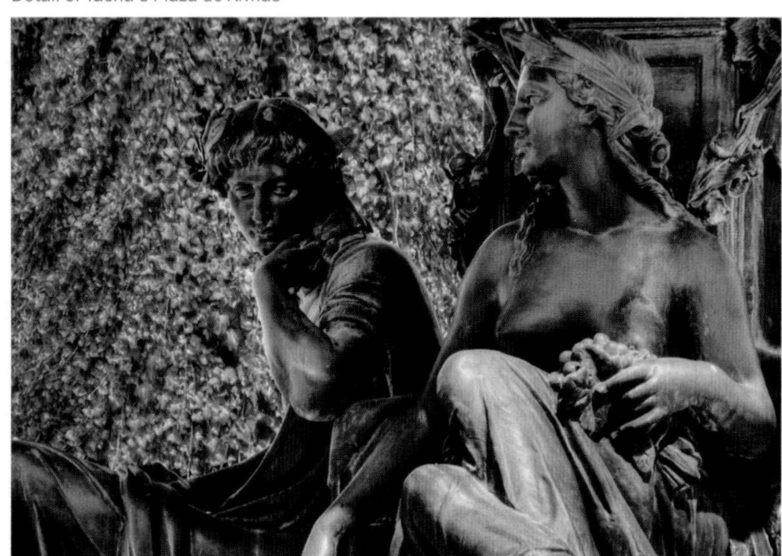

ACCOMMODATIONS

Colonial Arequipa, countryside haciendas and holiday resorts along the coast, are the main draws to this part of Peru. Pisco and Ica suffered gravely from the 2007 earthquake, and reconstruction has been slow. Paracas or Arequipa are better options, and they are reasonable distances from many of the most attractive sites.

Accommodations price categories

Prices are for one night's accommodation in a standard double room (unless otherwise specified)

$ = below US$20
$$ = US$20–40
$$$ = US$40–60
$$$$ = US$60–100
$$$$$ = over US$100

Arequipa

Casablanca Hostal
Puente Bolognesi 104
Tel: 054-221-327
www.casablancahostal.com
This is a pleasant hotel in a recently renovated colonial-style house. There are comfortable, antique-style rooms, hot water, and internet facilities. As the hostel is located close to the town center it is also close to many tourist attractions and restaurants. **$$$**

La Casa de Melgar
Calle Melgar 108
Tel: 054-222-459
www.lacasademelgar.com
A lovely hotel situated within the walls of the bishop of Arequipa's 18th-century home. There are several interior courtyards and quiet gardens, and the rooms are decorated with antiques. It isn't luxurious, but it is probably the most beautiful place to stay in Arequipa. **$$$$**

Hostal La Casa de Mi Abuela
Jerusalén 606
Tel: 054-241-206
www.lacasademiabuela.com
Consistently receives rave reviews for its friendly and efficient service. There's a large complex of bungalow-style rooms in a garden setting, a pool, and a colonial restaurant. Pisco sours are offered upon arrival. **$$$**

Hotel El Balcón
García Calderón 202, Vallecito
Tel: 054-286-998/9
Comfortable colonial-style hotel, located in a quiet area just outside the center of town. Most attractions can be easily reached by taxi. Friendly and helpful staff, pleasant and good value. **$$$**

Hotel Libertador Arequipa
Plaza Bolívar s/n, Selva Alegre
Tel: 054-215 110
Reservations in Lima: Tel: 01-518 6550
www.libertador.com.pe
The most traditional hotel in Arequipa, just out of town by Parque Selva Alegre, offering great breakfast out on the terrace. Swimming pool, soccer, jacuzzi, sauna, gym, and free internet. **$$$$$**

The poolside at the Libertador in Arequipa

Colca Lodge

Lula's B&B
Cerro San Jacinto, Cayma
Tel: 054-272-517/934-2660
www.bbaqpe.com
If you've had enough of hotels and you'd like somewhere that feels more like home, the lovely B&B run by multilingual Juana Lourdes Díaz Oviedo de Seelhofer, otherwise known as Lula, not far from the center, is a great option. As well as comfortable lodgings, Lula offers meals and Spanish lessons and is brimming with information about her city. **$$**

Canón del Colca

Colca Lodge
Fundo Puye-Yanque-Caylloma
Tel: 054-531-191
www.colca-lodge.com
This delightful country lodge is built of stone, mud-bricks and thatch, and is right in the heart of the Colca Valley, on the banks of the Colca River and next to wonderful hot springs. Stay here a night and you'll want to stay a week. **$$$$$**

Nazca

Hotel Alegría
Calle Lima 166
Tel: 056-522-497
www.hotelalegria.net
Forty-eight rooms are on offer here with a private bathroom, some with air conditioning. The hotel also features a quiet garden and swimming pool. This is one of the most popular hotels in Nazca, especially with backpackers. There is also a travel agency available to help you make arrangements to fly over the Nazca lines. **$$**

Hotel Majoro
Panamericana Sur, km 452, Vista Alegre
Tel: 056-522-481/490
www.hotelmajoro.com
A historical hacienda with a garden close to overflights to the Nazca lines. There are pools on site, a tennis court, and it offers friendly service and hot showers. Promotions available for all-inclusive tourist packages. **$$$$**

Paracas

El Carmelo
Crta Panamericana Sur, km 301.2
Tel: 056-232-191/232-553
Reservations in Lima: tel: 01-998-105-140
www.elcarmelohotelhacienda.com
Lovely hacienda-style country hotel built around a sunny, colorful garden and a swimming pool. The restaurant-café, in the outside patio, is a great place to dine on sunny days. Close to Ica on the Panamericana Sur. **$$$**

Hotel El Mirador
Crta Paracas, km 20
Tel: 056-545-086
Reservations in Lima: tel: 01-241-6803
www.elmiradorhotel.com
Set on the hill just above Paracas, this roomy old hotel is refreshingly breezy and cool, with a large beautiful garden and a pool at the rear. Some rooms offer a view of the sea. **$$$$**

RESTAURANTS

Pisco sours and *ceviche* are a staple in southern Peru, but there's more. Arequipa has maintained a reputation for style and affluence; there are a number of good restaurants around the Plaza de Armas, and cafés can be found in the first block of San Francisco. Paracas, Pisco, and Ica offer great seafood.

Restaurant price categories

Prices are for a three-course menu, including juice, but no wine or coffee

$ = below US$2
$$ = US$2–5
$$$ = US$6–10
$$$$ = over US$10

Arequipa

Café Casa Verde
Jerusalén 406
Tel: 054-226-376
Visit this pretty, quiet café not just for its good breakfasts, light meals, and snacks, but because the cost of your meal goes toward supporting a home for abandoned children. **$$**

Lakshmivan
Jerusalén 408
Tel: 054-228-768
Need a break from all the meat and traditional fare? Then this is the best spot to head to in Arequipa. The vegetarian menu here has lots of tofu, good salads, and delicious desserts. **$$$**

Ceviche mixto contains shellfish

Ras el Hanout y los 40 Sabores
San Francisco 227
Tel: 054-212 424
www.raselhanout40.com
This lovely restaurant with a peaceful inner courtyard plies you with the heady flavors of Moroccan and Mediterranean cooking. On a hot afternoon, a sweet mint tea in the shade is a delight. **$$$**

Sol de Mayo
Jerusalén 207
Tel: 054-254-148
www.restaurantsoldemayo.com
Good lunchtime menu of Peruvian specialties such as *rocoto relleno* (stuffed hot peppers), and *ocopa* (potatoes in a spicy sauce with cheese). *Tamales* (corn-based dough wrapped in a banana leaf) available on Sundays. **$$$$**

Wayrana
Calle Santa Catalina 210
Tel: 054-285-641
Funky interior design and a breezy outdoor courtyard give this place a cool edge. *Cuy* is the specialty here, and if you don't fancy eating your guinea pig whole, then try the fillet of *cuy* in asparagus, mushroom, and malt beer sauce. Yum! **$$$$**

Ica

Bodega El Catador
Fundo Tres Esquinas 102,
Urb. Subtanjalla
Tel: 056-403-295
A short taxi ride from town, Bodega El

Catador offers winery tours and wine and pisco tasting sessions. It also organizes wine pressing by foot in February and March. The restaurant features good Peruvian fare, and occasionally dancing. **$$**

Nazca

El Huarango
Jr. Arica 602
Tel: 056-522-141
This outlet is amongst the best restaurants in Nazca. The portions served are large, the meals are tasty, and, all in all, it's great value. Set over two floors, and there's a lovely rooftop garden, where you can enjoy gorgeous views. **$$$**

La Taberna
Jr. Lima 321
Tel: 056-521-411/523-803
Popular with gringos, La Taberna offers a diverse international menu, with vegetarian options, and there's often live music. Check out the graffiti left by other travelers. **$$$**

Paracas

Brisa Marina
Boulevard Turístico, El Chaco
Tel: 054-545-125
A seaside spot that's perfect after an Islas Ballestas cruise for a coffee, or a *ceviche* in the warmer months. Great seafood menu. **$$**

NIGHTLIFE AND ENTERTAINMENT

Arequipa has good nightlife during the weekend, and the old town hosts plenty of bars, discos, and restaurants. Check out Calle San Francisco, Santa Catalina, and Pasaje Catedral, behind the cathedral, for plenty more options. Southern nightlife has suffered from the 2007 earthquake, but Paracas enjoys the beach fun.

Arequipa

Déjà vu
San Francisco 319-B
Tel: 054-221-904
www.dejavu.com.pe

The happy hour, English-language movies shown on a big screen, and Latin music, make this place a favorite destination for foreigners.

Forum
San Francisco 317
Tel: 054-204-294
www.casonaforum.com
The liveliest club in town, Forum is a huge place with restaurant, bar, disco, and a concert hall. There are live bands Thursday through Saturday, and its repertoire of Latin music is popular among locals.

Mono Blanco
Ugarte 300, 2nd floor
Hosted in a light-blue colonial house, this French-owned bar is by far the best hang-out in town. Friendly staff, fussball tourna-ments, and good cocktails.

Try the local brew when you're out in Arequipa

SPORTS AND ACTIVITIES

Southern Peru has plenty to offer the adventurous, from kite surfing in Paracas to paragliding – a thrilling way to take in the Nazca lines or Paracas coastline. If you have no previous experience, you can join a trained instructor in a tandem flight. For flights over the Nazca lines in a light aircraft, reservations can be made with companies at Nazca airport, in town, or in Lima.

Kitesurfing

Perukite
Santo Domingo, L 36, Paracas
Tel: 099-456-7802/099-816-5464
www.perukite.com
Perukite can give you instructions on how to bring your own kit over to Peru, or rent it out to you. They also offer courses for beginners.

Nazca lines

Aero Cóndor
Panamericana Sur, km 447,
Hotel Nido del Cóndor, Nazca
Tel: 056-522-402
After office hours tel: 01-998-073-852
www.aerocondor.com.pe
Aero Cóndor also organizes tours from Lima (Av. Aramburu 858, Surquillo; tel: 01-421-3105/7014).

Aeroica
In Nazca airport, or at Hotel La Maison Suisse, Panamericana Sur, km 447, Nazca
Tel: 056-522-434
Booking in Lima: Trips and Travel, Diez Canseco 434 Of. 102, Miraflores
Tel: 01-445-0859
www.aeroica.net
Offers various trips to the Nazca lines, in light aircraft, from Lima, Pracas and Ica.

Aero Paracas
Av. Santa Fé 274, Lima
Tel: 01-265-8073/8173
www.aeroparacas.com
Conducts flights over the Nazca and Palpa lines from Maria Reiche airport.

Paragliding

Perufly
Various flying sites
Tel: 099-308-6795
www.perufly.com
Set up by a paragliding national champion, Perufly operates out of Lima, but has several flying sites. Call first to check the schedule.

Kitesurfing is one of the more exhilarating activities on offer

The incredible Nazca lines are best viewed from above

TOURS

You can join tours of Arequipa's beautiful colonial architecture, as well as day tours around the city, which include hiking around Colca Canyon, climbing the El Misti Volcano, and visiting the Cotahuasi Canyon. The following companies offer traditional and adventure tours around the region.

Colca Trek
Jerusalén 401B
Tel: 054-206-217
www.colcatrek.com.pe
Organizes treks to the Colca Canyon with practiced guides. These can include rafting, mountain biking, or climbing.

Condor Travel
Santa Catalina 210
Tel: 054-237-821
www.condortravel.com
Various tours of the region, including walking tours of Arequipa city, the countryside, and three- or four-night treks to Colca Canyon.

Giardino Tours
Jerusalén 604A
Tel: 054-200-100/231-010
www.giardinotours.com
Tours offered include a local cookery course. There are three-hour to 14-day tours (which include Lima and other areas).

Lima Tours
Mercaderes 193, Of. D-4
Tel: 054-225-759
www.limatours.com.pe
This company offers a four-day, three-night tour of Arequipa city which also includes an overland trip to Colca Valley.

Maravillas Peruanas Travel
Santa Catalina 102
Tel: 054-227-297
Email: maravillasperu@hotmail.com
Offers three- or four-day tours of Arequipa city and Colca Canyon.

Sky Viajes y Turismo
Calle Zela 301A
Tel: 054-205-124
www.skyperu.com
Operates gastro-tours and cultural tours, which can be organized in Arequipa, as well as half-day, or longer, tours to Colca Canyon.

FESTIVALS AND EVENTS

Many festivals are religious, and dates vary every year. Check with the Ministry of Tourism for more information: www.mincetur.gob.pe

February–March

Festival de Verano Negro

El Carmen, Chincha province

Afro-Peruvian dance contest, handicraft markets, and plenty of local fare and wines in this town just north of Pisco. To coincide with Carnival.

Carnival

San José, Camaná province

Masked horsemen, known as *guachanacos*, ride around the city three days before Carnival to invite everyone to celebrate.

Fiesta de la Vendimia

The grape harvest is celebrated with parades, dances, and revelry in the first half of March.

March–April

Holy Week

Festivities start on Palm Sunday and end on Easter Sunday with the parade that symbolizes the resurrection of Christ; flowers and arches decorate all the streets.

May

Cotahuasi anniversary

The largest fancy-dress festival around Arequipa is celebrated on May 4. There are bullfights and dance contests too.

August

Arequipa Day

Events take place all month and culminate on August 15 (the city's most happening event). Festivities include folkloric dances and handicraft markets, and end with fireworks.

October

El Señor de Luren

Thousands of pilgrims pay homage to the town patron in the Ica region, with the main procession on October 17, and various events between October 7–20.

Arequipa holds more than its fair share of festivals

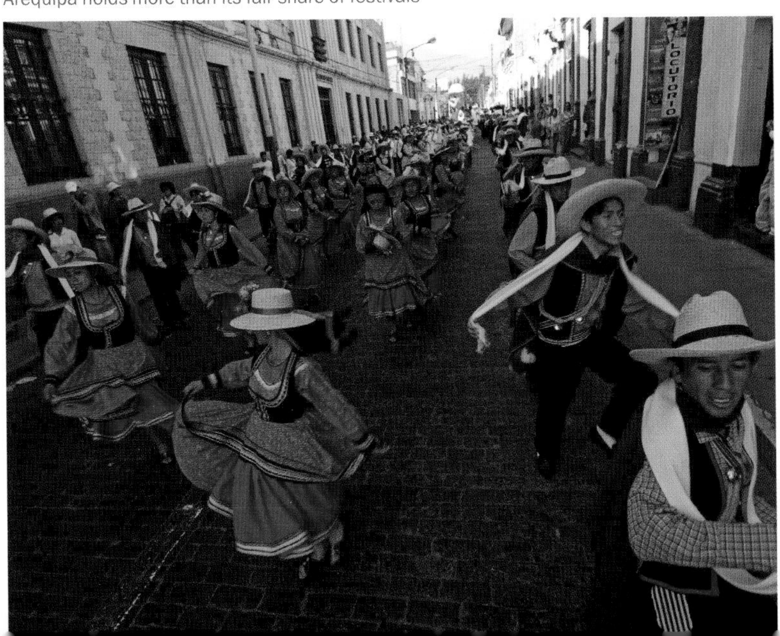

Cusco and the Sacred Valley

Cusco, the ancient capital of the Inca Empire, is a jewel of Inca and colonial architecture standing 3,330m (10,900ft) above sea level. It is also the starting point for expeditions to the magnificent fortresses of the Sacred Valley, the heartland of the last Inca, and to the breathtaking ruins of Machu Picchu.

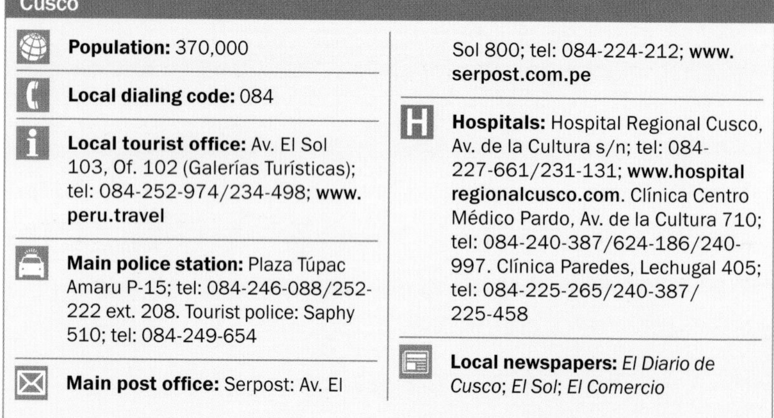

Cusco

Population: 370,000

Local dialing code: 084

Local tourist office: Av. El Sol 103, Of. 102 (Galerías Turísticas); tel: 084-252-974/234-498; **www.peru.travel**

Main police station: Plaza Túpac Amaru P-15; tel: 084-246-088/252-222 ext. 208. Tourist police: Saphy 510; tel: 084-249-654

Main post office: Serpost: Av. El Sol 800; tel: 084-224-212; **www.serpost.com.pe**

Hospitals: Hospital Regional Cusco, Av. de la Cultura s/n; tel: 084-227-661/231-131; **www.hospitalregionalcusco.com**. Clínica Centro Médico Pardo, Av. de la Cultura 710; tel: 084-240-387/624-186/240-997. Clínica Paredes, Lechugal 405; tel: 084-225-265/240-387/225-458

Local newspapers: *El Diario de Cusco*; *El Sol*; *El Comercio*

A 40-minute flight from Lima takes travelers straight into the heart of the Andes, to the former capital of the Inca Empire, **Cusco** ❶. Apart from its own attractions, Cusco serves as a base to visit the fortresses of Sacsayhuamán and Ollantaytambo in the Inca heartland of the Sacred Valley, and the most famous site on the continent, Machu Picchu. Cusco is also a starting point for expeditions into the Amazon jungle *(see p.154)*.

The Inca Empire came into being during the reign of Inca Pachacutec Yupanqui, who began a great expansion, imposing Quechua as the common language, conquering other native nations, and creating a state religion. It was Pachacutec who transformed Cusco from a city of clay and straw into a thriving metropolis with grand stone buildings in the second half of the 15th century. When Francisco Pizarro and his soldiers arrived in 1533, they found a glittering capital able to rival many European cities.

The Spaniards were impressed by its order and magnificence. In addition to palaces and gold-filled temples, they found sophisticated water systems, paved streets, indestructible foundations, and advanced medical techniques. But the cultural achievements of the Inca were a minor distraction in comparison with the lure of their treasures: conquistadors greedily pushed their way into ancient temples and seized their gold and silver artworks, which they promptly melted into bullion. The Inca nobility, initially respected by the conquerors, lost their social status in the wake of several indigenous rebellions, and the Sacred Valley passed into the hands of Spanish owners.

Cusco retained a level of importance for the first few decades after the Spanish conquest, but by 1535 its wealth had been stripped and the capital of this new Spanish colony had been set up in Lima. After centuries of provincial obscurity, the rediscovery of Machu Picchu in 1911 and the subsequent construction of a road up to the mountaintop citadel in 1948 transformed Cusco into the jumping-off point for visits to one of South America's best-known tourist attractions.

Backpackers exploring Plaza de Armas in the early hours

Local children relax beside archeological ruins from the Inca era

Cusco

Before you start to explore this intriguing city and its environs, remember that it is more than 3,330m (10,900ft) above sea level, so take it easy until you get acclimatized. Also, don't forget to buy a Cusco Visitor Ticket *(see p.154)*, which is essential for visits to historic sites in Cusco and the Sacred Valley.

The most startling and curious characteristic of Cusco at first glance is its architecture. Huge walls of intricately laid stone pay testimony to the civilization that 500 years ago controlled much of this continent. The Spaniards' attempts to eradicate every trace of the 'pagan' Inca civilization

Cusco transport

Airport: Aeropuerto Internacional Alejandro Velasco (CUZ); tel: 084-222-611; **www.corpac.gob.pe**

Bus station: Terminal Terrestre, Av. Vía de Evitamiento 429, Ovalo de Pachacutec; tel: 084-224-471. Public bus: buses and VW vans are common but pickpockets are a problem, particularly at peak times. They charge S./0.6

Taxis: Taxis to the center and Urubamba cost S./5. Train station: Peru Rail; tel: 084-238-722 ext 318, 319 or 320; **www.perurail.com.** To Puno: Estación del Sur/Wanchaq; Av. Pachacuteq s/n. To Machu Picchu: Poroy, west of Cusco. Taxis are plentiful and charge an average S./2.50 – S./3 in the center. Recommended companies include Lo Cusco; tel: 084-222-222. Llama Taxi; tel: 084-222-000. Okarina; tel: 084-255-000. Turismo; tel: 084-245-000

Car rental: Hertz (G&G); tel: 084-248-800; cel: 084-984-620-510; **www.gygrentacar.com.** Manu Rent a Car; tel: 084-233-382; cel: 084-9849-45414; **www. manurentacar.com**

proved too ambitious a task; the Europeans ended up putting their own buildings on the mammoth foundations of the Inca ones, often using the same stones that had been cut and rounded by Inca masons. When a massive earthquake shook the city in March 1650, the colonial walls came crashing down but the Inca foundations remained intact.

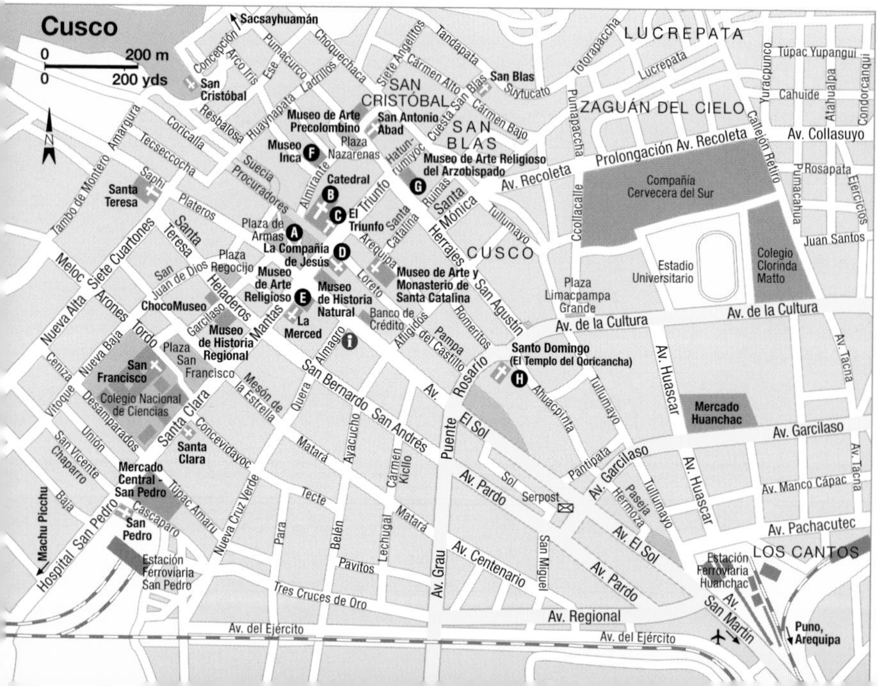

One of several ornate altars in Cusco's cathedral

Plaza de Armas

The **Plaza de Armas** Ⓐ is a perfect place to start exploring the city. In Inca times it was not only the exact center of the empire, but was also twice as large as it is now. Samples of soil from each of the conquered areas of the empire were joined at this spot, and the plaza itself, flanked by Inca palaces, was surfaced with white sand mixed with tiny shells, bits of gold, silver, and coral. This was the spot where important Inca religious and military ceremonies were staged. During the early days of Spanish control, the plaza was the scene of much violence and bloodletting. These days, things are quieter on this, one of the most superb colonial squares in Latin America. Tourists study the handicrafts for sale as insistent local women sitting under blankets beneath the colonial arcades chant '*cómprame*', or 'buy from me.' The most spectacular view of the plaza comes after nightfall when dramatic lighting transforms the square.

Catedral and El Triunfo

Cusco's magnificent **Catedral** Ⓑ (daily 10am–6pm, Mass at 10am; charge) is flanked by the 18th-century church of Jesús María, to the right and the Renaissance El Triunfo – the city's first Christian church – to the left. Built on what once was the palace of Inca Wiracocha, and made in part from stones hauled from the fortress of Sacsayhuamán outside the city, the cathedral mixes Spanish Baroque architecture with Inca stonework. Begun in 1559, it took a century to build. The cathedral also contains magnificent examples of Escuela

Cash for photos

It's always a good idea to have a fair amount of small change handy while traveling in Latin America. In Cusco, girls and women in fancy indigenous dress – often 'armed' with irresistible puppies or other baby animals – are a favorite picture opportunity, but also constantly on the lookout to sneak into your photo and charge you. Make sure the terms are pretty clear before pressing the button, and just say *'no gracias'* if you're not interested.

Cusqueña (School of Cusco, *see p.130*) paintings, including some by Diego Quispe Tito, the 17th-century Indian painter widely regarded as the master of the school. In the corner next to the sacristy is a painting by Marcos Zapata of the Last Supper, with Christ and his Apostles dining on roast guinea pig *(cuy)*, hot peppers, and Andean cheese.

The city's most venerated statue is the crucified Christ known as Nuestro Señor de los Temblores (Our Lord of the Earthquakes), depicted in a painting beside the main altar, which is of solid silver. The statue was paraded around the city during the 1650 earthquake, and after the tremors eventually stopped it was credited with miraculously bringing about the end of seismic activity. This gift to the New World from Spain, sent by Holy Roman Emperor Charles V, is still paraded around Cusco during Easter. The cathedral's María Angola bell in the north tower can be heard up to 40km (25 miles) away. Made of a ton of gold, silver, and bronze, the bell, which is more than 300 years old, is reportedly the continent's largest.

ChocoMuseo

For a break from the hustle and bustle, the ChocoMuseo at Garcilaso 210, in a lovely old colonial house, has upstairs balconies from which to observe events on the shaded Plaza Regocijo, a block west of the Plaza de Armas. Sit back with fair-trade chocolate – or learn how to make your own. The museum also has a store with organic chocolates and crafts and a little factory in which it produces chocolates from tropical Quillabamba, a town on the descent to Amazonia.

A mother and daughter taking in the view of Cusco

El Triunfo Ⓒ (opening hours as for the cathedral), which means 'the triumph,' was built to mark the Spanish victory over the Indians in the great rebellion of 1536. The uprising was led by Manco Inca, a descendant of an Inca leader, who the Spaniards assumed would be their political puppet. They were surprised, then, to find Manco and his army of followers surrounding the city. Cusco was under siege for many months, but the Inca

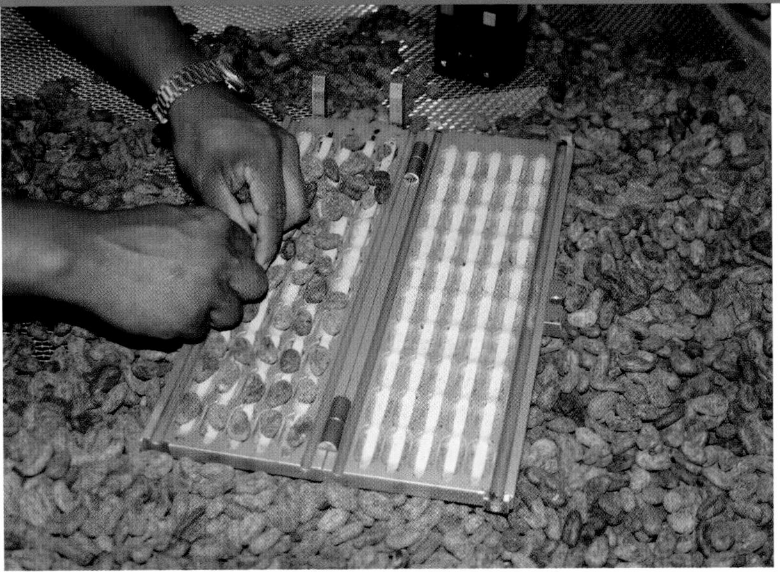

A member of staff at the ChocoMuseo checking beans for their quality

were finally defeated at Sacsayhuamán *(see p.133)*.

La Compañía de Jesús

In a city with so many churches, it is an honor to be dubbed the 'most beautiful.' That distinction belongs to **La Compañía de Jesús** Ⓓ (Sun–Thur 9–11.30am, 1–5.30pm, Fri and Sat 9–11.30am, 1–3.30pm; charge), on the southeast corner of the Plaza de Armas. The Jesuit church, with its Baroque facade, intricate interior, finely carved balconies, and altars covered in gold leaf, was started in 1571 and took nearly 100 years to complete, in part because of damage in the 1650 earthquake.

A few yards down the street, just past the Plaza de Armas, is the **Iglesia de la Merced** (Mon–Sat 8am–-12.30pm, 2–5.30pm; charge). Destroyed by the massive earthquake in 1650, this church was erected for a second time four years later. It contains the remains of Francisco Pizarro's brother Gonzalo, and of Pizarro's fellow conquistador Diego de Almagro, who returned to Peru after an unsuccessful search for riches in Chile, and was executed here after his failed coup attempt. There is a connected monastery and another **Museo de Arte Religioso** Ⓔ (opening hours as for the church), not to be confused with the museum of the same name in the Archbishop's Palace. This one contains several fine paintings, including a Rubens, and ornate gold and silver altarpieces.

Just north of the Plaza de Armas, on the corner of Calle Tucumán and Calle Ataúd you will find the **Museo Inca** Ⓕ (Mon–Fri 8am–5pm, Sat 9am–4pm; charge), also known as the **Admiral's Palace** because it was once the home of Admiral Francisco Aldrete Maldonado. There are some strange architectural features: an optical illusion is found in a corner window column, which looks like a bearded man from the inside and a nude woman from the outside, and there are mythical creatures guarding the main stairway. The building is well worth seeing for itself, as well as for the museum's newly expanded collection of pottery, textiles, and gold artifacts. Another splendid museum has opened at the Casa Cabrera in Plaza Nazarenas, the **Museo de Arte Precolumbino** (daily 9am–11pm; charge).

Calle Hatunrumyioc

One block up from El Triunfo, on the corner of **Calle Hatunrumiyoc**, literally 'the Street of the Big Stones', and Calle Palacio is the **Museo de Arte Religioso del Arzobispado** G (Mon–Sat 8am–6pm, Sun from 10am; charge). This Moorish building with complicated carvings on its doors and balconies was constructed on the site of the 15th-century palace of Inca Roca, under whose rule Cusco's schools were initiated. The museum houses an impressive collection of religious paintings of the Cusco School, including some by Diego Quispe Tito.

A little further north, the **Iglesia de San Blas** (Mon–Sat 8am–6pm, Sun from 10am; charge), a simple church by Latin American standards, has a beautifully carved pulpit, said to be one of the world's finest pieces of woodwork. The streets around San Blas form Cusco's artists' quarter, with galleries, studios, and small shops, hostels, and restaurants, and the workshops of the prolific Mendival family.

Iglesia Santo Domingo

A traditional dancer in the cloisters of Iglesia Santo Domingo

Temple of the Sun

Take any of the streets leading southeast from the Plaza de Armas and you will find your way to the most important place of worship in the Inca Empire. Now a church, the **Iglesia Santo Domingo** Ⓗ (Mon–Sat 8.30am–5.30pm, Sun 2–5pm; charge) was once **El Templo del Qoricancha** – the Temple of the Sun, and the most magnificent complex in Cusco. Walls there were covered in 700 sheets of gold studded with emeralds and turquoise, and windows were constructed so the sun would enter and cast a nearly blinding reflection off the precious metals inside. The mummified bodies of deceased Inca leaders, dressed in fine clothing and adornments, were kept on thrones of gold, tended by women selected for that honor. In the same room, a huge gold disk representing the sun covered one full wall while a sister disk of silver, to reflect the moonlight, was positioned on another.

Spanish chronicles describe a fabulous Hall of the Sun in Qoricancha and four chapels dedicated to lesser gods, including the moon, stars, thunder, and the rainbow. The rainbow had special significance for the Inca, which was why the Inca flag displayed all the colors of the *arco iris*, and it remains a good omen today. The chronicles also recall the Europeans' astonishment when they saw Qoricancha's patio filled with life-size gold and silver statues of llamas, trees, flowers, and handcrafted butterflies. Current excavations at the Temple of the Sun promise to reveal more of its mysteries.

Mercado Central

A cheap and convenient place to stock up on snacks while mingling with the locals is the large, open-air Mercado Central, on the fringe of the old town a block west of Plaza San Francisco. Do a little haggling and don't forget to ask for *la yapa* when the deal is closed to get a little something extra. Stalls overflow with sweets, chocolates, cheeses, and fruits, and you can get shoes shined or a little tailoring done on the side.

THE CUSCO SCHOOL

Pre-Hispanic temples and artifacts are Peru's main artistic claim, but beautiful cities like Arequipa, Cajamarca, and especially Cusco showcase the creativity that emerged under the new colonial regime. Indigenous craftsmen created sculptures and paintings that went well beyond just copying European models, originating their own imagery and styles. Recently, art collectors have shown increasing interest in the school's works.

One of the Spanish conquest's main concerns was to Christianize the many new subjects of the crown. The Inca had no written language, and literacy was rare among the conquerors too – limited mostly to clerics. Much as in Europe, the faithful had to be educated in the traditions and legends of the Church via powerful religious imagery. Spain sent teachers from the motherland to instruct the talented native craftsmen, and a school of art emerged soon after 1540 – the first in the New World, before schools in Quito and Potosí. Unsurprisingly, the overwhelming majority of its works are religious.

Italian Jesuit Bernardo Bitti, who arrived in 1584, is believed to have introduced painting to Cusco. What sets the works from Cusco and its environs in colonial Peru apart is the liberal use of perspective and color. Similar to European Mannerists,

A painting from the Cusco School

painters stretched proportions and depicted very stylized poses, preferring blue, red, and gold leaf, although also sometimes using bright green, ochre, and white. They also painted infants in a more natural way, even earlier than in Europe, and inserted native Andean objects such as corn or guinea pigs, famously featured in the *Last Supper* in Cusco's cathedral, which has one of the largest collections of the school's paintings.

A series of zodiac paintings there, of which nine have survived, merged the pre-Christian worship of sun and moon via the constellations to the Catholic faith. In these paintings inspired by a Flemish original, the school's most famous artist, Diego Quispe Tito (1611–81), applied parables from the life of Jesus to individual zodiac signs. Quispe included Andean landscapes and Amazonian birds, particularly parrots, in many of his paintings. The house he inhabited in San Sebastián, near Cusco, still exists, complete with his coat of arms on the door.

Most of the school's artists remained anonymous, but other important Cusco painters were Diego Cusihuamán, Luis de Riaño, Gregorio Gamarra, Basilio Santa Cruz Pumacallao, Antonio Sinchi Roca Inka, and particularly Marcos Zapata, who worked in the 18th century. Paintings from the school were exported to other parts of Spanish South America. The best places to see them are Cusco's cathedral and the MALI museum in Lima.

Diego Quispe Tito's *Virgin of Carmel Saving Souls in Purgatory*

Cusco's cathedral is the best place to see works from the Cusco School

Although the temple's wealth can only be imagined, its Inca architecture can still be appreciated. Visible from inside is the perfectly fitted curved stone wall that has survived at least two major earthquakes.

Museo de Arte y Monasterio de Santa Catalina

On Calle Arequipa is another Christian enclave that was formerly an Inca holy place. Centuries ago, the **Museo de Arte y Monasterio de Santa Catalina** (Mon–Thur 9am–5pm, Fri until 5.30pm, Sat 9am–5pm; charge) housed a different group of cloistered females, some 3,000 Chosen Women who dedicated their lives to the sun god. Foremost among these were the *mamaconas*, consecrated women who taught religion to selected virgins – called *acllas*. The *acllas* were taught to prepare *chicha* for use in religious ceremonies, to weave, and to pray. They made the fine robes that the Inca wore – only once – out of vicuña, alpaca, and even a silky fabric that was made from bat skins.

Attached to the convent is a museum containing religious art. An important contribution to the art world grew out of Cusco's mixing of the Indian and Spanish cultures in the often violent and bloody paintings of the School of Cusco. In many of these paintings archangels are dressed as Spaniards carrying European guns, but surrounded by cherubs with Indian faces, or Christ is accompanied by indigenous Apostles. The Virgin Mary wears local Peruvian dress, and Christ hangs on a cross decorated with Indian symbols.

The Museo de Arte, attached to the Monasterio de Santa Catalina

Traditionally attired woman at a market in the Sacred Valley

Plaza San Francisco

A couple of blocks south of the Plaza de Armas, the **Plaza San Francisco** has been planted entirely with Andean flora, including amaranth grain. Here, too, is Cusco's coat of arms, featuring a castle surrounded by eight condors. The castle represents Sacsayhuamán, and the emblem refers to the bloody battle fought there in 1536 as the Inca tried to defeat the Spanish conquerors *(see p.134)*. The condors flying over the castle vividly recall the scores of flesh-eating birds that, according to legend, circled over the Inca fort as the bodies of the dead piled up.

Flanking one side of the plaza is the 16th-century church and monastery, the **Iglesia de San Francisco** (Mon–Sat 9am–3.30pm). Simple in comparison with other houses of worship in the city, it has an extensive collection of colonial art, including a painting – said to be one of the largest canvases in South America – showing the family tree of St Francis of Assisi.

The Sacred Valley

The heartland of the last Inca, the Sacred Valley is home to the awe-inspiring fortresses of Sacsayhuamán and Ollantaytambo. The valley is a delightful place: the climate is pleasant, the people are agreeable, the agricultural terracing is a marvel, and there are a number of welcoming little *hostales* in which to spend the night. Sacsayhuamán is the Inca settlement closest to Cusco. You can walk or take a bus from the city to the first four sites, or you could use Pisac, a good base for exploring all the valley's ruins. All Sacred Valley sites are open daily 7am–6pm.

Sacsayhuamán

The overwhelming fortress of **Sacsayhuamán** ❷ is a bold demonstration of ancient construction skills. Made of massive stones weighing up to 17,000kg (125 tons), this military complex overlooking Cusco has a double wall in a zigzag shape – some say to imitate the teeth of the puma figure whose head the fort may have formed. Others say it represents the god of lightning. The fort also once had at least three huge towers, and a labyrinth of rooms large enough for a garrison of 5,000 Inca soldiers. It marks the birthplace of the river that runs under Cusco, channeled through stone conduits cut to give the city an invisible water supply.

Sacsayhuamán was the focus of the Great Rebellion led by Manco Inca against the Spanish in 1536. From here, the Inca besieged Cusco for 10 months. Historians say that if Manco Inca had defeated the Spanish in Cusco, he might have saved the empire. But, no matter how valiantly his troops fought and died, the Spanish eventually wrested back control of the fort, of the old Inca capital of Cusco, and ultimately of all Peru.

Archeologists estimate that tens of thousands of workers labored on this massive structure for up to seven decades, hauling the immense stone blocks that make up its double outside walls, and erecting the nearly indestructible buildings that transformed the complex into one of the most wondrous in all the empire. Although the outer walls remain intact, the buildings in the complex have been destroyed – in part to provide building stones for many of Cusco's structures. Even so, visitors to the fortress can still see the so-called **Inca's Throne** from which it is said parading troops were reviewed.

This is one of the area's most spectacular spots at which to take dawn photos, and, like much of Cusco, it provides a startling contrast of Indian and Christian cultures. Beside this complex is a giant white statue of Christ donated to the city in 1944

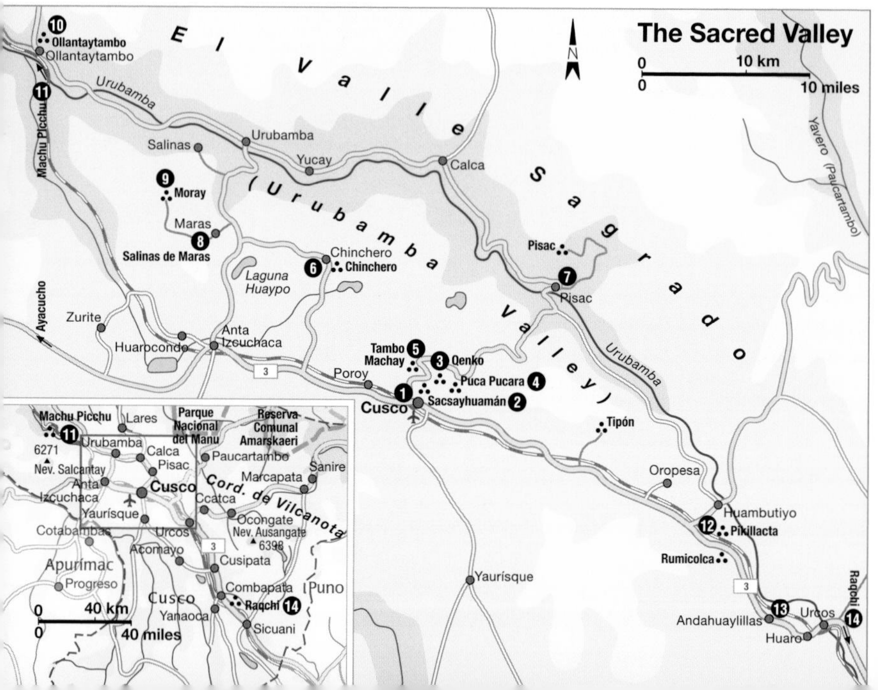

The Inca fortress of Sacsayhuamán

by grateful Palestinian refugees, his arms outstretched over Cusco in the valley below. It's a good place for a picnic lunch, too: perched on almost any stone you'll have an amazing view of the red-tiled roofs of Cusco and the lush fields of the surrounding valley.

Qenko

Some 7km (4 miles) from Sacsayhuamán is **Qenko** ❸, an Inca shrine with a circular amphitheater and a 5m (18ft) stone block that is said to represent a puma. This ceremonial center – dedicated to the worship of Mother Earth (Pacha Mama) – includes water canals cut into solid rock, and a subterranean room. Unlike Sacsayhuamán, which is a complex made up of huge stone blocks transported to the spot and assembled there, Qenko was carved from a huge limestone formation found at the site. Into its walls were carved typical Inca-style niches and alcoves used to display gold and holy items in pre-Hispanic times. The

Excavations and restorations

There are new excavations and restorations under way all the time. Among the most picturesque sights to have recently entered the visitors' circuit are the circular terraces of **Moray** and the salt pans at **Salinas de Maras**. A detour from Urubamba is well worth it, and Moray is included in the Cusco/ Sacred Valley visitors' ticket. The terraces form an amphitheater in the center and may well have been used by the Inca to plant different plants at each level: the site's protection from wind means that temperatures vary from terrace to terrace, with the warmest at the perfectly circular bottom, the largest of three such circles. Some researchers estimate that this may even have been an Inca agricultural laboratory.

At Maras, hundreds of salt pans fed by a river have been worked by locals for generations to extract salt. It's an extraordinary moonscape, startling amid the Andean scenery.

shrine also contains drawings etched laboriously into its stone, among them a puma, a condor, and a llama.

Puca Pucara

Farther along the road to Pisac is a smaller fortress, **Puca Pucara ❹**, which is believed to have guarded the road to the Sacred Valley of the Inca. Like Machu Picchu, this pink stone complex has hillside terraces, stairways, tunnels, and towers. To the north is **Tambo Machay ❺**, the sacred bathing place for the Inca rulers and the royal women. A hydraulic engineering marvel, its aqueduct system still feeds crystalline water into a series of showers where water rituals were once held. The ruins now consist of three massive walls of Inca stonework tucked into a hillside.

Chinchero

Chinchero ❻ is an attractive village with Inca ruins, which can be visited by bus from Cusco. It has a lively market on Tuesday, Thursday, and Sunday. It is said that Chinchero was one of the favorite spots of Inca Tupac Yupanqui, who built a palace and had agricultural terraces cultivated here at the mouth of the Río Vilcanota. Other historians say it was an important population center in Inca times and that Tupac Inca, the son of Pachacutec, had an estate here. If the Inca royalty were lured to Chinchero, it might have been by the view of snow-capped mountains and the river below. If you are here for the Sunday market, the best day to go, you will notice that local people use it as an opportunity to socialize as much as to buy goods.

Archeological ruins at Pisac

Local women selling vegetables at Pisac's Sunday market

This 'town of the rainbow,' as it was known in pre-Hispanic days, has kept many of its ancient customs and traditional ways.

Pisac

Pisac ❼ makes a good base for exploring the Sacred Valley. It is a friendly village known for its good fishing, busy Sunday market, and the ruins above the town; it lies about 32km (20 miles) from Cusco on a curving but decent road. There is a road up to the ruins, and you can sometimes get a ride in a taxi, but otherwise you can climb there past the mountainside terraces (local children will serve as guides for a small fee) or hire a horse from beside the village church. Tours from Cusco will take you closer to the ruins, but you will still need to hike up to the ruins; save some water for the walk.

Steep terraces and dramatic architecture mark this one-time fortress city, whose many features include ritual baths fed by aqueducts and one of the largest known Inca cemeteries. The stones making up Pisac's buildings are smaller than those at Sacsayhuamán, but the precision with which they are cut in Inca imperial style at the citadel is amazing. Pisac was probably built around 1440 by the Inca Pachacutec to fortify control over the Sacred Valley, possibly to defend it against the aggressive Antis from the Amazon. The site overlooks Inca terracing that provided food to the priests, warriors, and other residents of the fortress town spread out along a ridge.

Pisac's **Sunday market** is a riotous affair in a town where the people work hard and – apparently – play hard. The beer tent is the favorite haunt of the motley brass band that adds an increasingly out-of-tune touch to the town's festivities. There is a less touristy market held on Tuesday and Thursday.

Urubamba

From Pisac, follow the road and the river about 40km (25 miles) through the picturesque village of Yucay to **Urubamba**, which lies at the center of the valley. In recent years this has become a popular place to stay. The

Looking out over Ollantaytambo from its fortress

weather is milder than in Cusco, it is closer to Machu Picchu, and it makes a good center for visiting other places of interest. There are a number of hotels, cheap and not so cheap, in Urubamba itself and scattered along the valley.

Urubamba is a bustling place with a strong indigenous flavor. The coat of arms on the City Hall is sufficient evidence of this; no Spanish symbols are found in the emblem, which bears pumas, snakes, and trees. From here you can make trips to the salt pans at **Salinas de Maras** ❽ and the circular Inca agricultural terracing at **Moray** ❾. You can take a bus for the first part of the way, but after that it's a hike.

Ollantaytambo

Strategically placed at the northern end of the Sacred Valley is the mighty fortress of **Ollantaytambo** ❿, a place of great sacred and military importance to the Inca. The elegant and intricate walled complex containing seven rose-

Qhapaq Ñan

A whopping 15,000km (9,320 miles) of Inca roads have been surveyed in the early 21st century as countries from Colombia to Argentina push to have the Qhapaq Ñan, the whole of the Andean network, given World Heritage status by Unesco.

The infrastructure, also called the Inca Royal Road, was based on constructions made by pre-Inca cultures, but the Inca expanded it in just a century. Paved with stone, in many places it negotiated steep hillsides with a width of just 1m (3ft), crossing ravines over rope bridges. Fleet-footed *chasqui* runners traveled from *tambo* (inn) to *tambo*, providing crucial administrative orders and information. Today, it is most visible over the vast distance between Quito, Ecuador, and Mendoza, Argentina.

colored granite monoliths puzzles scientists, who say that the stone is not mined in the valley. A steep stairway enters the group of buildings, among which the best known is the so-called **Temple of the Sun** – an unfinished construction in front of a wall of enormous boulders. Portions of the original carvings on these huge worn stones can still be seen, although it is unclear if they really are pumas, as some claim. The complex also has plazas with sacred niches, shrines, an area of stone stocks where prisoners were tied by their hands, and ritual shower areas, including the **Princess's Bath**, or Baño de la Ñusta.

Ollantaytambo is the best preserved of all the Inca settlements. The old walls of the houses are still standing, and water still runs through original channels in narrow streets that are believed to date from the 15th century. In the nearby river stand the remains of an Inca bridge, and *campesinos* around the settlement live in houses that have changed very little since Pizarro's arrival. The **CATCCO Museum** (daily 9am–7pm; charge) has information about local history, culture, and architecture.

The world-famous ruins at Machu Picchu

Machu Picchu
N
Uña Huayna Picchu
Sacred Rock
Central Plaza
Common District
Intihuatana
Mortar Building
Sacristy
Temple of the Condor
Intimachay
Principal Temple
Royal Sector
Temple of the Three Windows
Main Fountain
Fountains
Fountain Caretaker's House
rocks
Temple of the Sun
Dry Moat
Agricultural Terraces
Palace of the Princess
Agricultural Sector
House of the Terrace Caretakers
Agricultural Terraces
Main entrance
Funeral Rock
Inca Trail
Hotel, train & bus stations

A mist surrounding the mountains at the lost city of the Inca

After exploring the Sacred Valley, most visitors head for the **Inca Trail** and **Machu Picchu ⓫**. You can get a train from Ollantaytambo (either the tourist train or the local one), or take a train from Cusco and get off at Aguas Calientes (Machu Picchu Pueblo). *For more information see p.255.*

Machu Picchu

When American archeologist Hiram Bingham and his party rediscovered **Machu Picchu** in 1911, he was actually searching for the ruins of Vilcabamba, the remote stronghold of the last Inca. Today we know that he had almost certainly found Vilcabamba, without realizing it, when he stumbled across the jungle-covered ruins of Espíritu Pampa, some 100km (60 miles) west of Machu Picchu, two months before making his spectacular find on the Urubamba Gorge. Machu Picchu – Ancient Peak – was what the local people called the mountain above the saddle-ridge where these spectacular ruins were located. Bingham carried out further explorations between 1911 and 1915, discovering a string of other ruins and a major Inca highway to the south of Machu Picchu, now known as the Inca Trail.

Inca Trail

Of all the popular treks in South America, the three- to five-day **Inca Trail** is the one that most travelers

Coming home

Hiram Bingham may be celebrated for his scientific discovery of Machu Picchu, but the crates full of artifacts from the site he sent to Yale University in the US later became bones of contention. In time for centennial celebrations, in late March 2011 Yale began to send home some of the artifacts, and a new museum to house them is being planned. More than 4,000 objects are to be sent back in all. What will come back is still a bit of a mystery: Peru claims they include objects made from precious metals, ceramics, and other artistic works, as well as mummies, while Yale says the objects are mostly fragments, some of which have been pieced together again.

want to do. The adventure begins with a four-hour train ride along the Río Urubamba. Legions of early-rising *campesinos*, loading and unloading their marketable goods at every station along the way, crowd together in what begins to look more like a cattle car than a passenger train. At Qorihuayrachina, **Kilometer 88**, the hikers' trail begins. It is no longer possible to walk the Inca Trail independently; you must prearrange the trip either at home or in Cusco, but preferably weeks in advance *(see p.154)*.

If you don't plan to walk the Inca Trail, your journey to Machu Picchu will be by train, and there are various ways to do this, depending on your budget. PeruRail (tel: 084-238-722; www.perurail.com) runs efficient daily services from Huanchac (Wanchac) train station on Av. Pachacutec in Cusco. Buy your ticket at the station a few days beforehand, if possible, as services usually fill up. You'll need to show your passport. If you're keen to see Machu Picchu in the early morning mist, the first services are the 6am and 6.15am Vistadome trains, which offer spectacular views, and the Backpacker service that leaves at 7am. You can also board these services at Ollantaytambo. For truly five-star travel, take the *Hiram Bingham* from Poroy station, just outside Cusco, at 9am. With elegant meals, top-notch guiding, and live entertainment on the return journey, this Pullman-style experience is worth the extra cost. Once passengers from all trains arrive in Aguas Calientes, buses whisk them up the switchback to the ruins.

The four-hour train journey to Machu Picchu offers magnificent views

Two explorers take in the awe-inspiring view at Machu Picchu

Touring the ruins

To understand the ruins best, you can hire one of the certified multilingual guides who offer their services at the entrance to the ruins. Enter the ruins through the House of the Terrace Caretakers, which flanks the **Agricultural Sector** Ⓐ. This great area of terracing was undoubtedly for agricultural purposes, and may have made the city self-sufficient in crops. The terraces end in a **Dry Moat**, beyond which lies the city itself. Straight ahead are the **Fountains**, which are actually small waterfalls, in a chain of 16 little 'baths,' varying in the quality of their construction. These were probably for ritual, religious purposes relating to the worship of water. The **Main Fountain** Ⓑ, just above and to the left, is so called because it has the finest stonework and the most important location. Here, too, is the **Temple of the Sun** Ⓒ. This round, tapering tower features the most perfect stonework to be found in Machu Picchu. It contains sacred niches for holding idols or offerings, and the centerpiece is a great rock, part of the actual outcrop on which the temple is built. Recent archeo-astronomical studies have demonstrated how this temple would have served as an astronomical observatory. The rock in the center of the tower has a straight edge cut into it. This is precisely aligned through the adjacent window to the rising point of the sun on the morning of the June solstice. The pegs on the outside of the window may have been used to support a shadow-casting device, which would have made observation simpler.

The adjacent building has two stories and was obviously the house of someone important. Bingham suspected that the building would have housed a *ñusta*, or Inca princess, and named it the **Palace of the Princess**. Most impressive when seen from ground level, its exterior granite wall on the northwest corner rivals that of the Temple of the Sun for its craftsmanship and beauty (Bingham called it the 'most beautiful wall in all America').

Next to the Sun Temple, just above

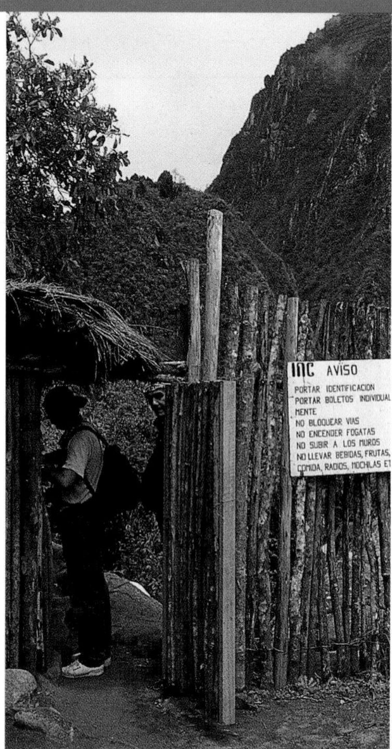

Walkers gear up for the ascent

the main fountain, is a three-walled house, which has been restored and had its roof thatched as an example of how these structures looked in Inca times. It is usually called the **Fountain Caretaker's House** – but it is unlikely to have been a house at all, since it is open to the elements on one side.

The structures directly opposite the Sun Temple, across the staircase, have been classified as the **Royal Sector** Ⓓ because of the roominess of the buildings, and also for the huge rock lintels (weighing up to 3,050kg or 3 tons) that in Inca architecture generally characterized the homes of the mighty.

At the top of the agricultural terraces, standing high above the city, is a lone hut, which is a great place for an overall view of the ruins. Just a few meters from the hut lies a curiously shaped carved rock, called the **Funeral Rock**. Bingham speculated that this had been used as a place of lying-in-state for the dead, or as a kind of mortician's slab, on which bodies were eviscerated and then left to be dried by the sun for mummification.

At the top of the staircase leading up from the fountains you come to a great jumble of rocks that served as a quarry for the Inca masons. Follow the ridge away from the quarry with your back to the staircase, and you come to one of the most interesting areas of the city. Here is the **Temple of the Three Windows** Ⓔ. Its east wall is built on a single huge rock; the trapezoidal windows are partly cut into it. On the empty side of this three-walled building stands a stone pillar that once supported the roof. On the ground by this pillar is a rock bearing the sacred step-motif common to many other Inca and pre-Inca temples.

Next to this site stands the **Principal Temple** Ⓕ, another three-walled building with immense foundation rocks and artfully cut masonry. It is named for its size and quality, and also because it is the only temple with a kind of sub-temple attached to it. This is generally called the **Sacristy**, because it seems a suitable place for the priests to have prepared themselves before sacred rites.

Ascending the mound beyond this temple leads to what was probably the most important of all the many shrines at Machu Picchu, the **Intihuatana** Ⓖ, the so-called 'Hitching Post of the Sun.' This term was popularized by the American traveler Ephraim Squier in the 19th century, but nobody has ever unraveled the mystery of how this stone and others like it were used. Every major Inca center had one. It seems likely that the stones somehow served for making astronomical observations and calculating the passing seasons.

The group of buildings across the large grassy plaza below forms another, more utilitarian sector of the city. At the north end, farthest from the entrance to the ruins, you find two three-sided buildings opening onto a small plaza, which is backed by a huge rock generally called the **Sacred Rock**. An intriguing aspect of this plaza is that the outline of the great flat rock erected at the northeast edge is shaped to form a visual tracing of the mountain skyline behind it. Then, if you step behind the *masma* (three-sided hut) on the southeast edge and look northwest, you find another rock that echoes in the same way the skyline of the small outcrop named **Uña Huayna Picchu**.

Walking back toward the main entrance along the east flank of the ridge, you pass through a large district of cruder constructions that has been labeled the **Common District**. At the end of this sector you reach a structure known as the **Mortar Building**, with two curious disk-shapes cut into the stone of the floor. Each is about 30cm (1ft) in diameter, flat, with a low rim carved around the edge.

The Temple of the Condor at Machu Picchu

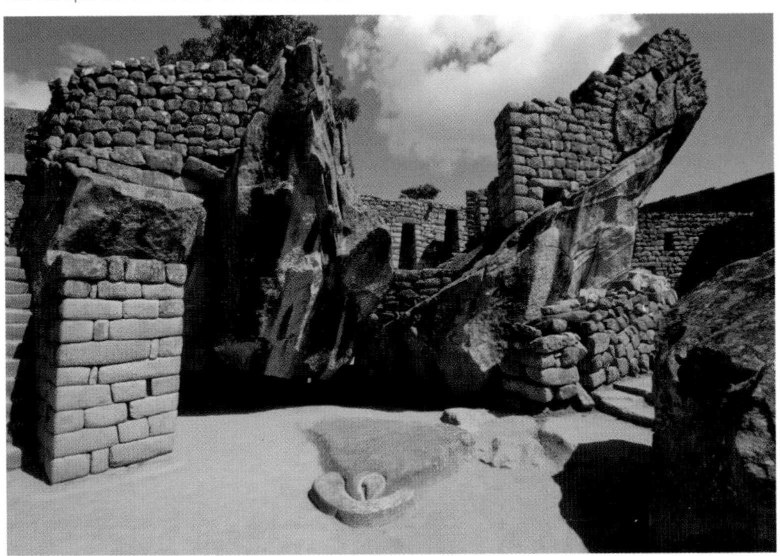

Just across the next staircase you come to a deep hollow, surrounded by walls and niches, which is known as the **Temple of the Condor** Ⓗ. A rock at the bottom of this hollow bears a stylized carving, apparently a condor, with the shape of the head and the ruff at the neck clearly discernible.

There is a small cave known as **Intimachay** above and to the east of the Condor Temple, which has been identified as a solar observatory for marking the December solstice. The cave is faced with coursed masonry and features a window carved out of a boulder that forms part of the front wall. This window is precisely aligned with the winter solstice sunrise, so that morning light falls on the back wall of the cave for 10 days before and after that date.

Southeast of Cusco

Lesser known but fascinating sites can be found heading east and southeast of Cusco toward Urcos (frequent buses leave from near the Puno railway station).

Tipón, near Oropesa, some 20km (13 miles) from the center of Cusco and built in the second half of the 15th century, has Inca terracing and the largest remaining network of Inca water channels cascading down walls and streaming downhill in zigzagging masonry.

Pikillacta ⓬, some 30km (18 miles) from Cusco, pre-dates the Inca: it is a large, unrestored ruin, with rough red stone walls more than 3m (10ft) high. The fortified town – it has just two entrance ways – goes back to the Wari (or Huari) period, around 500BC, but was occupied until

The Inca terracing at Tipón

Raqchi is home to the largest roofed Inca building

around 1532 and abandoned after the Spanish conquest. Streets running through the ruins lead to identifiable warehouses, administrative and residential neighborhoods.

About 1km (½ mile) farther on is **Rumicolca**, the Inca gateway to the Cusco Valley. In order to control access to the city, the Inca built, on Wari foundations, a wall of stone at the point where the valley narrows.

About 8km (5 miles) farther on is **Andahuaylillas** ⓭, a little village with some interesting colonial houses and the 17th-century Jesuit church of San Pedro, so extraordinarily ornate the locals call it 'Peru's Sistine Chapel.' It contains some particularly fine murals painted on the adobe walls in the Cusco School style by Lima painter Luis de Riaño (daily 7.30am–5.30pm; charge). The exuberant Baroque columns and altars are covered in gold leaf. It also has historic organs restored in 2008. The church may have been built on an Inca temple, as some of the old foundations remain visible.

Huaro, 4km (2½ miles) farther on, is another tiny village whose church (daily 8am–noon, 1–7pm; charge) has some marvelous 17th-century murals, painted by Tadeo Escalante, and a Renaissance altar among the oldest in Peru.

Raqchi ⓮, near the town of Sicuani, is in a valley along the Urubamba River 112km (70 miles) from Cusco. Farmers grow wheat at one of the most unusual Inca sites, built and used in the final years of the empire. The site's distinguishing feature is what was the largest roofed building of the Inca, the massive, two-story temple of Viracocha, the god of creation.

The adobe walls still standing on their Inca stone foundations are reminders of the giant building that spanned 92m (302ft) by 25.5m (84ft), supported by round pillars, and part of a large settlement with administrative quarters and residential areas, one of the empire's main *tambos*. Along with the walls, the ruins have ceremonial baths where the water still flows, and an extraordinary group of dozens of oddly circular storehouses called *qolqas* bunched together.

ACCOMMODATIONS

Don't be daunted by the number of hotels in Cusco. The competition is high and so is the quality. However, even with the large number of mid-range to budget accommodations, it is wise to book in advance, especially in June and August. When choosing a room, bear in mind that the traffic in Cusco is noisy; car horns start honking around 5.30am.

Accomodations price categories

Prices are for one night's accommodation in a standard double room (unless otherwise specified)

$ = below US$20
$$ = US$20–40
$$$ = US$40–60
$$$$ = US$60–100
$$$$$ = over US$100

Cusco

Amaru Hostal I
Cuesta de San Blas 541
Tel: 084-225-933
www.amaruhostal.com
Clean and friendly hotel, with a large central patio and balconies with great views of the city. Rooms come with or without a private bathroom and hot water all day. Good value. **$$$**

Amaru Hostal II
Calle Chihuampata 642, San Blas
Tel: 084-223-521
www.amaruhostal2.com
This is a very pretty hotel set in an old house and built around a green garden. There are also good views over the rooftops of Cusco. Rooms are rustic and comfortable, and the place looks gorgeous when lit up at night. **$$$**

Hotel Libertador

Hostal Corihuasi
Suecia 561
Tel: 084-232-233
www.corihuasi.com
Attractive colonial-style house near the Plaza de Armas, with warm and quiet rooms. It offers friendly service, free WiFi access, and hot water. Great views are on offer from the breakfast hall. Pay more for the two rooms with a great panoramic view of the city. **$$$**

Hostal El Balcón
Tambo de Montero 222
Tel: 084-236-738
www.balconcusco.com
This beautiful old house has been converted into a wonderful, rustic hotel, set around a garden with lovely views of the city. There's a cozy restaurant and WiFi access. **$$$$**

Hostal Monarca
Recoleta and Pumapaccha 290
Tel: 084-226-145
Close to the center of Cusco, just three blocks from the Plaza de Armas, this *hostal* is set in a pretty, historic building with sunny terraces. Rooms are modern, cozy, and carpeted. There's also a good restaurant. **$$$**

Hotel Libertador Palacio del Inka Cusco
Plazoleta Santo Domingo 259
Tel: 084-231-961
Reservations in the US/Canada:
Tel: 1877-778-2281
www.libertador.com.pe

A top-class hotel in a 380-year-old building. It is well furnished and efficiently run, with a bar, shops, a gym, and a Jacuzzi. The Inti Raymi restaurant serves *novo-andina* food. **$$$$$**

Hotel Los Andes de América
Calle Garcilaso 150
Tel: 084-606-060/70
www.cuscoandes.com
Part of the Best Western hotel chain, this hotel features centrally heated, comfortable rooms arranged around an interior courtyard. Staff are helpful, and an excellent buffet breakfast is included. **$$$$$**

Hotel Los Niños
Meloq 442
Tel: 084-231-424
www.ninoshotel.com
An attractive, renovated colonial building with a courtyard. Friendly, clean and very popular – so book well in advance. There is a sister hotel and apartments in Cusco, plus a comfortable hacienda just outside the city. Profits fund projects to help street children. **$$$**

Hotel Royal Inka I
Plaza Regocijo 299
Tel: 084-263-276
Reservations in the US: tel: 866-554-6028
www.royalinkahotel.com
Close to the main plaza, this hotel is housed in a National Historical Monument. Francisca *La Mariscala* Gamarra, the wife of one of Peru's first presidents and one of the country's most famous women, lived here in the 19th century. **$$$$**

Hotel Royal Inka II
Santa Teresa 335
Tel: 084-222-284/231-067
www.royalinkahotel.com
Attractively situated on the upper plaza, with good service. More comfortable than Royal Inka I, it has a sauna and Jacuzzi. Its restaurant, which can cater to large groups, has a large mural with the history of Cusco. **$$$$**

Machu Picchu Sanctuary Lodge

Hotel Sueños del Inka
Alabado 119, San Blas
Tel: 084-242-299
www.suenosdelinka.com
Located in the artists' quarter of San Blas, this hillside hotel has panoramic views over the city. Rooms are slightly dated, but warm and comfortable. Friendly service, free internet. **$$$$$**

Sonesta Hotel Cusco
Av. El Sol 954
Tel: 084-581-200
www.sonesta.com
This hotel was initially built as the Cusco Savoy, but was completely renovated and reopened to the public again in early 2010. It now features modern decor and a restaurant which serves classic Peruvian cuisine. **$$$$$**

Machu Picchu

Machu Picchu Sanctuary Lodge
By Machu Picchu ruins
Tel: 084-984-816-956
Reservations in Lima:
tel: 01-610-8300
http://machupicchu.orient-express.com
Luxurious modern hotel next to the entrance to the ruins – this is an extremely expensive hotel. Used by many large tour groups. It has two restaurants, one of which has great views over the surrounding valley. **$$$$$**

Gringo Bill's

Aguas Calientes

Gringo Bill's

Colla Raymi 104, just off Plaza de Armas
Tel: 084-211-046
www.gringobills.com

Set up in 1979 by a US-Peruvian couple, William (Gringo Bill) and Margarita, this hotel is very relaxed. Rooms come with or without a private bathroom, and have spectacular views of the surrounding mountains. **$$$$**

Hostal Machu Picchu

Av. Imperio de los Inkas 135
Tel: 084-211-065
Reservations in the US: tel: 888-790-5264
www.hostalmachupicchu.com

A cheaper option in Aguas Calientes, this *hostal* is good, basic, and clean. It has private bathrooms with hot water, and rooms with a balcony overlook the Vilcanota River. It is located next to the railway line. **$$$**

Inti Inn Machu Picchu

Pachacutec and Viracocha
Tel: 084-211-360
www.grupointi.com

Close to the Plaza de Armas, this hotel has clean, light-filled, and cozy rooms, with wrought-iron bed heads, terracotta floor tiles, and en suite bathrooms with plenty of hot water. **$$$$$**

Ollantaytambo

El Albergue

Next to Ollantaytambo rail station
Tel: 084-204-014/049
www.elalbergue.com

Ollantaytambo's oldest *hostal* is also known as the 'train station hotel' on account of its handy location. Simple and relaxing *hostal*, with eight rooms stylishly decorated by the artist-owner. Has a sauna and very pretty gardens. Staff can organize activities in the area. **$$$$**

Pisac

Pisaq Inn

Plaza de Armas
Tel: 084-203-062
www.hotelpisaq.com

A delightful hotel which overlooks Pisac's main square. It is brightly decorated with hand-painted murals and has a friendly, family atmosphere. Also on offer is a café serving simple Peruvian fare, a hot rock sauna, a massage service, a pizza oven, and a laundry service. **$$$**

Urubamba

Hostal Los Jardines

Jr. Convención 459
Tel: 084-632-425

Set in a quiet corner of this small town, this is a simple but welcoming hostel that has lovely sunny gardens. The owners also conveniently run mountain bike tours in the Sacred Valley. **$$**

Sol y Luna Lodge and Spa

Fundo Huincho Lote A-5 (1km/½ mile outside Urubamba)
Tel: 084-201-620/2
www.hotelsolyluna.com

This lovely lodge is made up of comfortable round bungalows set around a large and burgeoning garden. There's a spa on site with t'ai chi and yoga classes, and the lodge arranges all manner of activities, like trekking, mountain biking, and horseback riding. **$$$$$**

RESTAURANTS

Restaurant price categories

Prices are for a three-course menu including juice but no wine or coffee

$ = below US$2
$$ = US$2–5
$$$ = US$6–10
$$$$ = over US$10

The overwhelming majority of travelers' food on offer may initially appear to be along the lines of dubious pizza, but, fortunately, a large number of good-quality restaurants have opened their doors to local and foreign patrons, ranging from folksy Andean to sophisticated cuisine. Tempting as it may be to indulge, it's best to eat lightly and avoid alcohol until you are acclimatized to the altitude.

Cusco

A Mi Manera
Triunfo 393
Tel: 084-222-219
www.amimaneraperu.com
Just a block-and-a half from the Plaza de Armas, this is one of Cusco's premier *novoandino* restaurants, yet its dishes are attractively priced. The menu will appeal to lovers of Andean meats with alpaca and guinea pig, but *ceviches* are also on offer. It's all served in a lively atmosphere. **$$**

El Ayllu
Almagro 133
Tel: 084-232-357
www.inkaworld.org/cafeayllu
Ayllu is the Quechua word for community. This Cusco institution honors its name – popular with older *cusqueños*, it has tasteful decor and background classical and jazz music. Excellent breakfasts, cakes, and coffees. There is a new outlet at Marqués 263. **$$$**

Granja Heidi
Cuesta San Blas 525
Tel: 084-238-383
This German-owned restaurant offers excellent soups, salads, quiches, and pastas, mostly organic and homemade, with dairy products from the owner's farm. Leave some space for the excellent desserts. **$$$**

Greens Organic
Santa Catalina Angosta 135
Tel: 084-243-379
Upstairs from Incanto *(see below)*, this is the best place in town for vegetarians. Beautiful, natural food served by friendly staff. Try the Peruvian-style mushroom stir-fry, and don't forget their delicious juices. **$$$**

Incanto Ristorante
Santa Catalina Angosta 135
Tel: 084-254-753
This smart Italian restaurant with a Peruvian twist offers some interesting dishes. The *carpaccio de lomo* is highly recommended. You can enjoy great people-watching over the Plaza de Armas from the tables close to the windows. **$$$$**

KinTaro
Plateros 334, 2nd floor
Tel: 084-260-638
www.cuscokintaro.com
Serving cheap, excellent Japanese food, Kin-Taro offers lunch and dinner menus as well as à la carte sushi rolls and salads. Good

Fine dining in an upmarket restaurant

selection of juices. Also try their sake cocktails. Free WiFi and complimentary tea. **$$$**

Trotamundos
Portal de Comercio 177, 2nd floor
Tel: 084-239-590
With good coffee, juices, sandwiches, and meals, this place is very popular among backpackers. It has a fine view of the cathedral and a large fireplace to keep warm. A selection of wines is available for purchase. **$$$$**

El Truco
Plaza Regocijo 261
Tel: 084-235-295
http://restauranteltruco.com
With its high colonial ceilings and large spaces, El Truco caters to large tour groups. It offers a popular and elaborate nightly dinner and show. Good value. **$$$$**

Ollantaytambo

El Albergue
Ollantaytambo train station
Tel: 084-204-014
www.elalbergue.com
Homemade pasta and Peruvian food cooked with organic ingredients from the Sacred Valley, including from its own garden. It also offers very early breakfast for Machu Picchu travelers. **$$**

Café Alcazar
Calle del Medio (Chaupicalle) s/n
Tel: 084-204-034
A small, laidback café in the old Inca heart of Ollantaytambo. Serves vegetarian options, as well as meaty Peruvian staples and pasta dishes. Good juices and great pisco sours. **$$**

Hearts Café
Plaza de Armas s/n
Tel: 084-204-078
www.heartscafe.org
English food is as exotic in Peru as Peruvian cuisine in England, but you will find it on the menu at Hearts Café, along with vegetarian and light dishes. It's part of an initiative to support small farmers and workers in the Sacred Valley. **$**

Panaka Grill
Plaza de Armas s/n
Tel: 084-204-047
Situated right on Ollantaytambo's pretty Plaza de Armas, this restaurant has beautiful views and good service. It serves excellent meat grills and tasty oven-baked pizzas. Dining space upstairs is cozier. **$$$–$$$$**

Pisac

Mullu
Plaza Constitución 352
Tel: 084-203-073
Overlooking the plaza, this artsy, avant-garde café is just the place to hang out while sipping a refreshing juice or one of the excellent coffees. It also serves good light meals and snacks. **$$$**

Urubamba

Casa Orihuela
Ctra. Cusco–Urubamba km 64
Tel: 084-226-241
Located on the hacienda Huayoccari, this is a great place to stop on the journey between Pisac and Ollantaytambo. The menu features good Peruvian staples, and the restaurant has a lovely countryside atmosphere. **$$$$**

The Green House
Jr. Arica and Jr. Comercio 160
Cel: 084-974 955 977
http://greenhouseurubamba.com
Cozy nighttime hangout and Italian restaurant with fine pasta and pizzas, but it also serves lunch menus. **$**

El Huacatay
Jr. Arica 620
Tel: 084-201-790/967-6876

Casa Orihuela decor

Multicolored corn at Pisac Sunday market

www.elhuacatay.com
A quiet and appealing place with a garden, perfect for outdoor dining on mild evenings. The chef makes excellent food – a fusion of Mediterranean and Asian cuisine – cooked with the best local ingredients. **$$$$**

Killa Wasi
Hotel Sol y Luna, Huincho s/n (1km/½ mile outside Urubamba)
Tel: 084-201-621
This fabulous poolside restaurant decorated with terracotta tiles can be found at a smart country hotel outside Urubamba. Its varied menu features *novoandino* specialties such as curried alpaca and fried yucca, as well as tasty chicken, trout, and seafood dishes. **$$$$**

NIGHTLIFE AND ENTERTAINMENT

Cusco has some of the best *peñas* in South America, with a range of Andean styles (some of the bands are internationally known). They're mostly around the Plaza de Armas and easy to find because of the blaring music. The north and south sides of the Plaza de Armas are the best places to start off on a pub crawl. Several restaurants around the plaza, such as El Truco *(see left)*, also offer live music – just stroll around and listen. Many of the larger hotels stage folkloric shows.

Cross Keys Pub
Triunfo 350
Tel: 084-229-727
www.cross-keys-pub-cusco-peru.com
A typically British pub, with darts and good pub grub – a great meeting place.

Kamikaze
Plaza Regocijo 274
A live band plays at around 11pm, followed by rock, pop, reggae, and salsa music. There is also a happy hour before the live band.

Mama Africa
Portal de Panes 109
Tel: 084-246-544
www.mamaafricaclub.com
Offers movies, an internet café, hip music, and great cocktails. For those in search of an interesting evening out, this venue also offers live performances, such as fire dancing.

Los Perros
Tecsecocha 436
Tel: 084-241-447
This is a trendy bar that welcomes patrons with its comfy couches – perfect for sitting back, enjoying cocktails, and sipping beer. It also offers a great mix of music.

Ukukus
Plateros 316
Tel: 084-254-911
www.ukukusbar.com
Ukukus shows late afternoon movies and also features live local band, followed by a disco and folkloric music.

TOURS

On arrival in Cusco, the first thing to do is to purchase a Visitor Ticket – a combination entry pass to all the historic buildings of note in Cusco and the Sacred Valley. Tour operators in Cusco fall into two categories: those offering standard tours of Cusco and the surrounding ruins and market villages, and those operating adventure tours such as trekking, climbing, river running, horseback riding and jungle expeditions. The four-day Inca Trail to Machu Picchu is an extremely popular excursion, and it's mandatory to book well before you arrive in Cusco (it is forbidden to walk the trail independently).

Cultural tours

Condor Travel
Saphy 848A
Tel: 084-248-181
www.condortravel.com
Offers tailor-made excursions or set tours. It also runs a good selection of adventure trips.

Inka Natura Travel
Ricardo Palma J-1, Urb. Santa Mónica
Tel: 084-243-408/255-255
www.inkanatura.com
Organizes short and longer excursions on the Inca Trail to Machu Picchu.

Lima Tours
Jr. Machu Picchu D24, Urb. Manuel Prado
Tel: 084-228-431
www.limatours.com.pe
Expeditions offered include arts and culture tours, and longer treks lasting up to 17 nights.

Adventure tours

Amazonas Explorer
Av. Collasuyo 910, Urb. Miravalle
Tel: 084-252-846/984-765-448
www.amazonas-explorer.com
Organizes first-class rafting and mountain-biking expeditions. The English/Swiss owners are experts in alternative adventure.

A stunning backdrop in Pisac

Explorandes
Av. Garcilazo 316A
Tel: 084-238-380
www.explorandes.com
Offers river rafting in Cusco, zip lining and treks along the Inca Trail.

Peruvian Andean Treks
Av. Pardo 705
Tel: 084-600-500
www.andeantreks.com
Trips offered from Cusco include a 10-day trip with camping, exploring the Inca sites in Cusco, and a one-day trek on the Inca Trail to Machu Picchu.

Trekperu
Av. República de Chile B-15, Parque Industrial Wanchac
Tel: 084-261-501
www.trekperu.com
This company offers a varied range of tours for explorers, including one from Cusco to Lake Titicaca, and a jungle experience tour. It also organizes volunteering opportunities.

FESTIVALS AND EVENTS

With a mixture of Catholic holidays and Andean traditions that go back to Inca times, Cusco and its surroundings offer plenty of interesting festivals.

March/April

Semana Santa (Easter/Holy Week)

Among the nationwide commemorations is the spectacular procession in Cusco in honor of El Señor de los Temblores, held on Holy Monday and Maundy Thursday.

June

Corpus Christi

Cusco

One of the most beautiful displays of religious folklore, the Procession of the Consecrated Host is accompanied by statues of saints from churches all over Cusco. It takes place in mid-June.

Inti Raymi (Festival of the Sun)

Sacsayhuamán

This ancient festival is staged on June 24 at the Sacsayhuamán fortress, and involves Inca rituals, parades, folk dances, and contests.

July

La Virgen del Carmen

Festivities are held July 15–17 throughout the highlands and are especially colorful in Paucartambo, 255km (160 miles) from Cusco. The festival often includes a procession.

October

Unu Urco Festival

Urcos and Calca (near Cusco)

Music, dancing, and parades on October 19.

December

Festival of Santu Rantikuy

Cusco

Andean toy and handicrafts fair in the main plaza on December 24.

Group in traditional costume at Inti Raymi

Lake Titicaca

Straddling the borders of Peru and Bolivia, the highest navigable lake in the world is the legendary birthplace of the first Inca. At 174km (108 miles) long and up to 64km (40 miles) wide, Titicaca is South America's largest lake. Its floating reed islands are populated by fascinating indigenous communities who still ply its sapphire waters in *totora* reed canoes.

Puno

Population: 120,300

Local dialling code: 051

Local tourist office: Plaza de Armas at Jr. Deustua and Jr. Lima; tel: 051-365-088; **www.peru.travel**

Main police station: Jr. Deustua 530; tel: 051-353-988. Tourist police: Jr. Deustua 558; tel: 051-354-764

Main post office: Serpost: Jr. Moquegua 269; tel: 051-351-141

Hospitals: Hospital Nacional Manuel Núñez Butrón; Av. El Sol 1022; tel: 051-369-696/351-021

Local newspapers: *Los Andes*

Lake Titicaca is the world's highest navigable lake and the center of a region where thousands of subsistence farmers eke out a living fishing in its icy waters, growing potatoes in the rocky land at its edge, or herding llama and alpaca at altitudes that leave Europeans and North Americans gasping for air. It is also where traces of the rich pre-Hispanic past still stubbornly cling, resisting in past centuries the Spanish conquistadors' aggressive campaign to erase Inca and pre-Inca cultures and, in recent times, the lure of modernization.

The turquoise-blue lake was the most sacred body of water in the Inca Empire, and is now the natural separation between Peru and Bolivia; it has a surface area exceeding 8,000 sq km (3,100 sq miles), not counting its more than 30 islands. At 3,856m (12,725ft) above sea level, it has two climates: chilly and rainy or chilly and dry. It gets cold in the evenings, dropping below freezing June through August. During the day the sun is intense, so take care.

The area's first major town when coming from Cusco is **Juliaca**, a busy but unattractive place where passengers coming by air will arrive. From here the road and rail tracks continue to Puno, the town on the lakeshore. The *Andean Explorer* luxury train from Cusco is a wonderful way to arrive here (tickets can be purchased at Huanchac/Wanchac station in Cusco or from PeruRail; www.perurail.com). Luxury buses also offer tours taking in sites between Cusco and Puno, the base for tours in and around the lake.

Shopping in Puno

The streets of Puno are full of handicrafts and goods of cheap value but dubious origin. You can buy fair-trade items at the Casa del Corregidor (Deusta 576; Mon–Fri 10am–9pm, Sat–Sun 10am–8pm; www.casadelcorregidor.pe), one of the few remaining colonial mansions in the city. Its inside patio has a café with food from the local market, and the *casa* also hosts lectures and art expositions.

A group of female dancers in colorful traditional dress

Puno

At an altitude of 3,830m (12,630ft), **Puno ❶** is the capital of Peru's Altiplano – the harsh highland region much better suited to roaming vicuñas and alpacas than to people. During the colonial period it was one of the continent's richest cities because of its proximity to the Laykakota silver mines discovered in 1657. Puno is also Peru's folklore center, with a rich array of handicrafts, costumes, fiestas, legends, and, most importantly, more than 300 different ethnic dances.

Puno's sights

Little of Puno's colonial heritage is visible, but there remains a handful of buildings worth seeing. The **Catedral San Carlos Borromeo** is a magnificent stone structure, dating back to 1757, with a weather-beaten Baroque-style exterior and a surprisingly spartan interior – except for its center altar of carved marble, which is plated in silver. Over a side altar to the right of the church is the icon of the Lord of Agony, commonly known as El Señor de la Bala (Lord of the Bullet). Beside the cathedral

Boats moored on Lake Titicaca, the highest navigable lake in the world

is the Balcony of the Count of Lemos found on an old house on the corners of Deústua and Conde de Lemos streets.

On the **Plaza de Armas** are the **Biblioteca** (Library) and the municipal **Pinacoteca** (Art Gallery), and half a block off the plaza is the **Museo Carlos Dreyer**, displaying a collection of Nazca, Tiahuanaco, Paracas, Chimu, and Inca artifacts bequeathed to the city on the death of their owner, for whom the museum is named. One of the museum's most valuable pieces is an Aymara *aribalo*, the delicate pointed-bottomed pottery whose wide belly curves up to a narrow neck.

Three blocks uphill from the plaza is the Parque Huajsapata, a hill that figures in the lyrics of local songs, and an excellent spot for a panoramic view of Puno. Huajsapata is topped by a huge white statue of Manco Capac, gazing down at the lake from which he is said to have sprung. Another lookout point is found beside Parque Pino, at the city's north side, in the plaza four blocks up Calle Lima from the Plaza de Armas, in which stands the Arco Deústua, a monument honoring those killed in the decisive independence battles of Junín and Ayacucho. The park is also called Parque San Juan, after the San Juan Bautista church within its limits; at its main altar is a statue of the patron saint of Puno, the Virgin of Candelaria.

Two blocks down Calle F. Arbul from Parque Pino is the city market, a colorful collection of people, goods, and food. Tourists should keep their eyes on their money and

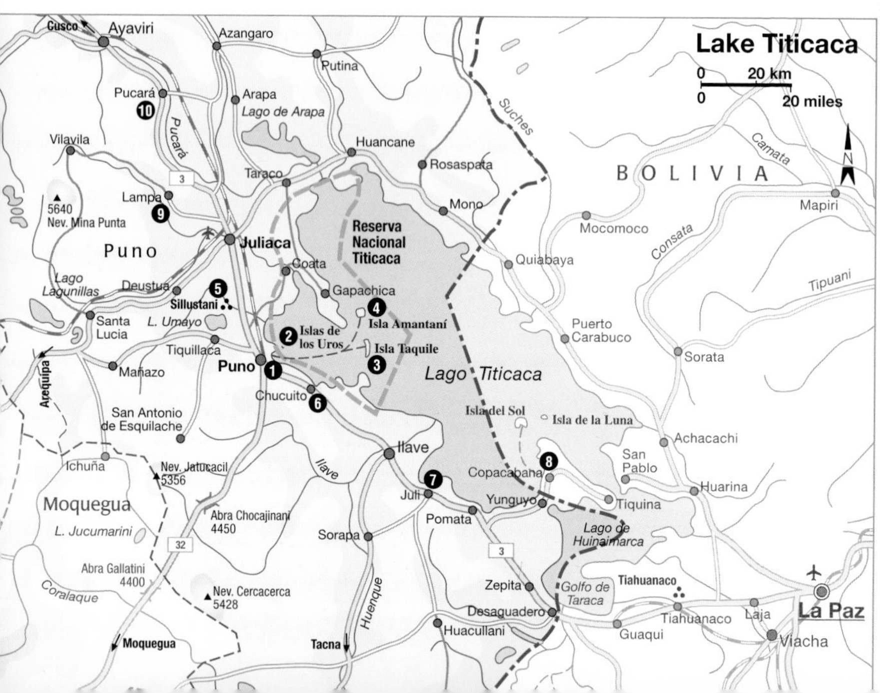

Uros islanders out for a lakeside promenade

cameras, but it is worth a stop to see the wide selection of products – especially the amazing variety of potatoes, ranging from the hard, freeze-dried *papa seca* that looks like gravel, to the purple potatoes and yellow- and orange-speckled *olluco* tubers. Woolen goods, colorful blankets, and ponchos are on sale here, along with miniature versions of the reed boats that ply Lake Titicaca.

Exploring the lake

The main reason for coming to Puno is that it is the stepping-off point for exploring Lake Titicaca and its amazing islands, native inhabitants, and colorful traditions. Small motorboats can be hired for island visits or fishing trips – although fish stocks have declined in recent years and most lake trout is now farmed.

Islands of the lake

The best known of the islands dotting Lake Titicaca are the **Islas de los Uros ❷**, 40 or so artificial floating islands of reed named after the

Puno transport

Airport: Puno is served by the Inca Manco Capac airport (JUL) in Juliaca; **www.corpac.gob.pe**; the one-hour taxi trip to Puno costs S./90

Bus station: Terminal Terrestre; Jr. Primero de Mayo 703, Barrio Magisterial; tel: 051-364-733

Taxis: Recommended taxi companies include Radio Taxi Milenium; tel: 051–353-134. Radio Taxi Fon Car Titikaka; tel: 051-368-000

Train station: Perú Rail; Av. La Torre 224; tel: 051-351-041/369-179; **www.perurail.com**

Port: Capitanía de Puerto Lacustre Puno; Av. Titicaca s/n; tel: 051-595-306. Boat travel to the Island of the Sun in Bolivia is possible from Copacabana, Bolivia; Transturin hydrofoils to Bolivia depart from Juli

Car rental: Del Sur Rent a Car; tel: 051-322-325; cel: 951-660-191. Drews Rent a Car; cel: 051-951-844-392/051-951-731-414

natives who inhabited them. Legends described the Uro islanders as people incapable of drowning, 'like the fish and the birds of the water.' Their original language is practically extinct, with most now speaking Aymara. The hilly island of Taquile, 35km (22 miles) east of Puno, is a very special place: the earth is rich, reddish brown, the color that predominates in the women's clothes, and the lake a glorious vivid blue. Life has changed very little over the centuries: the earth is farmed with traditional implements, and trout, the best in Peru, are fished from the lake. Even further away from Puno than Taquile, Amantaní is graced with Inca ruins. The island is dominated by two mountain peaks, both of which offer views across the lake that are particularly beautiful at sunset.

The Yavari steamship

A fascinating relic of a bygone era is the **Yavari steamship** (daily 8am–5pm; www.yavari.org). Built by the British in 1862 and carried up, piece by piece, by hardy mules, it plied the lake until 1975, and is now a floating museum moored in the Bay of Puno by the Sonesta Posada del Inca. It's a great spot to take a break and look over the great lake, sipping coffee to fight the cold. Overnight stays are also possible. In the longer run, the idea is to get it back up and running for cruises.

Taquile

An island that typically lures tourists is **Isla Taquile** ❸, the home of skilled weavers and a spot where travelers can buy well-made woolen and alpaca goods, as well as colorful garments whose patterns and designs bear hidden messages about the wearer's

Visitors to Isla Taquile stay with local residents as there are no hotels

A man knitting the traditional woolen hats that are native to Taquile

social standing or marital status. Prices of these goods may be higher than on the mainland, but the quality is very good. The residents of this island run their own tourism operations in the hope of maintaining a degree of control over tourism and ensuring that the visits of outsiders do not destroy their delicate culture.

There are no hotels on Taquile, but the Quechua-speaking islanders open their homes to tourists interested in an overnight stay. Arrangements for such accommodations can be made with local people, who wait at the top of the steep stone staircase where the boats dock. You will find several places to eat, mostly serving simple but tasty fish and rice dishes.

You can visit Taquile in one day, combined with a trip to the Uros, but it means spending much of the day on a boat, and an overnight stay is recommended.

Isla Amantaní

Handicrafts also play an important role in life on **Isla Amantaní** ❹, a lovely, peaceful island, where alpaca graze the terraced hillsides. It has opened its doors to outsiders who are willing to live for a few days as the Aymara-speaking islanders do – and that means sleeping on beds made of long hard reeds and eating potatoes at every meal. There is no running water, and nighttime temperatures drop to freezing even in the summer. But those happy to rough it catch a glimpse of an Andean agricultural community that has maintained the same traditions for centuries. Some Amantaní residents live and die without ever leaving the island.

Journeys to Amantaní and Taquile commence at the Puno docks. At the end of the three-hour trip, visitors are registered as guests and then assigned to a host family, who show the way to a mud-brick or reed home set around an open courtyard decorated with white pebbles spelling out the family's name. The socializing begins when a family member, who may speak a little English, offers a guided walk around the island, from where the views are absolutely spectacular.

UROS ISLANDERS

One of the world's most unusual human communities lives among the reeds of Lake Titicaca. The Uros islanders ply the waters on reed boats and construct their entire living environment from their natural surroundings. Tourism is helping the Uros people continue a way of life that has survived for centuries, despite the attractions of the modern world on the mainland shore. The gold-colored boats and islands make for a gorgeous contrast of colors with the sapphire lake and deep blue Andean sky.

No image of the great Lake Titicaca is complete without the distinct island culture of the Uros. Early Spanish chroniclers relate that the *totora* reeds that form the basis of their unique way of life grew profusely in the lake's shallow waters, as they still do today just west of Puno's port. The reeds grow 2–3m (6–9ft) high and supply the Uros with material for their transportation, homes, and even food. Dried and cut, the stalks float because their insides are hollow, making them excellent, quick-growing material for the construction of rafts and canoes in dry areas where wood is at a premium. Some of their boats even have two prows and small cabins.

Today's Uros have mostly lost knowledge of their original language,

The Uros people live on artificial islands made from *totora* reeds

speaking Aymara and/or Spanish instead, and many have moved to the mainland to try to escape poverty. Nevertheless, Peruvian genetic research has provided strong evidence that those who still live there are direct descendants of the pre-Hispanic Uros. Fishing, weaving, and tourism help today's Uros to make ends meet.

Man-made islands

There are still dozens of the floating *totora* islands in the lake, as there have been since before the time of the Inca. Everything on the islands, from the ground to the huts and observation towers, is made from the reeds. Cut and stacked blocks of the reeds are used to make the spongy ground. Gases emanate from the stalks as they rot, helping the islands to stay afloat. The islands are highly flammable, and to protect them from damage the local people build a heap of stones that separate fires from the dry reeds. There are also two churches and schools; electricity is generated by solar panels.

The lower part of the stalks, cut open, are a source of iodine and eaten; but they can also be used to make wraps that serve as painkillers. Uros also make a tea out of the reeds' flowers.

The community may originally have taken to living this way to escape violence on the mainland. Ethnically related groups of Uros live elsewhere in Bolivia, but this way of life is so far reserved for Lake Titicaca.

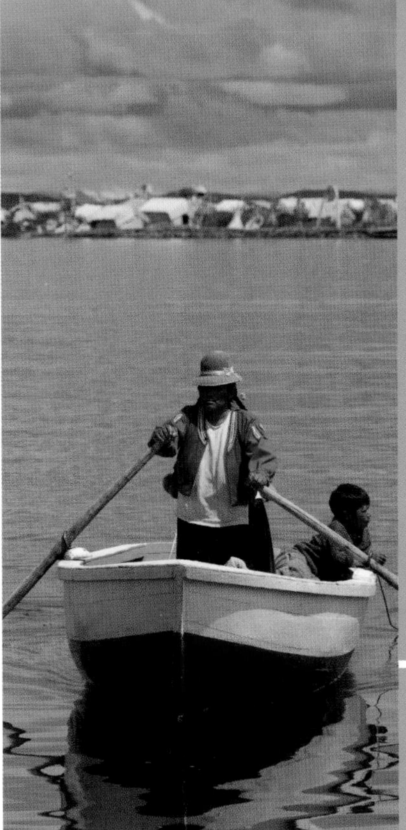

Two islanders making their way across the calm waters of Lake Titicaca

The locals use *totora* reeds to build their homes and canoes

Sleeping on the islands

On a clear, moonless night, the view of the star-filled sky from one of the islands on the lake is unforgettable. There are a handful of options for fantastic overnight stays. Reed cabins are available on Tupirmarka (tel: 051-835-016; www.urostupirmarka.com) and Khantati, and cabins on Anapia Island. Book the last two through Red Tur Comunitario, Jr. Cajamarca 206, Puno; tel: 051-364-329; www.redturcomunitario.com. The luxury option is the Suasi eco-hotel on a private island, which can be booked through All Ways Tours (Deustua 576, Puno; tel: 051-353-979; www.titicacaperu.com).

Excursions from Puno

Besides the lake, the Puno area sports a number of important archeological sites and Baroque colonial architecture within easy reach. Drier and – despite the high altitude – flatter than the Sacred Valley, the area is a melting pot of ancient cultures. Visitors have different options to move about, whether they want to travel on foot, bicycle, or on horseback, and there are fewer inclines than other parts of the Andes.

Sillustani

Some 35km (20 miles) from Puno is **Sillustani** ❺, with its circular burial towers or *chullpas* overlooking **Lago Umayo.** The age of the funeral towers, which are up to 12m (40ft) high, remains a puzzle. A Spanish chronicler described them as 'recently finished' in 1549, although some look as if they were never completed. They were built by people of the Colla civilization, who spoke Aymara, and whose architecture was considered more sophisticated than that of the Inca, but who had been conquered by the Inca about a century before the Spanish arrived. The *chullpas* were apparently

Inside Juli's San Juan Bautista church

A mother and son befriend a vicuña in Sillustani

used as burial chambers for members of the nobility, who were entombed together with their entire families and possessions to take with them to the next world. This is a stunningly beautiful spot with a wealth of birdlife, and guinea pigs scuttling across the paths.

Chucuito

Not far away (about 20km/12 miles from Puno) is **Chucuito** ❻, an Altiplano village that sits upon what was once an Inca settlement and which has an Inca sundial in the plaza. Close to the village stands the ancient fertility temple of the same name, whose most notable feature is an enclosure of giant stone phalluses. Have a look at the **Iglesia Santo Domingo** with its small museum; the church of **La Asunción** is also worth visiting.

Juli

Juli ❼ (about 80km/50 miles southeast of Puno), once the capital of the lake area, has four beautiful colonial churches. The largest – and oldest – of Juli's ornate churches is **San Juan Bautista**, with rich colonial paintings tracing the life of its patron saint, John the Baptist.

From the courtyard of the **Iglesia La Asunción** there is a captivating view of the lake. The other churches in the city are **San Pedro**, once the principal place of worship, in which a 400-strong Indian choir used to sing on Sunday, and **Santa Cruz**, which is just beside the city's old cemetery, and is currently in the worst state of repair. Santa Cruz was originally a Jesuit church upon the front of which indigenous stonemasons carved a huge sun – the Inca god – along with more traditional Christian symbols.

Inside Bolivia

Divided between two countries by the whims of Latin American history, the great lake's Andean history shared by the Quechua and Aymara living in and around it. Sites across the border in Bolivia are accessible (and stunning), and the views from Peru will already be a temptation. Nearby Tiahuanaco was the seat of one of the great pre-Hispanic cultures of the Americas.

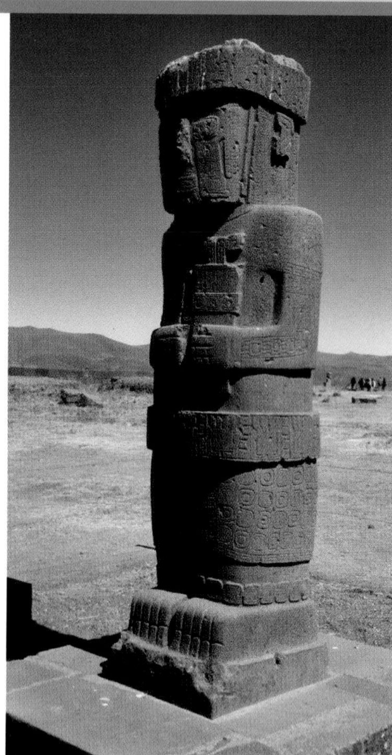

A large archeological relic dominates the skyline in Tiahuanaco

Copacabana

Copacabana ❽, a pleasant and friendly little town on the Bolivian side of the lake, can be reached by taking a minibus ride from Puno (via Yunguyo) around the side of the lake, passing the reeds waving in the wind, shy but curious children at the bends in the road, and the ever-present brilliant blue of Titicaca. This pleasant trip sometimes involves a short ferry ride at the **Strait of Tiquina**. As a pilgrimage site, Copacabana is accustomed to tourists and has a number of modest but clean restaurants and hotels, and a couple of very comfortable ones, newly built by the lakeside. It is most famous for its basilica devoted to the Virgin Mary containing a 16th-century carved wooden figure of the Virgin of Copacabana, the Christian guardian of the lake. The statue, finished in 1583, was the work of sculptor Francisco Tito Yupanqui, a descendant of the Inca Huayna Capac. Except during Mass, the statue stands with its back to the congregation – but facing the lake so that it can keep an eye out for any approaching storms and earthquakes. One of the loveliest outings in Copacabana is a dawn or dusk walk along the waterfront, watching the sky explode into color with the sunrise, or slip into the blue-black of night at sunset.

Bolivian islands

From Copacabana, launches can be hired to visit the Bolivian islands on Lake Titicaca – the **Isla del Sol** and the **Isla de la Luna** (the Island of the Sun and the Island of the Moon). The former (also accessible via a public ferry) has a sacred Inca rock at one end and the ruins of Pilko Caima, with a portal dedicated to the sun god at the other. The Island of the Moon, which is also known as Coati, has ruins of an Inca temple and a cloister for the Chosen Women *(see p.132)*.

Tiahuanaco

Near the sourthern tip of the lake, Bolivia's greatest archeological site was the center of a civilization that dominated the Titicaca and Altiplano from around 600BC to AD1000, until climate change brought massive drought and Tiahuanaco's power quickly crumbled. Sadly quarried for centuries after the conquest, it's only a relic of its original glory, but visitors can still appreciate the fine stonework – above all of the great Sun Gate – that make it worth the trip.

North of Puno

The pink stone and adobe town of **Lampa** ❾, 34km (21 miles) northwest of Juliaca, makes a delightful stop off the much-traveled Cusco–Puno route. One of the best-preserved colonial towns in the whole of Peru, it has imposing rose or ochre villas, including the **Casona Chukiwanka**, from which independence hero Simón Bolívar once rallied the townspeople against the Spanish. Its largest church, on the main square, **Santiago Apóstol,** built in the late 17th century, has Cusco School art, including a lovely carved pulpit. A more morbid attraction is the funeral chapel where Enrique Torres Belón, a local mining engineer who made it big in politics in Lima, had himself and his wife laid to rest, surrounded by skulls and bones extracted from tunnels under the church. Lampa also has a small sculpture and ceramics museum, the **Museo Kampac**. There are also nearby *chullpas* and caves.

Still pockmarked by an attack made by Shining Path guerrillas, the domed Baroque church of **Pucará** ❿ (meaning fortress), 64km (40 miles) north of Juliaca, was marked by, but survived Peru's violent recent past. Its interior is in dire need of restoration. The village is most famous for its production of ceramic bull figurines *(see p.57)* and also has a small **Lithic Museum** with artifacts from its nearby ruin, **Qalasaya** (www.pukara.org). The site was the center of a regional culture that flourished before Tiahuanaco, between 250BC and AD380, where a ceremonial center with nine pyramids can still be discerned.

A woman selling her wares to passersby

ACCOMMODATIONS

Puno may not be nearly as beautiful as Cusco, but it has numerous cozy hotel options to stay in where you can beat the frigid high-altitude nights and relax after excursions on the lake.

Puno

Casa Andina Classic – Puno Plaza
Jr. Grau 270
Tel: 051-367-520
www.casa-andina.com
A modern and cozy hotel near Puno's main square, with 35 rooms offering bed and breakfast facilities. Friendly and helpful staff; coca tea always available to help out against altitude sickness. **$$$$**

Casa Andina Classic – Puno Tikarani
Jr. Independencia 143
Tel: 051-367-803
www.casa-andina.com
Just five minutes away from the shores of Lake Titicaca, but still close to the center of Puno. This hotel has simple, comfortable rooms and a log fire to keep you warm. **$$$**

Casa Andina Private Collection – Isla Suasi
Isla Suasi
Tel: 051-9513-10070
www.casa-andina.com
A solar-powered lodge on the only privately owned island in the Lake Titicaca, on the northeast shore. Spa, canoes, and a gourmet restaurant. **$$$$$**

Lake Titicaca vista

Accomodations price categories

Prices are for one night's accommodation in a standard double room (unless otherwise specified)

$ = below US$20
$$ = US$20–40
$$$ = US$40–60
$$$$ = US$60–100
$$$$$ = over US$100

Colón Inn
Jr. Tacna 290
Tel: 051-351-432
www.coloninn.com
Hosted in a renovated elegant house that dates back to the 19th century, this hotel is warm and comfortable, despite the dated decor. Pleasant restaurant open for dinner, free internet. **$$$**

Hostal Europa Inn
Alfonso Ugarte 112
Tel: 051-353-026
www.europashotel.com
Located in a modern building only a few minutes away from Puno's main square, this *hostal* is quite popular with backpackers. Breakfast is served on the fifth floor, with a nice view over Lake Titicaca. **$$**

Hostal Pukara
Jr. Libertad 328
Tel: 051-368-448
Email: pukara@terra.com.pe
Friendly, comfortable, family-owned small hotel in the center of the city. It has hot water and heating – a luxury in the cold Puno nights. Lots of stairs, so make sure to check on which floor your room is. **$$**

Hotel Hacienda Puno
Jr. Deustua 297
Tel: 051-356-109
www.lahaciendapuno.com
Attractive hotel, with the feel of an old colonial house. Well decorated and comfortable, with good service. Buffet breakfast, free WiFi, restaurant with view available on the sixth floor. **$$$$**

Hotel Libertador Lago Titicaca Puno
Isla Esteves s/n
Tel: 051-367-780
www.libertador.com.pe
Large, modern, and luxurious hotel on the shores of Lake Titicaca. It has a private jetty, gym, Jacuzzi, and outdoor pool, as well as several restaurants and bars. **$$$$$**

Miski Wasi Inn
Jr. Santiago Giraldo 117
Tel: 051-365-861
Email: miskiwasiinn@hotmail.com
This is a quiet, friendly, family-run hotel, not far from the Plaza de Armas. There's plenty of hot water 24 hours a day, and good heating to keep you warm through the cold nights. **$$**

Sonesta Posada del Inca
Sesqui Centenario 610, Sector Huaje-Puno
Tel: 051-364-111
www.sonesta.com
Located 5km (3 miles) outside Puno, on Lake Titicaca, with great panoramic views. **$$$$$**

Totorani Inn
Av. La Torre 463
Tel: 051-364-535
www.totorani.com
Whilst this hotel is no great thing of beauty, the rooms are comfortable, and the owners are kind and helpful and will help arrange tours. Free internet access and laundry service. **$$**

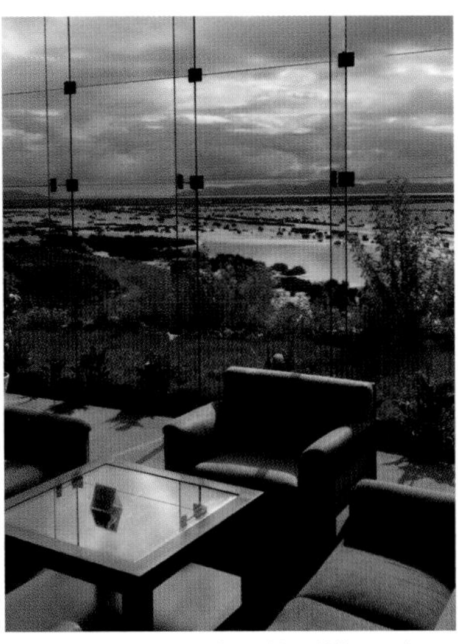

Overlooking the lake from Hotel Libertador

RESTAURANTS

This far from the Pacific Ocean, lake fish – particularly freshly caught trout – replaces the seafood of Peru's coastal areas. Andean food with a strong dash of Aymara culture is the main culinary attraction here, accompanied by a fair amount of international food catering to visitors, including some vegetarian meals.

Restaurant price categories

Prices are for a three-course menu including juice but no wine or coffee

$ = below US$2
$$ = US$2–5
$$$ = US$6–10
$$$$ = over US$10

Puno

Don Piero
Jr. Lima 356
Tel: 051-365-943/364-877
www.restaurantdonpiero.com
Popular with locals and gringos; its touristy menu has a choice of international and Peruvian dishes. It serves breakfast and vegetarian food. Live music some evenings. **$$$**

Mojsa
Jr. Lima 635, 2nd floor
Tel: 051-363-182
www.mojsarestaurant.com

Making *ceviche mixto*

Mojsa is an Aymara word that means sweet or delicious. A nice mixture of traditional Peruvian, international and *novoandino* food. Good breakfasts and excellent-value meals right through the day, including noteworthy pizzas. **$$$**

Pizzeria del Buho
Jr. Libertad 386
Tel: 051-356-223/367-771
Cozy small restaurant specializing in wood oven-baked pizzas. Extremely popular with foreigners. The menu also offers pastas and soups. Also at Jr. Lima 430. **$$$**

Restaurant Giorgio
Jr. Lima 430
Tel: 051-367-771
www.restaurantegiorgio.com
This large restaurant serves fusion Peruvian and international cuisine, like guinea pig with Greek-style potatoes and *ocopa* sauce. Most nights it also has floorshows of traditional dancing from the Altiplano. **$$$**

Tradiciones del Lago
Jr. Lima 418
Tel: 051-368-140
As the name suggests, this cozy restaurant offers food prepared to local recipes, but it also has some international dishes. Lake fish features prominently on the menu. Don't miss the *ceviche*. **$$$**

Ukuku's
Pasaje Grau 172, 2nd floor
Tel: 051-367-373
With huge portions of Peruvian and international fare, this is truly good value for money; interesting photos of the area adorn the walls. Another branch can be found at Libertad 216. **$$$**

NIGHTLIFE AND ENTERTAINMENT

Not much happens in Puno after dark. The few bars and discos around are mostly located along the pedestrian street, Jr. Lima.

Apu Salkantay
Jr. Lima 425
Tel: 051-351-962
A good place to warm up after a chilly day on the lake, this bar offers hot drinks and has a fireplace where you can hang out.

Café Bar Ekekos
Jr. Arequipa 655
Tel: 051-365-614
www.casonaplazahotel.com
This bar, located at the bottom of a hotel, has a small dance floor and large TV screens to watch soccer games. Happy hour every day between 5 and 9pm.

Kamizaraky Rock Pub
Pasaje Grau 148

Considered by most the best night place in Puno, it serves excellent cocktails and has occasional live rock music.

Positive Bar
Pasaje Lima 378
Tel: 095-131-0615/130-1381
www.positive-bar.com
This self-declared rock 'n' reggae hangout is mainly for the reggae aficionados out there. Friendly and young staff; previously known as Positive Vibrations.

TOURS

The Bolivian border cuts right through Lake Titicaca, but crossing the border is relatively straightforward. Tours can be taken around the lake, including to the Uros floating islands, to the ruins at Sillustani and Chucuito, and the town of Juli. You can also opt for a more adventurous way to explore the lake, by going on a bike tour or on a kayak trip. These agencies offer a variety of tours.

Edgar Adventures
Jr. Lima 328
Tel: 051-353-444
www.edgaradventures.com
One of the most experienced sustainable tourism agencies in Puno. Tours include archeological sites around Lake Titicaca, island communities, and plying the lake in kayaks. Options for volunteers are available.

Käfer Viajes y Turismo
Jr. Arequipa 179
Tel: 051-354-742
www.kafer-titicaca.com
Tour agency offering trips on the lake including the remote Suasi Island, as well as destinations further from Puno like the lovely colonial towns of Lampa and Pomata.

FESTIVALS AND EVENTS

Puno is known as the folkloric capital of Peru, due to its wealth of artistic and cultural expressions, particularly dance. Around Lake Titicaca there are many indigenous cultures and traditions to be observed.

February

Virgen de la Candelaria
'La Mamita Candicha,' the patron of Puno, is honored with folklore demonstrations. Thousands take part in parades, dances, fireworks, and music at this religious event.

Carnival
This pre-Lenten carnival is celebrated throughout Peru every mid-February, but in Puno it is especially big, with La Pandilla dancing and traditional festivities.

May

Las Alasitas
This important exhibition and sale of miniature handicrafts takes place from May 2–4. People buy miniature versions of the objects they wish to obtain in the future, such as houses and cars.

November

Puno Jubilee Week
Every November 1–7, Puno celebrates its founding by the Spanish, followed by a reenactment of the emergence of the legendary founders of the Inca Empire, Manco Capac and Mama Ocllo, from the waters of Lake Titicaca. Jubilee Week sees the best of Puno's folkloric festivities.

Central Sierra

Isolated for years by geography and terrorism, a breathtaking highway now links Lima to the church-filled city of Ayacucho, in the heart of the central Andes. This relatively unexplored area, renowned for its handicrafts, is a wonderful place to experience a traditionally Peruvian way of life and enjoy some spectacular mountain scenery.

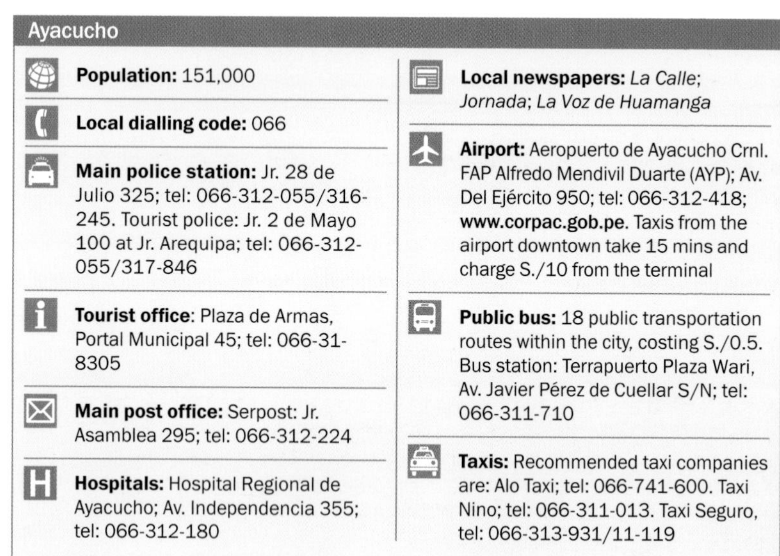

Ayacucho

Population: 151,000

Local dialling code: 066

Main police station: Jr. 28 de Julio 325; tel: 066-312-055/316-245. Tourist police: Jr. 2 de Mayo 100 at Jr. Arequipa; tel: 066-312-055/317-846

Tourist office: Plaza de Armas, Portal Municipal 45; tel: 066-31-8305

Main post office: Serpost: Jr. Asamblea 295; tel: 066-312-224

Hospitals: Hospital Regional de Ayacucho; Av. Independencia 355; tel: 066-312-180

Local newspapers: *La Calle*; *Jornada*; *La Voz de Huamanga*

Airport: Aeropuerto de Ayacucho Crnl. FAP Alfredo Mendivil Duarte (AYP); Av. Del Ejército 950; tel: 066-312-418; **www.corpac.gob.pe**. Taxis from the airport downtown take 15 mins and charge S./10 from the terminal

Public bus: 18 public transportation routes within the city, costing S./0.5. Bus station: Terrapuerto Plaza Wari, Av. Javier Pérez de Cuellar S/N; tel: 066-311-710

Taxis: Recommended taxi companies are: Alo Taxi; tel: 066-741-600. Taxi Nino; tel: 066-311-013. Taxi Seguro, tel: 066-313-931/11-119

Historically, Ayacucho and the central highlands have been the link between Lima and Cusco. It is here that much of Peru's mineral wealth is to be found, which brought both riches and hardship to the area. In the 1980s, terrorism and emergency military rule made the highland provinces unsafe and unwelcoming, but with the return of peace and the building of a new highway from Lima, the area is once again welcoming travelers who enjoy its traditional way of life, handicrafts, and often spectacular mountain scenery.

These mountains contain caves where, as at Pikimachay, traces have been found of the first known inhabitants dating back to over 15,000 years ago. Ayacucho was also important during the Wari (or Huari) culture, which dominated the region for several centuries before falling to the Inca in the 14th century. Mining in the area continues, as it has done for centuries, with the giant Cerro de Pasco mine still being one of the world's most important producers of copper. To the north are the imposing peaks of the Cordillera Occidental and the mysterious rock formations at Marcahuasi.

Ayacucho

Ayacucho ❶ was founded by Francisco Pizarro in 1540 as an important communications link between Lima and Cusco. Today, it is a major center for traditional handicrafts *(see p.59)*. Its reputation as a city with 'a church on every street corner' may be exaggerated, but it does have 33 churches, most of them still in regular use. The best times to visit are during Easter Week, which is given up entirely to processions and fiestas, or the week at the end of April, when Ayacucho's patron saint is remembered with more riotous celebrations.

Ayacucho is famed for its 33 churches, most still in regular use

Children tend their sheep in the highlands around Ayacucho

The center

The most impressive church in the city is the early Baroque **Catedral** Ⓐ, Nuestra Señora de las Nieves (Our Lady of the Snows; daily 10–11am, 5.30–7pm) on the Plaza Mayor de Huamanga, also known as Plaza de Armas. Begun in 1612, it has superb gilt altars, a silver tabernacle, and a beautifully carved pulpit. It

Local punch

While the herbal drinks sold in glasses are best left to the locals, the *ponche* (punch) is well worth a try. This is a milk-based punch flavored with peanut, sesame, clove, cinnamon, walnuts, and sugar, and spiked with pisco. You could accompany it with one of the hearty local dishes such as *puca picante*, a stew made of pieces of pork, potatoes, and toasted peanuts, served with rice and parsley.

also contains Stations of the Cross paintings brought from Rome. During the famous Semana Santa celebrations during Easter Week, this is one of the most visited churches in all Peru (*see p.44*). Another outstanding church, the Jesuit **Templo de la Compañía** Ⓑ (Mon–Sat 9am–noon, Sun 11am–1pm), built in 1605, boasts an unusual carved facade of orange-red stone and has a lovely gilded altar. The interior also has richly carved wood and 17th-century religious paintings.

A few blocks away up Jirón 9 de Diciembre stands the Renaissance church of **Santo Domingo** Ⓒ (Mass daily 7am and 6pm). It has an altar richly decorated with gold leaf, but it is this church's role in history that is most significant: bells in its small towers rang out the first peals of Peru's independence following the decisive Battle of Ayacucho. Round the corner on Jirón Callao, the finest carved pulpit of all Ayacucho's churches is to be found in the **Iglesia de San Francisco de Paula** (Mass daily 7am, Sun 9am).

Although Spanish colonial architecture is the pride of Ayacucho, this was an important area for many civilizations prior to the arrival of the Spaniards. Five hundred years before the Inca, the Wari empire dominated these highlands, and traces of that and other influences are to be found at the **Museo Hipólito Unanue** Ⓓ (Mon–Fri 9am–5pm, Sat until 1pm; charge), part of the **Instituto Nacional de Cultura** on Avenida Independencia. The museum's collection ranges from 1500BC stone carvings to Wari ceremonial bowls, Chancay textiles, and

The baroque altar in the Templo de la Compañía

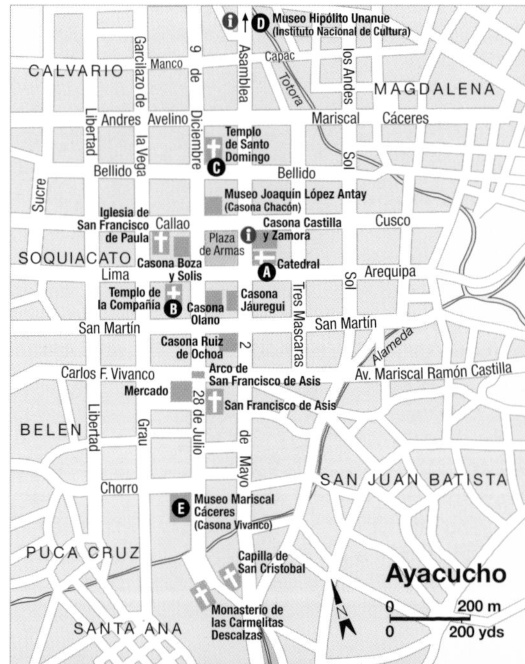

Stall at Ayacucho market

stone and ceramic Inca pieces.

Ayacucho has several other museums that are worth visiting. The **Museo Joaquín López Antay** (Mon–Sat 9.15am–1pm, 3–6.30pm; free) in the colonial **Casona Chacón** (now a bank) on the Plaza Mayor de Huamanga (also called Plaza de Armas, *see p.173*) has a good collection of local art, popular objects, and photographs of the city and its surroundings.

The **Museo Mariscal Cáceres** Ⓔ (daily 8am–noon, 2–6pm; charge), housed in the elegant 17th-century **Casona Vivanco** on Jirón 28 de Julio, has a fine display of colonial paintings and furnishings. The *casona* is one of the best preserved of the colonial mansions which are the hallmark of Ayacucho. Another splendid mansion is the **Casona Boza y Solis** (Mon–Fri 8am–6pm), the seat of the provincial prefecture. Built in 1740, it has a two-story interior courtyard and a wide staircase lined with beautiful imported colored tiles.

Shopping is also a lively experience at the city's sprawling **market**, a block south of Jirón San Martín. Here, stalls offer everything from handicrafts and hand-knitted sweaters, to rubber boots and hot peppers, and other medicinal herbs. Delicious freshly made bread, with cinnamon

TRAIN TO THE SKIES

Breathtaking views and altitudes make Peru's 'train to the skies' one of the world's greatest rail journeys. Crossing deep ravines over some of the highest railway bridges or climbing in switchbacks, it's hard to imagine a way to experience the beauty of traversing the Andes in greater comfort or at closer proximity. The steep inclines and frigid weather make the engineering feat all the more remarkable considering the 19th-century technology the thousands of workers used to toil up the mountains.

Access to Machu Picchu is limited to foot and rail traffic. That automatically makes the train ride to Aguas Calientes the most famous in the country – but beautiful as it may be, by far the greater trip is the spectacular 346km (215-mile) journey between Lima and Huancayo in the central Andes.

Polish engineer Ernest Malinowski proposed the railway in 1851, but it took until 1870 for the work to begin. Conditions were tough and the 10,000 workers, including Chinese from Macao and Chileans, suffered a significant mortality rate. Machinery, tracks, and pieces of bridges were imported from the UK, France, and the US. Under the leadership of US engineer Henry Meiggs the work initially went smoothly, but it was interrupted by the War of the Pacific *(see p.114)*. Construction resumed

Peru's mountainous scenery makes for some spectacular train journeys

in 1890 after financing was secured, and the railway finally reached Huancayo in 1908. Until the completion of the new Tibetan railway in 2006, it was the highest in the world, giving it the apt moniker 'train to the skies.' It is run by the private Ferrocarril Central Andino (FCCA), a US-owned company.

Dramatic climb

Most of the rail traffic is freight, but every two to three weeks, the 12-car, 500-passenger train pulls out of Lima's central Desamparados station. Starting along the Rimac River, it stops at Chosica and San Bartolomé before beginning its dramatic climb through the Yaulí Valley that will take it through 68 tunnels, over 61 bridges, and up nine switchbacks to a highest point of 4,782m (15,688ft) at the Galera station (which has a sign saying 15,881ft) after 172km (107 miles) and about eight hours. Both the cheaper *clásico* and the wood-paneled *turismo* cars carry oxygen. At Oruyo, the passenger trains head south through the picturesque Mantaro Valley before reaching Huancayo. From there, travelers can also continue via train to Huancavelica, 128km (80 miles) away, on the twice-daily *Tren Macho* (one per day on Sundays), restarted in December 2010. The FCCA also has ambitious plans for a $100 million refurbishment of its network, including a tunnel that would cut the journey time between Lima and Huancayo from 13 hours to 2½ hours.

For booking information see p.255.

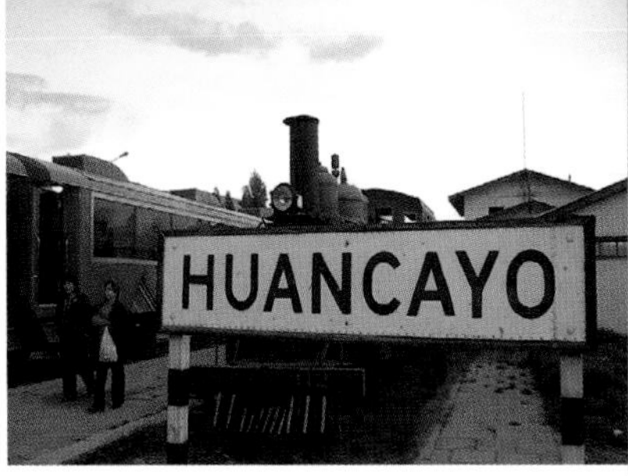

Pulling up at Huancayo station, the end of the journey

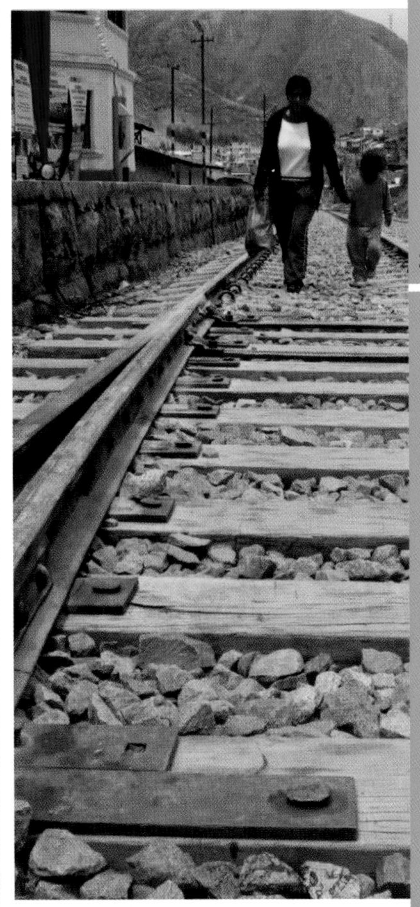

A mother and child taking a walk along the tracks

and aniseed, is sold from cloth-covered baskets.

Around Ayacucho

In the rolling hills 37km (22 miles) northeast of the city is the village of **Quinua ❷**. It was on the pampa (plain) 1km (½ mile) outside the village that the decisive Battle of Ayacucho was fought against the Spanish troops on December 9, 1824. Although outnumbered almost two to one, the Venezuelan general Antonio José de Sucre won the battle, the last fought by the Spaniards in Latin America. The place of the encounter is marked by a hulking 1970s obelisk some 44m (144ft) high, built with Venezuelan oil wealth. Its one redeeming feature is the spectacular scenery to be seen from its viewing platform. Each December, the victory is celebrated in an eight-day extravaganza.

The village of Quinua itself is a center for handicrafts. Almost all the red-tiled roofs are topped with good-luck symbols: small ceramic churches or pairs of bulls, made originally for festivals coinciding with the branding of cattle. These pieces are also on sale in the village's many stores, together with handmade guitars and sculptures in *huamanga* stone.

One stopover is the ruins about 20km (12 miles) outside Ayacucho on the way to Quinua. These extensive remains, in a landscape full of tuna cactuses, are thought to be the remains of the **Wari** (Huari) culture that flourished here between the 6th and 11th centuries. Ayacucho tour companies organize day trips of Quinua and the battlefield, and also a visit to **Vilcashuamán ❸**, interesting above all for the Spanish constructions built directly on top of Inca architecture. Vilcashuamán is a day trip 120km (75 miles) south of Ayacucho, about a four-hour drive. The village is most famous for its *usnu* or ceremonial pyramid, preserved almost intact. Inca remains are also to be found at nearby **Baños Intihuatana ❹** (a 30-minute walk from the highway). Next to a lagoon thought to have been constructed by the Inca, there are the remains of a palace, baths, a tower, a

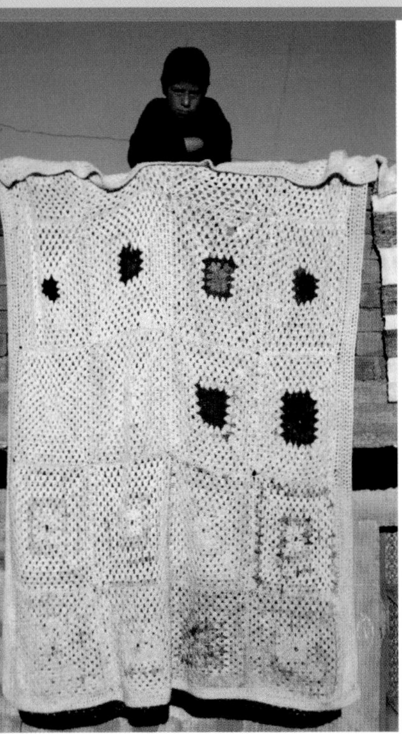

A Huancavelica boy selling quilts on a terrace

Temple of the Sun, a sacrificial stone, and a boulder carved with 17 angles.

North from Ayacucho

Ayacucho's nearest northern neighbors – although it takes several hours to reach them – are the historic towns of Huancavelica and Huancayo. The latter is the starting point for journeys to the Mantaro Valley, which has several places well worth a visit, including the old capital of Spanish Peru, Jauja, and the national park of Junín.

Huancavelica

Huancavelica has a lengthy past as one of Peru's main mining towns. Silver was discovered here soon after the Spanish conquest, and through the 17th and 18th centuries it was a great creator of wealth, though not for the indigenous people who worked in the mines. The mines at **Santa Barbara**, some 5km (3 miles) outside the city, can be visited. As in Ayacucho, some of this mining wealth was spent on the city's churches. The red sandstone-fronted **Catedral San Antonio** in the Plaza de Armas in the center of Huancavelica has a fine gilded altar and some Baroque paintings. Nearby, **San Francisco** shows how Spanish Baroque architecture became far more ornate in the 18th century, while the church and convent of **Santo Domingo** has paintings shipped especially from Rome.

Huancayo

More interesting is the bustling city of **Huancayo** ❺, situated some 400km

Precious metals

As the world market price for metals has continued to climb, so has the value of Peru's vast mineral deposits that make it one of the world's biggest producers of gold, silver, and copper, among others. Foreign mining companies have flocked to Peru, and booming metals exports have helped the economy grow at one of the fastest paces on the planet. Peru's dependence on world market prices for its metals makes it vulnerable, however, and the unequal distribution of wealth has contributed to unrest and the high number of votes captured by populist candidates in the 2011 elections.

A street vendor in Huancayo sprays water over her vegetables to keep them fresh

(250 miles) northwest of Ayacucho. The city's name means 'place of stones,' and from the remaining monuments it is easy to see why. Its main attraction is the **Capilla de la Merced** (Mon–Sun 9am–noon, 3–6.30pm), the colonial church where the Peruvian constitution was signed in 1839. The people of Huancayo are also very proud that it was in their city that slavery was abolished in Peru in 1854, and the statue in the main plaza honors Mariscal Ramón Castilla, who pushed the measure through.

There is also an interesting regional museum in the **Museo del Colegio Salesiano** (Mon–Fri 8am–noon, 2–6pm; charge) in the El Tambo district, while the Cerrito de la Libertad has panoramic views. A short walk farther on are the remarkable eroded stone towers known as the **Torre Torre**, which also give views over the town.

Mantaro Valley

About 8km (5 miles) from Huancayo is the village of **Cochas Chico**, where some of the best local handicrafts can be bargained for. There is also the **Convento de Santo Ocopa**. In the convent there is a precious library, with texts dating back to the 15th century. Further north, the **Santuario Warivilca** is a fortified ruin from the days of the Wari Empire.

The mountains here form the Cordillera Huaytapallana, which is 17km (11 miles) long and has five peaks over 5,000m (16,400ft) high, with many important glaciers. The highest of the peaks is the snow-covered Nevado Lasuntaysuyo.

Some 40km (25 miles) from Huancayo is the small town of **Jauja**, best known for being the capital of Spanish Peru before Lima was founded, and for the expression *país de Jauja*, referring to a never-never land of milk and honey. Its narrow streets and blue-painted houses seem to reflect hundreds of years of unhurried existence. Boats can be rented by the hour to take you to the nearby Laguna de Paca.

Some 170km (105 miles) north of Huancayo is a favorite destination for birdwatchers: the **Reserva Nacional de Junín**. The lakes here abound with aquatic birds and endemic Andean species.

Huánuco

Previously part of the Wari (or Huari) and then the Inca culture, the present city of Huánuco was founded by Gómez de Alvarado in 1539. It has always been the market center for a mainly agricultural and wooded region, and maintains much of its slow charm today. The central square or Plaza de Armas has a 19th-century sculpture by an Italian designer but, unlike many other Peruvian cities, its cathedral is modern, dating from 1966. Two older churches are the **Iglesia San Cristóbal** (open during Masses), the first built by the Spaniards, which is adorned with fine woodcarvings, and the **Iglesia de San Francisco** (daily 6–9am, 5–8pm), first constructed in 1560 but remodeled in the 18th century in neoclassical style.

Five km (3 miles) outside Huánuco stands **Kotosh** ❻ and its famous **Templo de las Manos Cruzadas.** As the name suggests, this temple, believed to be from about 2300 to 2000BC, making it one of the oldest of the Andes, has carvings of crossed hands on the walls. According to some archeologists, this is a sign that the ancient people who lived here had a dual vision of the universe.

Inca remains near Huánuco

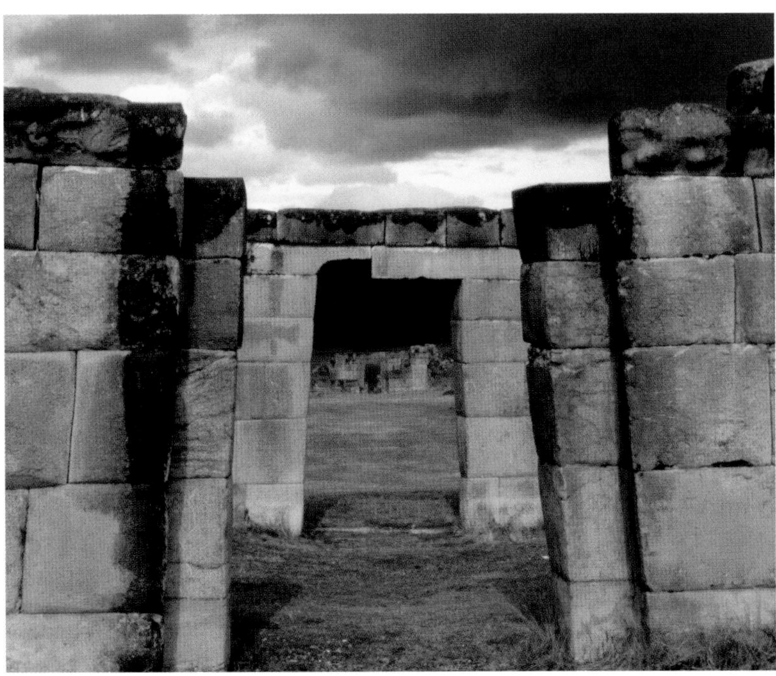

ACCOMMODATIONS

Ayacucho and its surroundings have a large choice of hotels. Most are rather basic, but good value. They tend to be full around Easter Week, so it is necessary to book well in advance. It is worth checking whether your room faces the street, because these towns have a lot of traffic and the roads tend to be noisy.

Accommodations price categories

Prices are for one night's accommodation in a standard double room (unless otherwise specified)

$ = below US$20
$$ = US$20–40
$$$ = US$40–60
$$$$ = US$60–100
$$$$$ = over US$100

Ayacucho

Ayacucho Hotel Plaza
Jr. 9 de Diciembre 184
Tel: 066-312-202
www.bookingbox.org.uk/hotelplaza
Built around a courtyard on the Plaza de Armas, this hotel is popular with business travelers. As Ayacucho's largest hotel, it provides full services and amenities. Rooms are fairly plain, with high ceilings. **$$$$**

Hostal La Florida
Jr. Cusco 310
Tel: 066-312-565
www.bookingbox.org.uk/hostalflorida
This hotel's pretty courtyard, full of cacti and flowering plants, gives it a tranquil air. The rooms are plain, but clean and comfortable, with good views from the upper levels. WiFi available. **$**

Hotel Santa Rosa

Hotel Santa Rosa
Jr. Lima 166
Tel: 066-314-614/315-830
www.hotel-santarosa.com
Centrally situated, in a large colonial house with inner patio, this hotel offers spacious, clean and comfortable rooms and good service. As an added bonus, parking space (a rarity in Ayacucho) is available, and there is WiFi access. **$$$**

Huancavelica

Hotel Presidente
Plaza de Armas
Tel: 067-452-760
www.hoteles-del-centro.com
Set in an old stone building with wooden balconies, this is Huancavelica's top choice. Simple rooms, but there's reliable hot water and a range of facilities, including WiFi and laundry service. **$$–$$$$**

Huancayo

Hotel Presidente
Real 1138
Tel: 064-231-275
www.hoteles-del-centro.com
Situated in the heart of Huancayo, this businesslike hotel is smart, clean, and efficient – often used for conventions. Good facilities, including a restaurant that can cater to large groups. **$$$–$$$$**

RESTAURANTS

A meat-heavy, traditional restaurant scene greets you in the highlands, but vegetarian options are also available. Ayacucho has some very decent restaurants, and so does Huancayo, serving a number of local dishes such as the *papa a la Huancaína*, potato covered in a cheese and peanut sauce. *Pachamanca*, meat and vegetables cooked under hot stones in the earth, is also from these parts.

Restaurant price categories

Prices are for a three-course menu including juice but no wine or coffee

$ = below US$2
$$ = US$2–5
$$$ = US$6–10
$$$$ = over US$10

Ayacucho

Los Alamos
Jr. Cusco 215
Tel: 066-312-782
www.bookingbox.org/losalamos
Just off the Plaza de Armas, yet very quiet, thanks to its setting around a pretty courtyard. Outdoor seating in a vine-covered tent. Local chicken and meat dishes are a specialty. American-style breakfasts available. **$$**

Mia Pizza
Mariscal Cáceres 1045
Tel: 066-313-273
Sing like an Italian by grabbing the microphone at this cozy pizzeria plus karaoke bar. Open evenings only. **$**

Nino
9 de Diciembre 205
Tel: 066-814-537
A large old house, with some rooms containing huge paintings of Andean scenes, is the setting for this restaurant specializing in meats – particularly Peruvian chicken on a spit – and Italian food. It has a patio garden with an open fire. **$$**

Recreo las Flores
Jr. José Olaya 106, Plaza Conchopata
Tel: 066-316-349
Having celebrated its 30th anniversary in 2010, this may well be the best place to try guinea pig in all of the Peruvian Andes. For the less adventurous, there are also other meats such as suckling pig and trout. There are several patios at this old building slightly outside the center. **$**

Restaurant La Casona
Jr. Bellido 463
Tel: 066-312-733
www.bookingbox.org/lacasona
Pork dishes and highland food on this exclusively Peruvian menu. Recommended by travelers for its large portions and good value. Often has excellent live music at weekends. **$$**

Pachamanca is one of the region's specialty dishes

Huancayo

Detrás de la Catedral
Ancash 335
Tel: 064-212-969
As its name indicates, it's right behind the cathedral in an old building with colorful interiors and offering local dishes in a cozy atmosphere. It's hard to beat for value. **$**

Huancahuasi
Av. Mariscal Castilla 2222, El Tambo
Tel: 066-244-826
www.huancahuasi.com
Without doubt the best restaurant in Huancayo, and often packed with Peruvian tourists. On weekends it does a fine *pachamanca*. They have recently opened a new branch in Lima's Santa Catalina neighborhood. **$$$**

Huánuco

Pizzeria Don Sancho
Av. General Prado 645
Tel: 066-516-906
Good pizzas and a wide variety of pastas. A good choice for those looking for an alternative to the meat-heavy fare. Open late. **$$**

NIGHTLIFE AND ENTERTAINMENT

The towns in the area are relatively quiet during the week, but wake up during the weekends. Festivals are big here, and unmissable *(see section below)*.

Ayacucho

Los Balcones
Jr. Asamblea 187, 2nd floor
Tel: 066-814-139
This is a popular disco/*peña* among locals. It also occasionally hosts live Andean bands.

Taberna La Magia Negra
Jr. 9 de diciembre, corner Cáceres
Tel: 066-328-289
This is a great place to hang out, and it is popular with gringos. La Magia Negra offers pizzas and drinks in a relaxed atmosphere, with live music.

Huancayo

La Noche
Jr. San Antonio 241, San Carlos
Tel: 064-223-726
Friday is the biggest night out at La Noche, the self-proclaimed best place to party in town. This is a good choice for those looking for a livelier night out. It is best to take a taxi here, as it is not safe to walk.

TOURS

For tours in the Central Sierra, there are several travel agencies around Ayacucho's Plaza de Armas. In Huancayo there are also several other options for tours of Mantaro Valley.

Ayacucho

Morochucos Reps
9 de diciembre 136
Tel: 066-317-844
This reputable tour agency offers guides for local tours of the city center and day trips to the Ayacucho battlefield and village of Quinoa as well as the Wari archeological site.

Wari Tours
Jr. Lima 138, Of. B
Tel: 066-311-415
http://waritoursayacucho.blogspot.com
Offers a range of tours around Ayacucho.

Warpa Picchu
Portal Independencia 66

Tel: 066-315-191
Email: verbist@terra.com.pe
www.bookingbox.org/es-warpa-picchu.html
For adventure tourism, including mountain biking, horse riding, and four-wheel drive tours in the mountains, contact Pierre Verbist well in advance in order to organize tailored trips.

Huancayo

Incas del Perú
Av. Giraldez 652
Tel: 064-223-303
www.incasdelperu.org
Offers tours in the area, jungle trips, language courses, volunteering, and bike rentals.

FESTIVALS AND EVENTS

This area receives relatively few tourists, so festivals are still pretty genuine. And there are plenty of them throughout the year, with lots of dancing and music.

January

Reyes Magos
Ayacucho
On January 6 in Ayacucho's Belén neighborhood, groups of dancers celebrate the advent of the Three Kings by spending the night in a traditional *tijeras* dance competition.

Fiesta de los Negritos
Throughout January local dance groups, dressed in colorful costumes with black masks, perform traditional dances. It's especially popular in Huancayo.

February

Huaylarsh
The *huaylarsh* is a typical and colorful Andean dance from this area, which was once performed to coincide with the sowing and harvest of potatoes. It now overlaps with Carnival.

Carnaval
In Ayacucho, Carnival is celebrated with dances and water fights, and the throwing of unripe walnuts at young people. The celebrations are also very big in Huánuco.

March/April

Semana Santa
The Easter Week celebrations in Ayacucho are among the largest in Peru, with 10 days of processions and events. In Tarma, Semana Santa is celebrated with colorful processions on carpets of flowers.

July

Yawar Fiesta
Ayacucho and Apurímac
Yawar is a Quechua word that means blood, and this festival is definitely bloody. It originated in colonial times: a condor (symbolizing indigenous people) is tied to a bull (which symbolizes Spain) and the two fight for survival. The bull used to be killed with dynamite, but the festival is more regulated now.

August

Huaylas Trilla
Huancavelica
This August 30 festival coincides with the wheat harvest.

Palm Sunday procession

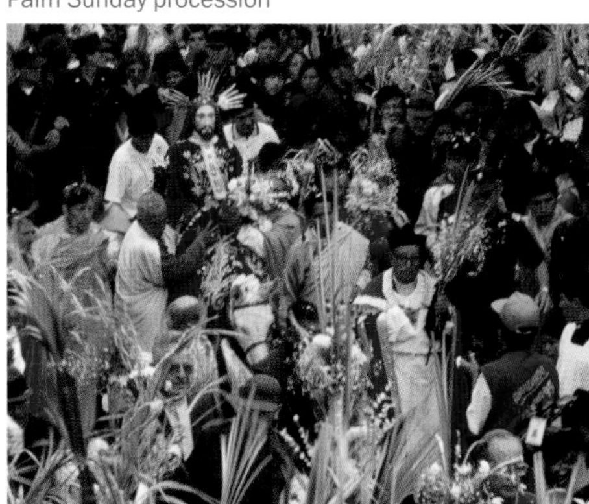

Huaraz and the Cordillera Blanca

The remote area around Huascarán, Peru's highest summit, and the Callejón de Huaylas valley, draws dedicated trekking and climbing enthusiasts, as well as those who are content to spend their days relaxing in a spectacular mountain setting and exploring the villages that sprawl the hillside.

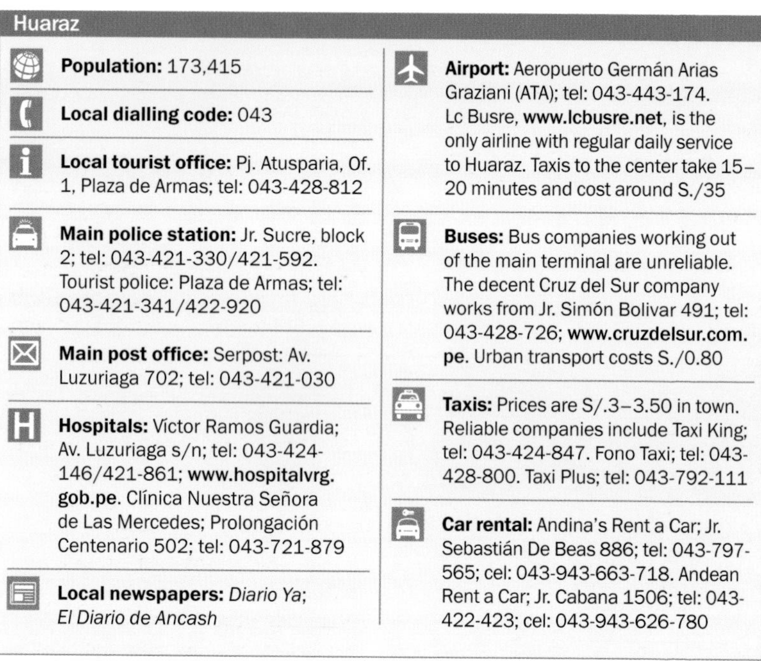

Huaraz

Population: 173,415

Local dialling code: 043

Local tourist office: Pj. Atusparia, Of. 1, Plaza de Armas; tel: 043-428-812

Main police station: Jr. Sucre, block 2; tel: 043-421-330/421-592. Tourist police: Plaza de Armas; tel: 043-421-341/422-920

Main post office: Serpost: Av. Luzuriaga 702; tel: 043-421-030

Hospitals: Víctor Ramos Guardia; Av. Luzuriaga s/n; tel: 043-424-146/421-861; **www.hospitalvrg.gob.pe**. Clínica Nuestra Señora de Las Mercedes; Prolongación Centenario 502; tel: 043-721-879

Local newspapers: *Diario Ya*; *El Diario de Ancash*

Airport: Aeropuerto Germán Arias Graziani (ATA); tel: 043-443-174. Lc Busre, **www.lcbusre.net**, is the only airline with regular daily service to Huaraz. Taxis to the center take 15–20 minutes and cost around S./35

Buses: Bus companies working out of the main terminal are unreliable. The decent Cruz del Sur company works from Jr. Simón Bolivar 491; tel: 043-428-726; **www.cruzdelsur.com.pe**. Urban transport costs S./0.80

Taxis: Prices are S/.3–3.50 in town. Reliable companies include Taxi King; tel: 043-424-847. Fono Taxi; tel: 043-428-800. Taxi Plus; tel: 043-792-111

Car rental: Andina's Rent a Car; Jr. Sebastián De Beas 886; tel: 043-797-565; cel: 043-943-663-718. Andean Rent a Car; Jr. Cabana 1506; tel: 043-422-423; cel: 043-943-626-780

Stretching for 160km (255 miles) and ranging in altitude from a mere 1,800m (5,900ft) to 4,080m (13,380ft), the valley known as the **Callejón de Huaylas** rates as one of the finest areas in all of South America for its superb mountain vistas and trekking opportunities. It is bordered on the east by the **Cordillera Blanca** (White Mountains) – a mountain range with the greatest number of 6,000m (20,000ft) peaks outside the Himalayas – and on the west by the lower range known as the Cordillera Negra (Black Mountains) for their sparseness of vegetation and complete lack of snow. To the north, the valley terminates with the Cañón del Pato, a narrow gorge of a canyon with sheer rock walls, steep precipices, and a dirt road winding its way through numerous crudely constructed tunnels down toward the coast.

Trekking on a glacier in the Cordillera Blanca

Huaraz

The center of most commercial activity and the common destination for visitors to the Callejón de Huaylas is the city of **Huaraz** ❶. There is an airport just outside the town, but flights from Lima are very unreliable, so most people get here by bus, from either Lima or Chimbote – both journeys take about eight hours on a paved road. There are frequent services, and the more expensive buses are quite comfortable. As the capital of the department of Ancash, and with a population of more than 80,000 inhabitants, Huaraz is well equipped to support the demands of tourism, and all necessities are readily available. Scores of low-cost hostels offer accommodations of varying kinds, some very

A brightly dressed festivalgoer in the Callejón de Huaylas

Huaraz cafés

Spacious and airy, **Café Andino** (Morales 75) is a great place to grab breakfast or step into for a mid-morning coffee. A charming travelers' hangout, with a beautiful view of the Cordillera Blanca from its outside balcony, it's also a great place to kick back beside the fireplace when the cold starts to descend in in the late afternoon. Both it and **California Café** (28 de Julio 562), around the corner from the Plaza de Armas, have libraries and board games and are good sources for last-minute trekking and climbing information.

basic, others very comfortable, and there are a few higher-priced hotels for those who would like a bit more comfort during their mountain retreat. From the city, some two dozen glistening white summits can be seen.

Before departing for remote regions, or after a long trek in the mountains, you'll find plenty of activity in the bustling town. Along the main street of Luzuriaga, vendors sell a wide selection of woolen goods, pan flutes, and ceramic replicas of the Chavín temple. Storefront tour companies set out brightly colored billboards promoting day trips to popular tourist sites and advertise an assortment of climbing and trekking gear for hire. Other traditionally dressed highlanders sell regional food specialties from wooden carts. Andean cheeses, rich honey, and *manjar blanco* (a milk-based fudge used as a dessert or filling) are a few tasty edibles that are worth trying. A wide range of restaurants caters to international tastes: pizzerias, Chinese food, and hamburgers are found alongside more typical dishes such as *lomo saltado* (strips of beef with potatoes), *pollos a la brasa* (griddled chicken), and *cuy* (roasted guinea pig).

Worth a visit is the **Museo Arqueológico** (Avenida Luzuriaga 762; Mon–Sat 8.15am–6.30pm, Sun 8.15am–5pm; charge), off the **Plaza de Armas**. It has an interesting collection and is considered noteworthy for its display of stone monoliths from the Recuay culture, which date from 400BC to AD600. Also on display are mummies, ceramics, and household utensils dating from the same period.

Alpaca yarn on sale at a market

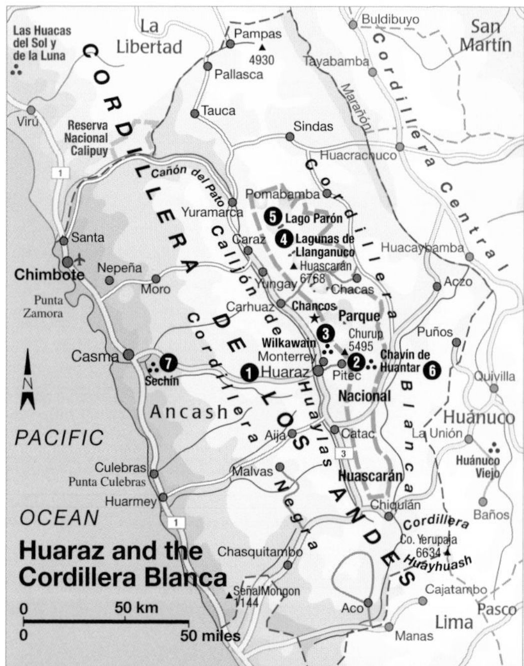

Watching an incredible sunset in the Cordillera Blanca

The outlying area of Huaraz offers numerous opportunities for day excursions. Footpaths lead to a number of small villages and agricultural areas within walking distance of the city center. Rataquenua, Unchus, Marían, and Pitec are just a few of the pueblos that can be visited in a few hours.

Trekking near Huaraz

The Huaraz area is a trekker's paradise. Just above the city is **El Mirador**, a scenic lookout marked by a huge white cross. The route heads uphill east along city streets, which eventually turn into a footpath beside an irrigation canal lined with eucalyptus trees. Fields of wheat ripening in the sun add a serene, pastoral feel. At the top, the highest mountain in Peru, **Huascarán** (6,768m/22,200ft), dominates the northern horizon; the lower Vallunaraju (5,680m/18,600ft) peeks out over the foothills to the east, and the city of Huaraz sprawls below.

Another popular choice is the **Pitec Trail to Laguna Churup** ❷. There is no public transportation to this small village 10km (6 miles) from the center of Huaraz, but often a taxi driver or someone driving a pick-up truck can be found at *el puente* (the bridge) at Huaraz who will navigate the rough road to Pitec. Walking is an option – it takes around two hours at a slowish pace – but it's nicer to be fresh at the trailhead and then walk back down to Huaraz afterwards.

The trail begins at the parking lot before the village of Pitec is reached.

A well-worn footpath heads north up a ridgeline, and the Churup massif rises just above 5,495m (18,000ft) in the distance. At the base of this mountain is the destination of the hike, Laguna Churup, fed by glacial melt-off and surrounded by huge boulders. A picnic lunch and a midday siesta in the warm sun reward the effort of getting here. A leisurely hike back to Huaraz follows a cobbled road through *campesino* (subsistence farmer) homesteads.

Wilkawain

About 8km (5 miles) north of Huaraz, and easily reached on foot, is the small pre-Inca ruin of **Wilkawain** ❸ (daily 8am–5pm; charge). Little is known about this three-storied structure which stands in the middle of an agricultural valley, but, because of the typical masonry style, it is thought to date from the expansionist period of the Wari-Tiahuanaco culture (AD200–700). The windowless inner chambers can be explored with a flashlight, or with candles proffered by any one of the hordes of schoolboys who haunt the site and offer their services as guides, for a small fee. Most of the rooms within the construction are inaccessible from the debris of centuries, but a few of them have been opened up to reveal a sophisticated ventilation system and skillful stone craftsmanship. Willkawain is a good walk for acclimatization when you first arrive in Huaraz.

Monterrey

The village of **Monterrey**, just 5km (3 miles) outside Huaraz, is worth a visit for its *baños termales* (hot springs). Two swimming pools of warm water,

Exploring the Santa Cruz Trail

Camping in a spectacular setting near Huaraz

and private baths of the steaming variety, are extremely inviting, especially after a rigorous trek in the mountains. About 35km (22 miles) farther up the valley is **Chancos**, which claims to have its own Fountain of Youth – more thermal baths with natural saunas and pools of flowing hot water.

Santa Cruz Trail

Buses frequently leave Huaraz, loaded with an assortment of *campesinos*, their chickens, *cuyes* (guinea pigs), and children, heading for the small village of **Yungay**, which lies north down the valley. This was completely destroyed by the 1970 earthquake. During the most recent rebuilding of Yungay, the village site was shifted a few kilometers north of its original location in the hope that it would now be out of the way of any future natural disasters. Yungay is the turn-off point for the popular two-hour ride up to the **Lagunas de Llanganuco ❹**. *Camionetas*, small pick-up trucks, wait in the plaza to transport hikers and sightseers up the valley to the dazzling, glacier-fed lakes. It is also one of the starting points for the **Llanganuco to Santa Cruz Loop** *(see p.25)*. One of the most frequently hiked trails in the region, this five-day route passes under a dozen peaks over 5,800m (19,000ft), and panoramic views abound.

Caraz is the end point of this loop, a pretty town that was fortunate enough to survive several recent earthquakes

Traditional dress

Throughout the Callejón de Huaylas, a lifestyle dating back centuries continues to thrive. The traditional dress of the villagers has not changed radically in many years. The women, especially, hold on to their heritage, wearing layers of colorful woolen skirts and embroidered blouses which developed during colonial times. In addition, each wears a hat whose style may vary significantly from village to village. The custom of hat-wearing can also be used to indicate marital status, as in the village of Carhuaz. There, a woman wearing a black band round her fedora is a widow, while a rose-colored band is worn by single women, and a white one shows that the wearer is married.

with relatively little damage. Fields of flowers line the road as you approach, and at the other side of town groves of orange trees sit beneath snowy mountain peaks. There are several small hotels and a few basic restaurants around the Plaza de Armas. If you choose to start, rather than finish, your trek here, you can get a bus from Huaraz, about 65km (40 miles) away. From Caraz you can take gentle walks in the nearby hills, or visit the stunning turquoise-blue **Lago Parón** ❺, some 30km (18 miles) up a rugged, winding road. It's a magnificent all-day hike, or a relatively inexpensive trip by taxi.

Huascarán National Park

Much of the Cordillera Blanca above 4,000m (13,000ft) and the area around Huascarán mountain falls within the confines of **Parque Nacional Huascarán.** The park is easily visited from Huaraz, and its office, where you can get information before your visit, is located there. Established in 1972, Huascarán National Park was formed to protect the Andean wildlife, archeological sites, geology, and natural beauty of an area threatened by mining and other commercial interests. An entrance fee is charged to help offset the cost of providing park guardians and preserving trails.

Of the more interesting wildlife that you can possibly see, with a little patience and a bit of luck, is the *vizcacha*, a small, hare-like animal with characteristics similar to the North American marmot; the vicuña, a cameloid cousin to the llama; and (much less frequently) the stealthy puma.

A daring climber takes on the Cordillera Blanca

The striking blue-and-black Tanager can be seen in this part of Peru

Chavín de Huantar

The region is less endowed with Inca ruins than the area around Cusco, but there is one extraordinary archeological site in the area: **Chavín de Huantar** ❻ (daily 8am–5pm; charge), one of the oldest major archeological sites in the Americas. The site is located across the mountains in the next valley to the east, near the village of Chavín, but is most accessible from Huaraz, from where tours can be arranged. There are regular buses, and the journey takes about three hours *(see pp.194–5)*.

Cordillera Huayhuash

Once a place where few outsiders dared to tread, the Cordillera Huayhuash is now considered one of the most scenic trekking areas in Peru *(see p.25)*. Until a few years ago, this isolated range to the south of the Callejón de Huaylas was the haunt of bandits, and home to just a handful of rugged mountain men. Sendero Luminoso guerillas used the area as a base in the 1980s and early 1990s, so until the late 1990s the Huayhuash remained largely undiscovered by Peruvians and foreigners alike, keeping it mysterious and unspoiled: a real zone for adventure.

Valley festivals

Ancient traditions live on in the valley's great variety of celebrations, which occur on any given month. The major festivals of San Juan (St John on June 24) and San Pedro and San Pablo (St Peter and St Paul on June 29) are particularly lively, especially since they fall at the same time as the national day that has been set aside to honor the *campesino*, and Inti Raymi, the Andean celebration of the winter solstice. On the eve of San Juan, fires are lit throughout the valley, burning the chaff from the harvest and the wild *ichu* grass on the hillsides. During Semana Santa, or Easter Week, processions carry finely adorned religious figures on litters, scenes of the Resurrection are depicted in flower petals on the ground, and folkloric bands play music throughout the villages.

CHAVÍN DE HUANTAR

Many visitors to the Callejón de Huaylas come not only for the majestic mountains but also to experience one of the oldest archeological sites in the Americas. At the temple complex of Chavín de Huantar lie the remains of one of the most important pre-Inca cultures. Dating from around 800 to 300BC, the Chavín culture created a highly developed artistic style and a culture whose influence lasted centuries.

Archeologists have been able to learn very little about the Chavín because they left no written records. Theories that have been put forward about this mysterious culture are mostly based on the study of this 7-hectare (17-acre) site containing a temple, plazas, and a multitude of stone carvings and drawings.

Based on discoveries here, it is widely accepted that, at the time the Chavín culture was emerging, mankind was moving from a hunter-gatherer way of life to a society based on agriculture, which gave people new-found leisure time to devote to cultural pursuits.

What first strikes most visitors upon their arrival is the quality of the stonework found in the temple walls and the plaza stairways. The granite blocks for its construction were brought here on rafts during the rainy season. The drystone masonry construction reflects surprising sophistication from a culture that flourished more than 3,000 years ago. Added to this are huge stone slabs with highly stylized carvings of jaguars, eagles, and anacondas.

The temple sits above a large, sunken plaza where it is believed pilgrims came to worship during certain

A gargoyle on a wall at Chavín de Huantar

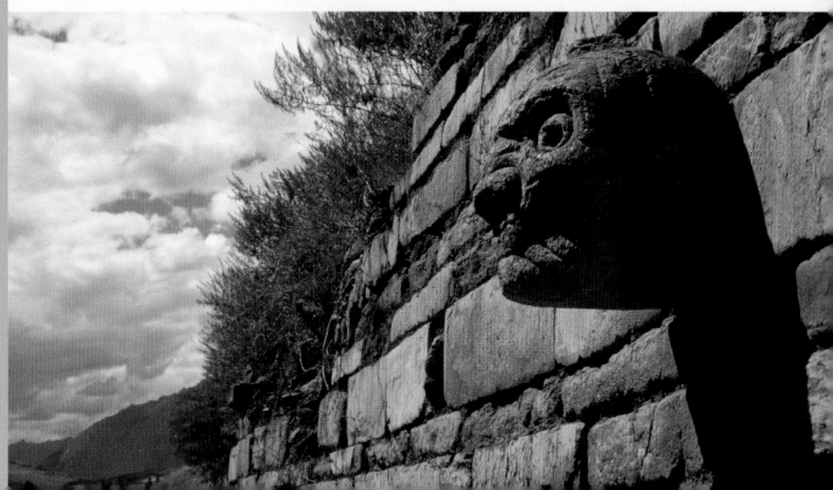

seasons. Two 3m (10ft) high stone portals overlook the plaza and represent the entryway into the interior of the temple. Finely etched bird-like figures, one male and one female, face each other across a stairway, symbolically divided into two halves – one painted black and the other white. Niches set around the outside of the temple walls originally held protruding sculpted stone heads, human in shape but with the snarling grin of a jaguar.

The interior is a subterranean labyrinth of passages and galleries set on at least three levels, connected by a series of ramps and stairs. Though there are no windows, a highly engineered ventilation system allows the continuous flow of fresh air throughout. Some of the rooms contain the remains of the sculpted heads and intricately carved slabs portraying Amazonian and highland animals.

At the heart of the underground complex, two narrow passageways cross, and at their junction stands the crowning glory of the Chavín religion – the Lanzón de Chavín. This 4m (13ft) high granite monolith is thought to be the principal god-image worshiped by this cult. Its Spanish name comes from the lance or dagger-like shape of the monolith, which appears to be stuck in the ground. A mythological image emerges from the elaborate stone carving, and its demeanor is in keeping with most of the terrifying god-images created by the Chavín. Its significance is a mystery, but the experience is unforgettable.

A stone fragment depicting a feline god, dating from 600BC

The Lanzón de Chavín is the crowning glory of the Chavín religion

Though there are several routes through the Huayhuash that allow walkers to see parts of it, the best way to visit this magnificent range is to do the full Circuito del Huayhuash, a 12- to 14-day trek of some 170km (102 miles). This route passes over a series of high passes (all well above 4,000m/13,300ft), overlooked by awe-inspiring, glacier-shrouded peaks.

The spine of the Huayhuash is made up of over 20 individual mountains, six of them at over 6,000m (19,800ft); Yerupaja, at 6,634m (21,836ft), is the second-highest peak in Peru. Slopes of rock and ice extend down into wide grassy valleys with azure-hued glacial lakes. From the mountain paths, the stone-walled, grass-roofed huts of the people who graze their animals here are just visible.

From April to early June the landscape is green and dotted with wild flowers; by July, it has dried to a yellowish hue for the coldest and driest part of the year, when there are nightly freezes and skies as clear as glass. This is the best time for trekking, as daytime temperatures are warm. By September the rains begin, and bitter snowdrifts come to the highest passes and valleys.

Sechín

West across the Cordillera Negra, in the Casma Valley not far from the Pacific Ocean, lies the other major ruin of the Ancash department, the name of the administrative district

Walking down a street in Huaraz

Earthquake tragedies

The Callejón de Huaylas is also well known for a history of natural disasters. Earthquakes and alluvions – the name given to floods of water combined with avalanches and landslides – have caused considerable damage over the past 300 recorded years. The capital city of Huaraz was severely damaged by an alluvion in 1941 when an avalanche caused Laguna Calcacocha to overflow. The most tragic disaster occurred in 1970, when an earthquake measuring 7.7 on the Richter scale devastated the entire region and was responsible for nearly 80,000 deaths.

Wall carving at Sechín depicting a warrior with a ceremonial axe

that covers both mountain ranges. **Sechín** ❼ is a 5-hectare (12½-acre) site that archeologists date back to the end of the Initial Period, before 1000BC, thus making it a millennium older than even Chavín de Huantar. Unique, 4m (12ft) carved monoliths depicting bellicose warriors and their hapless, dismembered victims close off the oldest adobe remains in a nearly perfectly square lower complex. It appears to have been a fortress protected by these warrior images. Unusually, the carvings depict humans and some undeciphered geometric figures, but no animals. Inside, a wall with ancient graffiti reveals more geometric symbols and mythological beings, some clearly influenced by the Chavín culture.

Despite the impressive stonework, almost nothing is known about the Sechín culture. The stone carvings have led researchers to describe their society as warlike and theocratic, possibly sacrificing prisoners. Nearby mounds are adobe pyramids worn down by the passing of centuries, making them look like small hills, but some still have identifiable masonry. The first excavation here was conducted by the eminent Peruvian archeologist Julio César Tello in the late 1930s. The site is still under excavation, but much of it is accessible, and there is an informative museum on the site (daily 9am–5pm; charge).

The site can also be reached by taking a bus from Lima, 350km (250 miles) to the south, to the nearby town of Casma, and from there taking a taxi or *colectivo* (bus) to the ruin.

ACCOMMODATIONS

Fitting for the mountain setting, accommodation in the Callejón de Huaylas often has a much more Alpine than Spanish or indigenous-style flair. That said, there are beautiful old haciendas offering overnight stays and backpackers' inns as well as some run by local indigenous communities.

Accommodations price categories

Prices are for one night's accommodation in a standard double room (unless otherwise specified)

$ = below US$20
$$ = US$20–40
$$$ = US$40–60
$$$$ = US$60–100
$$$$$ = over US$100

Huaraz

Albergue Churup
Jr. Amadeo Figueroa 1257
Tel: 043-422-584/424-200
www.churup.com
This small, family-run hotel looks like something out of the Swiss Alps and is beautifully furnished inside. There's a log fire on winter nights in a loft with a magnificent view. **$$**

B&B Mi Casa
Av. Tarapacá 773
Tel: 043-423-375
www.aventuraquechua.com
Small guesthouse run by friendly owners, with simple rooms set around an interior courtyard. Good breakfasts served. Plenty of travel and mountain advice available. **$$**

La Casa de Zarela
Jr. Julio Arguedas 1263
Tel: 043-421-694
www.lacasadezarela.com
A quiet, small hotel, with lovely decoration, interior courtyards, and terraces, plus a great café. En suite rooms available. Zarela is endlessly knowledgeable about the area and will help arrange climbing and trekking trips. **$$**

Edward's Inn
Bolognesi 121
Tel: 043-422-692
www.edwardsinn.com
Friendly family-run place, among the most popular hostels in Huaraz. Edward is a good source of information on climbing and trekking and rents out bikes and equipment. **$$$**

Hostal El Patio
Av. Monterrey, Crta. Huaraz Caraz, km 6
Tel: 043-424-965
www.elpatio.com.pe
Lovely, Andean hacienda-style hotel with 25 rooms, four cabins, interior patios, and gardens in a quiet spot near the thermal baths. Salons and cabins have fireplaces. **$$$$**

Llanganuco Lodge
Lake Keushu (at the entrance of the Llanganuco Valley)
Tel: 043-943-688-791
www.llanganucolodge.com
This modern lodge in the mountains outside Huaraz is a perfect luxury base for day adventures, or for a few days' acclimatization before a climb. **$$$$$**

Olaza's Guest House
Jr. Julio Arguedas 1242
Tel: 043-422-529
www.andeanexplorer.com/olaza
This is a clean, pleasant guesthouse, with lovely rooftop terraces and amazing views of the mountains. The owners are specialists in mountain-bike adventures. **$$**

Peruvian table setting

RESTAURANTS

While food in the Andean Sierra goes heavy on pork and potatoes, the influence of the tourism trade has brought a great deal of international variety to Huaraz restaurants. Cuisine cooked up in the outlying villages, however, is still very much traditionally Peruvian, with plenty of fresh trout.

Restaurant price categories

Prices are for a three-course menu including juice but no wine or coffee

$ = below US$2
$$ = US$2–5
$$$ = US$6–10
$$$$ = over US$10

Huaraz

Amma y Tequila
Parque Ginebra (next to the Casa de Guías)
Tel: 043-840-553
This cozy place has a wood oven and grill under which it cooks all of its mouthwatering meats. It does a fantastic teriyaki spatch-cocked chicken and serves fine margaritas. **$$$**

Bistro de los Andes
Jr. Julián de Morales 823
Tel: 043-429-556
Known for good Peruvian food with a French twist, among other influences, and a good place to breakfast with a view of the Plaza de Armas. Thoughtful decor makes this one of the prettier places to eat in Huaraz. **$$$**

La Brasa Roja
Av. Luzuriaga 919
Tel: 043-427-738
Pasta, pizza, and chicken from the grill, plus great hamburgers and good vegetarian options. Great value. This place is popular with locals and deservedly so. **$$$**

Encuentro
Av. Luzuriaga 6ta cuadra (Parque del Periodista)
Tel: 043-427-971
Though there are three Encuentros in Huaraz, this is the best for its tranquil location on the square known as Parque del Periodista. They do a lot more than pastas and coffee and are just the spot for a light meal. **$$$**

El Horno
Av. Luzuriaga 6ta cuadra (Parque del Periodista)
Tel: 043-424-617
BBQ meats, salads, pasta, and vegetarian dishes. They do an excellent lasagne, and pizzas are baked in their wood oven. **$$$$**

Monte Rosa
Jr. José de la Mar 661
Tel: 043-421-447
This restaurant serves great Argentine beef, bountiful salads, and good pizzas and pastas. It even does a mean Swiss cheese fondue. **$$$$**

NIGHTLIFE

Huaraz nightlife has plenty to offer. *Peñas*, or folklore nightclubs, entertain with traditional Andean musical groups in the early evening, and switch to disco later on for serious high-altitude dancing. For a night of fun, El Tambo Discoteca is among the most popular and is packed on weekends and during high season.

Makondos
Jr. La Mar 812 and Av. Simon Bolivar
Popular place for dancing to pop music, with a bar and restaurant attached to the disco.

El Tambo Discoteca
Jr José de la Mar 776
Tel: 043-423-417
Not the most innovative music, but that's the point in this disco that's wildly popular with locals and tourists.

Vagamundo
Av. Julián de Morales 753
Tel: 043-614-374
Relaxing backpackers' hangout with snacks, fussball tables, and movies.

X-Treme
Av. Luzurriaga and Gabino Uribe
Tel: 043-682-115
As the name hints, rock music bar with plenty of good cocktails.

Huaraz at dusk

ENTERTAINMENT

Despite the destruction suffered by Huaraz in its major earthquake, the city is vibrant beyond tourism, and has a cultural scene influenced by both local tradition and the influx of foreigners who have set up shop locally.

Instituto Nacional de Cultura de Ancash
Av. Luzuriaga 76
Tel: 043-421-829
www.huaraz.info/inc
The most important cultural center in Huaraz, the INC is home to an art gallery as well as resident dance, ballet, and theater companies.

SPORTS, ACTIVITIES, AND TOURS

In a country rich in outdoor athletic activities, the Callejón de Huaylas stands at the pinnacle. All manner of adventure sports from glacier skiing to kayaking are practiced here, and there are many knowledgeable outfitters and agencies. For some of the more exotic sports and advanced athletes, it's probably best to bring your own gear, however, as there are limited quantities of top rental goods and few importers.

Huaraz

Enrique Expedition Tours
Av. Luzuriaga 464 Piso 2 Of. 0
Tel: 043-425-362
www.enriqueexpedition.com
Experienced touring agency with dozens of outings, including ice climbing and mountaineering and six ski tours in the Cordillera Blanca.

Explorandes
Av. Centenario 489
Tel: 043-421-960
Fax: 043-428-071
www.explorandes.com
Huaraz branch of the reputable adventure travel company with excellent 'green' credentials and multi-day, multi-sport activities. Tours throughout Peru available.

Shelek Trek
Av. Confraternidad Internacional Oeste 674
Tel: 043-424-676
www.shelektrek.com
Huaraz agency specializing in tours in the Cordillera Blanca, Cordillera Negra, and Cordillera Huayhuash. Bungee jumping, mountain biking, and kayaking also offered.

Siex Perú
Jr. Huaylas 139
Tel: 043-426-529
www.siexperu.com
This agency specializing in rock climbing and trekking is owned by experienced mountain guide Hugo Sifuentes Maguiña. The outfit also runs tours to the Llanganuco lakes and the Chavín de Huantar ruins.

FESTIVALS AND EVENTS

The Callejón de Huaylas has plenty of traditional festivals, mostly linked to religious events that nonetheless normally end up as raucous celebrations – residents save for months to hold a proper party. At the same time, the area's importance to Peru's outdoor tourism has made it a center for events tied to adventure sports.

January

Virgen de Chiquinquirá
Huaylas-Caraz
Between January 18–21 is this traditional religious festival for the Patron of Huaylas, but with cultural and musical events, folkcloric music, and fireworks.

February/March

Carnaval Huaracino
Huaraz
Carnival festivities in Huaraz include parades of decorated floats through the city.

April

Semana Santa (Easter Week)
Throughout the Callejón de Huaylas there are numerous religious processions for Holy Week.

June/July

Adventure Festival
From June 28–July 1 there are numerous international sporting competitions and demonstrations throughout the valley, including ice and rock climbing, canyoneering, kayaking, cross-country running and orienteering, mountain biking, triathlons, and free riding. These are accompanied by food and crafts fairs.

July

Santa Isabel
Huaylas
One of the most ostentatious of the Huaylas fiestas: taking place between July 6–9, it includes numerous bands, dancers, and guests who enjoy the fun day and night.

September

Semana Turística de Carhuaz – Virgen de las Mercedes
Carhuaz
Every September 23–7, Carhuaz hosts this traditional festival, incorporating a mix of religious, entertainment, cultural, and sporting events: the celebrations include afternoon bullfights, fireworks, bands, dances, and folk groups.

October

Semana Turística de Yungay
Yungay
This major festive event includes parades, contests, fairs, sports, and civic activities. The action takes place between October 25–30.

The north

The relaxed city of Trujillo is full of colonial charm and is the perfect spot from which to explore Peru's gentle north. From here, hugging the coast to Ecuador, the Panamericana Highway is strung with archeological sites and fine beaches. Journeys inland to the Andean highlands are more difficult, but the rewards are breathtaking scenery and more spectacular remains, including the jungle-covered ruins of Kuélap.

Trujillo

Population: 312,000

Local dialing code: 044

Tourist office: Jr. Diego de Almagro 420 on Plaza de Armas; tel: 044-294-561; **www.peru.travel**

Main police station: Jr. Bolognesi 428; tel: 044-291-438/232-552. Tourist police: Jr. Independencia 630; tel: 044-291-705

Main post office: Serpost: Jr. Independencia 286; tel: 044-246-131/245-941

Hospitals: Hospital Regional Docente de Trujillo; Av. Mansiche 795; tel: 044-231-581. Clínica Sánchez Ferrer, Los Laureles No. 436, Urb. California; tel: 044-482-900; **www.pyrushd.com**

Local newspapers: *Nuevo Norte*

Airport: Aeropuerto Martínez de Pinillos (TRU); Via a Huanchaco s/n; tel: 044-464-013/464-324, near Huanchaco, is 10km (7 miles) north of the center of Trujillo. A taxi downtown takes 15 minutes and costs S./20

Public bus: Local transport consists of combis and buses. Rates vary depending on destination. Urban routes and transport to the entrance of Chan Chan cost S./1; routes to the Temples of the Sun and Moon cost S./1.30 and to Huanchaco S./1.50. Bus station: Trujillo has no main long-distance bus station. Recommended lines include: Transportes Línea, which has a terminal at Av. América Sur 2855; tel: 044-258-994/297-399; TEPSA departs from Jr. Amazonas 468; tel: 044-201-626

Car rental: Aero Trujillo; Reforma 172, El Cortijo; tel: 044-788-878; cell: 044-949-924-156. Ruby Car Perú; Husares de Junín, La Merced; tel: 044-9494-72677/47818

Taxis: On the main routes, fares in the historic center cost S./3; from the center to the Temples of the Sun and the Moon S./12; from the center to Chan Chan or Huanchaco S./15

Vast and largely diverse, Peru's north has a staggering amount of attractions for visitors that may be less famous and less visited than those of the southeast, but hardly less significant. The country's warmest waters lap at the laidback beaches among Peru's top destinations for swimmers and, above all, world-class surfers. But the beaches also offer a break for those lapping up the ancient and colonial cultural relics, including the brightly painted walls of the Huaca de la Luna, the spectacular museum for the Lord of Sipán – Peru's Tutankhamun – and the vast adobe city of Chan Chan. Trujillo, meanwhile, may be Peru's second-biggest city, but the city of eternal springtime remains agreeably provincial and free of skyscrapers. See its colonial heritage and that of Cajamarca in the Andes, whose beauty allows it to rival Unesco World Heritage towns elsewhere in South America. The city has its Inca landmarks, too, including the Ransom Room that epitomizes the tragedy and greed of the Spanish conquest. Heading out from Cajamarca, the uppermost reaches of the Amazon hold the mysterious Kuélap ruins that rival those of Machu Picchu in scale.

Chan Chan

The colonial-style building which houses the City Hall in Trujillo

Trujillo

The coastal city of **Trujillo** ❶, about 570km (354 miles) north of Lima on the coast road, is the second-largest city in Peru. Founded in 1535 and named after Francisco Pizarro's birthplace in Spain, Trujillo was the resting place for Spaniards journeying between Lima and Quito. It soon

Museo del Juguete

Trujillo's eclectic, playful museum of old toys, the Museo del Juguete, is located in a restored blue Trujillo town home (Independencia 701 and Junín, two blocks from the Plaza de Armas), on the ground floor. It has an attractive old bar and café adorned with antique furnishings and photographs of Mario Vargas Llosa and other Peruvian intellectuals who have visited the café over the last decade. The bohemian haunt is owned by local painter Gerardo Chávez, who calls it his 'little Paris.'

merited the title 'Lordliest City,' and its well-preserved colonial homes with intricate wooden Andalusian-style balconies and window grills pay testimony to an elegant past. The best way to visit the city center is on foot *(see Trujillo Tour, p.206)*.

North coast

The north coast of Peru is not visited as much as the area around Lima, but it has much to offer, including several archeological sites near Trujillo, as well as some lovely beach resorts. Regular buses ply the Panamericana north from the capital to the border with Ecuador and beyond.

Around Trujillo

About 10km (6 miles) southeast of Trujillo lie the **Huacas del Sol y de la Luna** ❷ (Temples of the Sun and the Moon; daily 9am–4.30pm; charge). You can get there by minibus from Trujillo, or go with a guide on an organized tour. These two pyramidal temples were built by the Moche people (100BC–AD850)

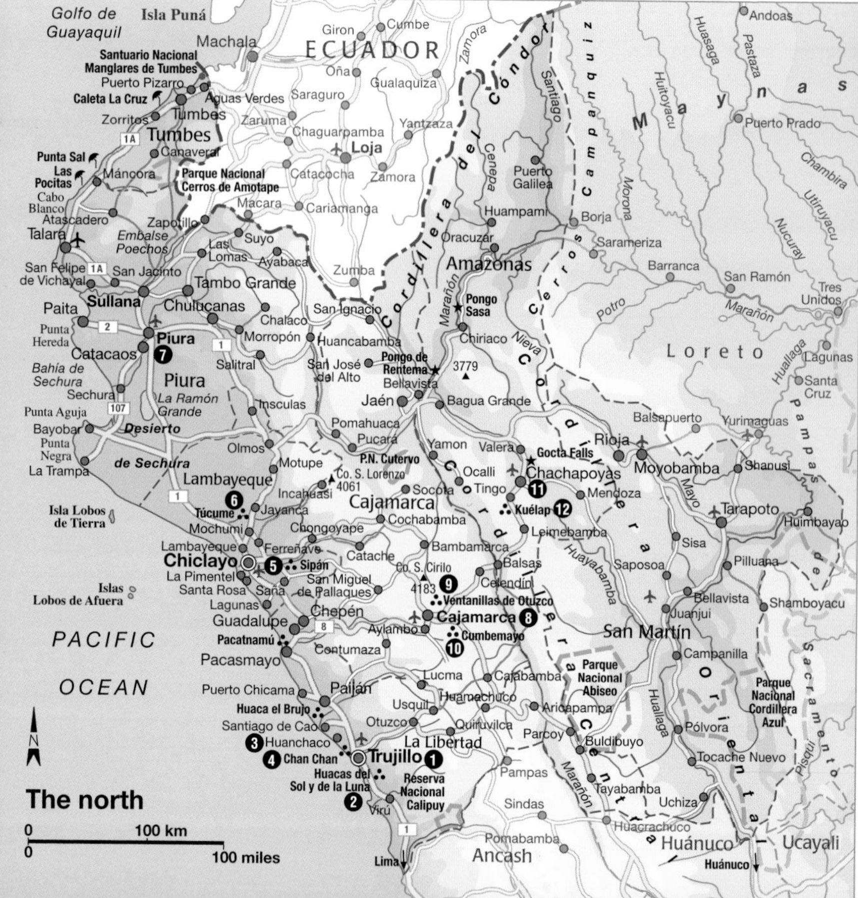

Exploring the Huacas del Sol y de la Luna, southeast of Trujillo

over several generations. The Huaca del Sol (arguably the largest pre-Columbian building in the Americas) is currently being excavated, but at the smaller Huaca de la Luna, years of archeological work have begun to unveil a series of temples superimposed on one another to form a pyramid covered in beautiful, brightly colored murals. A new site museum was inaugurated in 2010.

Another short trip (about 15km/10 miles) from Trujillo is to the seaside village of **Huanchaco** ❸, which has been improved by the restoration of its Baroque church and by landscaping. Today Huanchaco is a popular destination for surfers and beach lovers, although it still retains a village air. Sun-bronzed fishermen head out each morning with their nets tucked into *caballitos de totora*, literally 'little horses' woven from *totora* reed, just as they have for many centuries. The design of these peapod-shaped boats is not very different from that of the craft used by pre-Inca people, and the *caballitos* contrast startlingly with the brightly colored surfboards that now share the Pacific waves.

Chan Chan

Just northwest of Trujillo (take one of the frequent minibuses or *colectivos* from Trujillo), only 600m/yds from the ocean are the monumental ruins of **Chan Chan** ❹ (daily 9am–4.30pm; charge), the world's largest adobe city and one-time capital of the Chimú Empire. Its citizens fished, farmed, and worshiped the moon, but left no written records – leaving it to archeologists to unravel their secrets. At its height in 1450, the sprawling mud-brick city covered 23 sq km (9 sq miles). There are nine rectangular compounds, each corresponding to a Chimú monarch. Each compound served as an administrative center as well as a palace, a royal storehouse, and, on the king's death, his mausoleum. Around the royal compound, in small, crowded dwellings lived a population of weavers, potters and metalsmiths who supplied the royal storehouses. Today the city is a bewildering labyrinth of ruined adobe walls, some 7.5m (25ft) high and stretching for 60m (200ft).

TOUR OF TRUJILLO

A half-day walk through the magnificent mansions and Baroque churches of Trujillo will take you back to the elegant days of Spain's colonies on the Pacific coast.

The best way to see this city is on foot. Start from the **Plaza de Armas** (also known as the the Plaza Mayor), the vast square in the middle of the old town, flanked by colonial mansions decorated with a torch-bearing statue of liberty in the center. The statue stands on disproportionately short legs, designed to appease officials who feared the monument would end up taller than the cathedral facing it. The mid-18th century **Catedral** (Mon–Fri 8am–12.30pm, 4–8pm, Sat 8am–1pm, Sun for Mass only), with two massive domed towers, now dominates the north corner of the square. The cathedral once had elaborate metal adornments and railings, like many of the colonial houses, but they were melted down for armaments during the War of Independence *(see p.273)*.

Consider having breakfast at luxurious **Hotel Libertador**, a gorgeous three-storied mansion with closed wooden balconies just across from the cathedral; dining in one of the rooms looking out over the plaza is a real treat and provides the perfect opportunity to people-watch.

Take Jr. Independencia on the left of the cathedral, where just past Gamarra, on the left side, is 18th-century **San Francisco** (Mon–Sat 7–9am, 4–8pm, Sun for Mass only); across the street is the **Casa de los Leones** (Mon–Fri 9am–1pm, 2–6pm, Sat 9am–1pm), which houses a small art gallery as well as the Policía de Turismo. Half a block onwards, on the corner with Jr. Junín, is the **Museo del Juguete** (Toy Museum), with its

Trujillo's cathedral dates from the mid-18th century

Trujillo's Museo de Arqueología is housed in a 17th-century colonial mansion

bohemian café downstairs, a good spot for a break. **Santa Clara**, a 19th-century church, is on the other side of the street.

Head right on Junín and right again on Pizarro, with Palacio Iturregui, where Trujillo's unilateral independence from Spain was declared in 1820, on the corner. On the next corner, the 1640s **Casa de la Emancipación** (Mon–Fri 10am–6pm) is one of the few mansions that still has original furniture. La Merced, from 1636 a few meters further down the street, has an elaborate rococo organ. A view of the Plaza de Armas opens up on the next corner. The yellow **Casona Orbegoso**, remarkable for its massive balconies, but no longer open to visitors, and blue and white **Casa de Urquiaga** (Mon–Fri 9am–3pm, Sat 10am–1.30pm; free), now owned by Banco de la Nación, are to the left on this block of Orbegoso.

From the facade of late 16th-century San Agustín, head left on Bolívar and walk three blocks to El Carmen, a fine late Renaissance church on the corner with Colón. Head right here and again right on Ayacucho, where the **Museo de Arqueología**, the museum of the National University of Trujillo (Mon–Fri 8am–2.45pm; charge), is on the next block. Among the artifacts in this fine frescoed colonial mansion are notable Moche and Chimú pottery and copies of some of the wall paintings found at the Huaca de la Luna *(see p.204)*. When leaving the museum, head right on Ayacucho and right on Almagro, which takes you back to the Plaza de Armas. A few meters left on Independencia, end the walk at **La Compañía**, the 1640 ochre and white Jesuit church.

Tips

- Distance: 2.6km (1½ miles)
- Time: Half a day
- Trujillo, Peru's coastal town of eternal spring, can be visited at any time. Much shuts down for lunch and a *siesta*, so either start early or late or plan for a lunch of fine *norteña* food *(see listings, p.225)*

An echoing silence surrounds visitors to this ancient city, whose walls bear carvings of sea otters, fish, seabirds, fishing nets, and moons.

An entrance ticket to Chan Chan also allows visitors to see the **Huaca del Dragón** – also known as the Huaca Arco Iris (the Rainbow Temple) – with its beautifully restored wall carvings, and the ruins of **Huaca La Esmeralda** nearby. Licensed guides can be hired at the ticket office. Tourists are advised to begin their visit in the morning and avoid going alone; the tourism police at Chan Chan frequently go home in mid-afternoon, and there have been a number of thefts at the site.

Archeology enthusiasts should also visit the **Huaca el Brujo** site, 60km (40 miles) north of Trujillo in the Chicama Valley and worth a visit for its colorful Moche reliefs. Ask at the Tourist Information Office for details.

Chiclayo

Some 200km (125 miles) up the Panamericana from Trujillo is the busy port of **Chiclayo** (there are regular bus services as well as frequent flights from Lima and Trujillo), a major commercial hub for northern Peru. The city is now mostly modern, except for some isolated remnants of colonialism in the winding streets. It is a lively and friendly spot with few pretensions.

One unmissable sight within the city is the extensive **Mercado de Brujos** (Witch Doctor's Market), one of the most comprehensive in South America. Here is an overwhelming choice of herbal medicines, potions, charms, and San Pedro cacti, from which a hallucinogenic drug is extracted and used by *curanderos* (healers) in traditional shamanic healing rituals.

A short distance away is the coastal resort of **Pimentel**, with

Caballitos de mar on the beach at Pimentel

A strawberry vendor weighs his produce at Chiclayo market

a good sandy beach – an excellent place to try the local specialty of *pescado seco*, a kind of rayfish known as *la guitarra*, which can often be found hanging out to dry in the sun in Chiclayo's market. Just south of Pimentel is **Santa Rosa**, where beautiful fishing boats can be seen drawn up on the beach.

Chiclayo is the starting point for visits to two of the continent's most exciting archeological digs. The greatest attention has been lavished on the Moche burial area at **Sipán** ❺ (daily 9am–5pm; charge; guided tours available), about 30km (18 miles) south of the city. Originally unearthed by grave robbers in 1987, the tomb of the Lord of Sipán, believed to be a ruler of the Moche period (*c.* AD100–700), yielded unimaginable riches: gold masks, turquoise and lapis lazuli jewelry, copper headdresses, ceramic pots, and domestic implements, and provided archeologists with vital information about the Moche way of life. The site is well worth visiting, but to see the stunning gold, silver, and ceramic artifacts taken from it you must visit the world-class **Museo Brüning** (daily 9am–5pm; charge), which is in **Lambayeque**, about 17km (10 miles) from Chiclayo. Lambayeque or **Sicán**, meaning 'home

The witch doctor's market

One of South America's most exotic markets is Chiclayo's **Mercado de Brujos** inside the Mercado Modelo on Arica, between Cuglievan and Balta, six blocks north of the main square. Patrons flock here to buy herbs and other ingredients for homemade medicines, but this market also has ingredients for any number of shamans' potions – tonics, animal bones and shark cartilage, amulets, snake skins, religious symbols, and, above all, the hallucinogenic San Pedro cactus. Sliced and boiled, it produces a potent brew used by shamans – *brujos* – to induce hallucinogenic visions. Beware, however, of sham artists approaching tourists offering shamanic cleansings, and pick any *brujo* carefully with local advice. One of the most famous is Víctor Bravo, who works in his house near the Tucume pyramids.

The north coast beaches are a surfer's paradise

of the moon,' is the name of the successor culture to the Moche, one which created some of the highest-quality gold artifacts of ancient Peru. The Lord of Sipán's tomb has been dated AD300–400; the Sicán culture, however, flourished around AD750–1375, before being conquered by the Chimú. In Ferreñafe, 20km (12 miles) from Chiclayo, the modern **Museo Nacional Sicán** (daily 9am–5pm; charge) holds exquisite gold and ceramics from tombs at archeological sites a bit further north.

From the town of Lambayeque you can also go on to the huge site at **Túcume** ❻, the last great Sicán site with numerous flat-topped adobe pyramids. The excavation here was originally directed by Norwegian Thor Heyerdahl, best known for his *Kon-Tiki* voyage. Although he recorded numerous graves containing silver figurines and textiles worked in tropical feathers, Heyerdahl showed most enthusiasm over artifacts supportive of his theory that ancient Americans were capable of long-distance navigation and were the first settlers in Polynesia. Chief among such finds were a wooden oar and a balsa raft frieze on a section of wall at the site.

Piura

Piura ❼ is a hot commercial city best known for its folk dance, the *tondero*, a lively barefoot Afro-Peruvian dance accompanied by strong rhythmic music and sashaying dancers in multicolored outfits. But many Peruvian visitors come to see more than the dancers. There are Lima business executives who travel

Coastal mangroves

Near Zarumilla on the border with Ecuador are Peru's only coastal mangroves, protected in the Santuario Nacional Manglares de Tumbes. Tours through the extraordinarily biodiverse 3,000-hectare (7,400-acre) preserve allow you to observe the four species of mangrove tree and more than 200 bird species, including frigate birds. If you're lucky, you may see howler monkeys, otters, and rare crab-eating racoons and American crocodiles (one of the world's biggest crocodile species). The preserve is best visited May through December.

here annually to consult the area's *brujos* – witch doctors and folk healers who use herbs and potions to cure patients.

Piura has a proud history, beginning with its foundation by the Spanish in 1532 – three years before Lima – and continuing through the War of the Pacific with Chile (1879–83). That war's most famous Peruvian hero was Admiral Miguel Grau, and his home on Jirón Tacna across from the Centro Cívico has been converted into a museum, the **Museo Naval Miguel Grau** (hours vary; free). Of interest there is the scale model of the British-built *Huascar*, the largest Peruvian warship in that conflict. Grau was commander of the vessel and used it to keep the invading Chilean forces at bay until he was forced to scuttle his ship in the Battle of Angamos, an event still remembered every year on October 8.

Beach resorts

North of Piura, on the way to the Ecuadorian border, lies Talara, a desert oasis and petroleum-producing center. Closer still to the northern border are some of the best and most fashionable beaches in Peru: **Máncora**, **Punta Sal**, and **Las Pocitas**. **Cabo Blanco** (south of Máncora) is a popular spot for marlin fishing, once frequented by Ernest Hemingway, but experts say the marlin have now been carried south by the Humboldt Current to Máncora. Peru's coast has some of the world's most spectacular waves, and Máncora is frequently the site of international surfing competitions *(see page 37)*.

Tumbes

About 140km (85 miles) north of Talara is **Tumbes**, a frontier town with a military post and immigration offices, although it is about

Museo Brüning

30km (18 miles) from the Ecuadorean border. Although there has been an ongoing effort to give this city a facelift, there continues to be a problem with theft – particularly affecting tourists – often occuring near the bus offices or at the colorful outdoor market. A few miles outside the city, at the actual border, known as **Aguas Verdes** on the Peruvian side, travelers are barraged by unscrupulous money-changers, porters, and over-friendly individuals with dubious motives. Police corruption is notorious here, although that is something which affects Peruvians far more than outsiders, and focuses on the widespread cross-border trafficking in contraband items.

Tumbes is also within spitting distance of the few Peruvian beaches that offer white sand and warm water for swimming year-round. **Caleta La Cruz**, which has an attractive fishing fleet, can be reached by taxi, in *colectivos*, or by combis heading north from Máncora, as can **Zorritos**, a larger fishing village with a couple of hotels. **Puerto Pizarro** has intriguing mangrove swamps around the village with some interesting birdlife, and boat tours can be arranged with fishermen in the port.

Northern Sierra

Journeys in the highlands are long and the roads are poor, but the rewards are colonial towns, breathtaking scenery, and some spectacular ruins. Cajamarca is the area's Baroque crown, studded with beautiful churches. There are Inca baths a short distance from Cajamarca. The largest ruin in the north, the Chachapoyan fortress of Kuélap, is much farther away. Not to be outdone, water thunders down one of the world's highest falls at Gocta

Cajamarca's cathedral presides over the Plaza de Armas

Kuélap is off the beaten track, but a highlight of the Northern Sierra

before continuing the long, long journey to the Atlantic Ocean.

Cajamarca

Across the dusty desert into the Andean highlands lies **Cajamarca** ❽. Now dotted with cattle herds and dairy farms, where Peru's best cheese is made, this was one of the largest cities in the Inca Empire and marks the site where the Inca people and the Spaniards had their first – and crucial – showdown. It was in Cajamarca that the Inca Atahualpa was taken prisoner and later executed *(see p.218)*.

Cajamarca can be reached by daily flights from Lima, by bus from Trujillo, which takes about nine hours, or Chiclayo (about seven hours), or on a better, faster road that turns off the Panamericana near Pacasmayo (about five hours).

The hub of this slow-paced city of some 120,000 inhabitants, built on the banks of the Río San Lucas, is the **Plaza de Armas**, the spot where Atahualpa was executed. It is still sometimes said that the pink grain on a stone slab, where the Inca was allegedly killed, is the indelible mark of his blood. The massive Inca palaces that stood here are gone, and the plaza is now ringed by colonial buildings, the cathedral, and the lovely San Francisco church. The center of the square is graced by an imposing stone fountain, frequented every evening by locals stopping for a chat with friends, and by birds dipping down for a drink throughout the day.

The Baroque **Catedral Santa Catalina** (Jirón Cruz de la Piedra; daily 8–11am, 6–9pm), founded in 1665, is the most noteworthy building on the plaza. Its carved wooden altars are covered in gold leaf, and its facade of intricately carved volcanic rock is impressive.

On the opposite side of the plaza is the **Iglesia San Francisco** (Church of San Francisco; Mon–Fri 9am–noon, 4–6pm), older and more ornate than the cathedral, and home to the **Museo de Arte Religioso** (Museum of Religious Art; Mon–Fri 2–5pm; charge), which is filled with colonial-era paintings and statues, often portraying violent

PASO HORSES

Versatile, hardy, and spirited yet possessing a remarkably soft step, Peru's Paso horses are enjoying a renaissance after modernization led them at risk of disappearing from their homeland. Beautiful haciendas all over the country now have these magnificent animals accompany visitors on excursions, from the beach to the high Andes around Cusco and Arequipa. Paso horses offer one of the most enjoyable riding experiences of any breed, particularly for visitors unused to the saddle.

Paso means step in Spanish and refers to the distinctive gait that gives these horses their name. This Peruvian breed, of a type called 'saddle horses,' has the naturally softest gait of any breed. For connoisseurs, the breed is a fascinating example of past centuries' careful selection of horses for specific traits. Cross-breeding of Spanish Jannets and Andalusians with Barbs, a North African desert horse, created horses suitable for traveling the great distances between haciendas. Paso horses are medium-sized with abundant manes, and might be bay, brown, black, chestnut, gray, or palomino in color.

The animals' great stamina and soft gait helped riders stand the many hours required over the difficult terrain. Cattle were mostly bred in other colonies, or harvested from feral livestock, so Peru didn't need fast horses for

A group navigating the rocky landscape on horseback

rodeos and roundups. A Paso rider is called a *chalán*; typical dress includes straw hats with long, tapered rims, white shirts and trousers, and elegant white ponchos striped with brown vicuña fibers. Saddles are typically highly decorated.

The horses were intimately associated with the rural economy of Peru from decades after colonization to the early 20th century. They inherited much of the communications role that Inca *chasqui* runners had played before the conquest. Road construction diminished their importance in the south. In the north, they held on until agrarian reform led to a breakup of great haciendas, and many were sold and sent to other countries.

Since the 1980s, however, Peru has made an effort to recover and protect the breed, with considerable success. Exports of the horses are restricted, and they have been declared part of Peru's heritage and its national horse.

For novices, the breed's amiable disposition makes it an excellent mount. Its hardiness allows it to withstand all manner of Peruvian climates, meaning haciendas throughout the country use Paso horses for tours.

The breeders' and owners' group **Asociación de Criadores y Propietarios de Caballos Peruanos de Paso** has daily demonstrations of Paso horsemanship near Trujillo at Km 569 of the Pan-American Highway (tel: 044-693-047). Tours on horseback and exhibitions are also available near Lima, including along the beach, via **Cabalgatas Perú** (tel: 01-221-0725; www.cabalgatas.com.pe).

Paso horses have great stamina and are the ideal way to travel across the terrain

The Paso horse once played a key role in the rural economy of Peru

and bloody subjects. A guided tour of the museum, which is a veritable storehouse of silver candelabras, gold altar vessels, jeweled vestments, and portraits of saints, includes entrance to the church's eerie catacombs – precursor to the present city cemetery.

A few blocks from the main plaza, on Avenida Amalia Puga, is **El Cuarto del Rescate** (The Ransom Room; Mon–Sat 9am–1pm, 3–6pm, Sun 9am–1pm; charge, which also gives admission to the Complejo Belén and the Ethnographic Museum, *see p.217*). This is the sole surviving Inca structure in the city, and there is some debate about whether it was where Atahualpa was imprisoned, or where the treasure collected from across the empire for his ransom was stored. As *rescate* means both 'ransom' and 'rescue' in Spanish, it could be either; whichever it was, it forges a very real link with a past that sometimes seems almost mythical.

Also close to the plaza, on Apurímac, is the **Teatro Municipal**, now known as the **Teatro Cajamarca**, rescued by this culture-loving city after being used first as a movie theater and then as a storehouse for industrial cleaners. Built by a wealthy German merchant, the theater has an impressive stamped metal ceiling, and its seating almost exactly duplicates that in the original plans. Ticket prices are kept low to entice students and less affluent *cajamarquinos*, but unfortunately performances are not staged on a regular basis.

Heading east along Junín from the theater you will come to

Three-wheeled taxi in Cajamarca

Looking down over the city

the **Complejo Belén** (Mon–Sat 9am–1pm, 3–6pm), housing the Institute of Culture, Cajamarca's most picturesque chapel, a museum, and an art gallery. The 17th-century Belén church is the city's loveliest, with elaborately carved stone and woodwork, and brightly colored statues and side altars. The small white carved dove suspended over the pulpit represents the Holy Spirit and allegedly gives those who stand under it the power of eloquence. Many visitors are fooled by the brilliantly painted details on the upper walls and ceiling of the church; these saints and cherubs are not made of painted wood or plaster, but intricately carved stone. More carving is found on the massive wooden doors in the church, most of them solid pieces of Nicaraguan cedar.

Connected to the church is the **Pinacoteca**, a gallery of local artists' work in what was once the kitchen of a hospital for men. Off the Pinacoteca is the former hospital ward, a room with alcoves along its side walls. The alcoves were the patients' 'bedrooms,' and the images of saints originally painted above them corresponded to their illnesses. The sickest were bedded closest to the altar, conveniently located near the door to the cemetery. Across the street, the **Museo Etnográfico y de Arqueología** (Ethnographic and Archeological Museum; Mon–Fri 8.30am–2.30pm) was once a maternity hospital. The only difference between the two hospitals was that from the tops of the women's alcoves dangled long scarves, which the patients pulled to help them when giving birth. The

Café Los Jazmines

Café Los Jazmines, with a pretty courtyard and a small hostel, is a good spot for a coffee break with tasty German cakes, one and a half blocks from the Plaza de Armas at Jr. Amazonas 775 (tel: 076-361-812). Los Jazmines is part of Projekt Cajamarca, which cares for about 300 children with mental and physical learning difficulties from the city and surrounding rural areas. Crafts made in the organization's three workshops are available at the store adjacent to the café.

An elegant colonial residence in Cajamarca

museum has an interesting collection of ceramics from indigenous cultures that dominated this region of Peru, various samples of local handicrafts, and costumes used during the annual Carnival celebrations – the most raucous in the country *(see p.229)*.

Across the street at the **Instituto Cultural**, a good selection of Spanish-language books and the area's best postcards are on sale. The institute has details of ongoing archeological digs that can be visited from October to May, before the highlands' rainy season begins.

For the physically fit, the best way to delight in Cajamarca's charms is from above. That means climbing steep **Cerro Apolonia** (daily 9am–1pm, 3–5pm; charge). Stone steps take climbers as far as a little chapel – a miniature version of Nôtre-Dame Cathedral, about halfway up the hillside – and the rest of the journey is on a curvy road bordered by cacti, flowers, and benches for the fatigued. Near the top is the **Silla del Inca** (the Inca's Chair), a rock cut into the shape of a throne where, it is said, the Inca Atahualpa sat and looked out over the valley. A bronze statue of the Inca, and parking for those who arrive by taxi or car, are at the top of the hill.

A king's ransom

In 1532 the Spanish conquistadors, led by Francisco Pizarro, arrived in Tumbes and marched to meet the Inca leader, Atahualpa, at Cajamarca. In an ambush on Plaza de Armas, the heavily armed Spaniards captured Atahualpa and massacred thousands of Inca subjects who were trying to protect him. A demand went out across the Inca Empire to assemble an outrageous ransom for Atahualpa's release. Leading llamas laden down by riches, groups of people from as far away as Cusco journeyed to Cajamarca, filling the 'Ransom Room' with valuable treasures – which the Spanish promptly melted down into bullion. But once the majority of the ransom had been collected, the conquistadors, afraid that the Inca would serve as a focal point for rebellion as long as he remained alive, had him garroted.

The view is of green, rain-fed fields, red-tiled roofs, and whitewashed houses. At night, the Cajamarca skies – which in daytime may switch in minutes from brilliant blue to stormy gray – are usually clear and star-studded. Early risers are in for a special treat: sunrises in these highlands are beautiful.

If you look out from the Cerro Apolonia by day, you may see a white mist hovering over the edge of the city. This is the steam rising from the **Baños del Inca** (daily 6am–6.30pm), reputedly the Inca's favorite bathing spot. A sign over a huge stone tub at the bubbling mineral springs claims that it was here that Atahualpa bathed with his family. The springs are so hot at their source that local people use them to boil eggs. Whether or not they are curative, as the locals believe, they are well worth a visit – you can get a bus or a *colectivo* from the center of the town.

The city has channeled the water from the springs into a lukewarm Olympic-sized outdoor pool, and built rustic cabañas where families or groups of friends can splash privately, and modern 'tourist baths' where one or two people can soak in tiled hot tubs. There is a minimal charge for the use of these facilities. At the springs, several tourist hostels have sprung up, all of them with bathtubs or swimming pools fed by the springs.

Around Cajamarca

Cajamarca and its environs are good places for buying ceramics. The Complejo Belén artisan shop and others near the Plaza de Armas are filled with pottery, as well as good-

Herb mixtures on sale

quality knitted sweaters, baskets, leather goods, and the gilt-framed mirrors popular in this northern region. But the most fascinating – and least expensive – spot to buy ceramics is a few kilometers to the south of the city at the village of **Aylambo**, where there is a series of ecologically balanced workshops. Sewage at the workshops is processed into natural gas, which is used to generate heat and light, and the students who learn their skills at the workshops collect kindling from the hillside to make their own heat-tolerant kiln tiles – in much the same way as their ancestors did.

Products here range from plates bearing traditional Indian motifs to teapots with modern glazes and the proceeds from pottery sales go to the people who work in the studios.

There are many possible excursions outside Cajamarca, all of which are best organized through a travel agency which can arrange transportation to the isolated area; there are several agencies in Cajamarca that provide these services. From here it is possible to visit the puzzling **Ventanillas de Otuzco** ❾ (about 8km/5 miles from town), the cliffside 'windows' that served as ancient Indian burial grounds. Anthropologists and archeologists still have not unraveled the mystery of how the pre-Inca people were able to open the burial holes on the sides of sheer cliffs, but they have counted the openings to get an idea of the population – and importance – of the area before the conquistadors' arrival.

Equally astonishing is the site of **Cumbemayo** ❿, about 24km (15 miles) from Cajamarca, a valley cut by an Inca irrigation ditch of carved rock. The sophistication and precision of the ditch's angles – hewn

Ventanillas de Otuzco

The astonishing Inca irrigation ditch carved into the rock at Cumbemayo

by stone tools – leave modern-day hydraulic engineers marveling. Sharp turns in the ditch prevent the water from rushing too fast, as do imperceptible inclines. In the same valley are Los Frailones (The Friars), huge rocks that have eroded into the shape of hooded monks – sparking a number of local legends – as well as some primitive petroglyphs and caves once used as places of worship.

Those who start their countryside ramblings early may have time to reach the dairy farm called **Hacienda La Colpa** before cow-calling time. Every day, just before 2pm, the cows at this cooperative are called by name – to the delight of the crowd that gathers to watch. The animals respond by sauntering up to the milking areas bearing their names. Colpa is an example of the many cooperative dairies outside Cajamarca, famous for its butter, cheese, and *manjar blanco* – a milky dessert. A hostel offers travelers a pastoral spot to spend the night, although most people, after admiring the nearby pretty village of Llacanora, head back to Cajamarca.

Chachapoyas

There is a rough but scenic route from Cajamarca, via the small city of Celendín, to **Chachapoyas** ⓫, heart of the pre-Inca culture of the same name. Little is known about the Chachapoyas period, which was roughly contemporary with the Chimú (*c.*1000–1400), but its people were certainly good at building cities and, judging by their fortifications, must have felt themselves under threat. There are buses to Celendín (about 120km/75 miles from Cajamarca) on a slow road, but from there on the usual method of transport is by truck. If your time is limited, or you visit during the rainy season when the road gets washed away, it's advisable to access Chachapoyas from Chiclayo. This road is in much better condition, and there are more buses. There are also flights from Lima to Chachapoyas.

Chachapoyas alone, although pleasant, would not be worth the long journey, but the spectacular surrounding area, the sense of visiting a spot which still sees few tourists, and the opportunity to visit the area's many hilltop ruins make it a trip worth taking. The effort needed to reach the remote **Gocta** waterfall, at 771m (2,530ft) the third-highest in the world, is most definitely a worthwhile one.

The best of the hilltop sites is **Kuélap ⓬**, a great pre-Inca walled city perched high above the Río Utcubamba. The location and its jungle-covered ruins are nothing short of spectacular, but they receive relatively few visitors. The extensive citadel was the principal administrative center of the Chachapoyas civilization (AD200–1475). The center is thought to have been a sanctuary for a powerful elite who administered agricultural production and religious practices. This enormous complex extends on a north–south-orientated platform for more than 600m (1,900ft), with stone walls measuring up to 19m (62ft) in height. Despite its grand dimensions, the city only has three narrow entrances, which served to control entry to the site and strengthen its defenses. Inside the complex are 335 circular buildings, some near complete, adorned with geometrical friezes. There's also an ingenious system for channeling rainwater.

Discovering Kuélap is a real off-the-beaten-track adventure that's worth the journey there. Minibuses leave in the morning for the village of **Tingo**, from where a road goes to within 15 minutes' walk of the ruins.

There are 335 circular buildings within the walled city of Kuélap

ACCOMMODATIONS

From beachfront hotels to Andean mansions, Peru's north has options for all budgets and tastes. Extraordinary diversity, even for Peru – it's the only region to share the coast, Andes, and Amazon – has increased its popularity, and you should book ahead for important festivals and Peruvian holidays.

Accommodations price categories

Prices are for one night's accommodation in a standard double room (unless otherwise specified)

$ = below US$20
$$ = US$20–40
$$$ = US$40–60
$$$$ = US$60–100
$$$$$ = over US$100

Trujillo

Casa De Clara Guest House
Cahuide 495, Santa María
Tel: 044-299-997/243-347
www.xanga.com/CasadeClara
Economical, multilingual backpackers' guesthouse seven blocks from the Plaza de Armas in a peaceful area overlooking a park. Includes free wireless internet, library, and advice on tours. **$–$$**

Los Conquistadores
Diego de Almagro 586
Tel: 044-481-660/481-650
www.losconquistadoreshotel.com
Comfortable hotel, with bar and restaurant half a block from the Plaza de Armas. Rooms that overlook the street can be noisy at night, so make sure to double-check. Free internet. **$$$$**

Gran Bolívar Hotel
Jr. Bolivar 957
Tel: 044-222-090
www.perunorte.com/granbolivar
This breezy hotel has good, clean rooms (some with attractive artwork) and pleasant communal areas. It constantly receives positive reviews for its helpful staff and good value. There's free WiFi access too. **$$$$**

Hotel Paraíso
San Martín 240–246
Tel: 044-201-909
www.hotelesparaiso.com.pe
Built in 2008, the Paraíso features modern, functional rooms with WiFi, a restaurant, and a location in the historic center. It also serves a good breakfast buffet. Suites come with a bathtub for two. **$$$$**

Libertador Trujillo Hotel
Jr. Independencia 485, Plaza de Armas
Tel: 044-232-741
www.libertador.com.pe
Good-value accommodation in a beautiful building in the town's main square. It comes with a gym, sauna, swimming pool, Jacuzzi, and free parking. Excellent Sunday buffet. A favorite among travelers. **$$$$$**

North coast

Costa Azul
Balneario de Zorritos, Zorritos
Tel: 072-544-135
www.costaazulperu.com
A small resort by the white-sand beach in the lovely seaside village of Zorritos just outside Tumbes. You can sunbathe on the beach, or hang out by the pool. There is a spa and a gym with views of the beach. Great value. **$$$$**

A friendly face at the Libertador Trujillo Hotel

Hotel Bracamonte
Los Olivos 503, Huanchaco
Tel: 044-461-162
www.hotelbracamonte.com.pe
Set up by a family that fell in love with Huanchaco after several holidays here, this hotel is a good place to stay with family and friends. It has a relaxed atmosphere, a pool, games room, and a restaurant. **$$$**

Hotel del Wawa
Pje 8 de Octubre s/n, Máncora
Tel: 073-258-427
www.delwawa.com
This hotel has changed administration in the past couple of years, which has improved its offerings. It has air-conditioned cabins with palm-leaf roofs right on the beach. It also features a surf school and a good restaurant. **$$**

McCallum Lodging House
Los Ficus 460, Huanchaco
Tel: 044-462-350
E-mail: mccallum-lodging-house@hotmail.com
http://mccallumlodginghouse.wordpress.com
Popular with the young crowd of surfers and backpackers, this hostel is just off Huanchaco's beach. It offers beds in dorms, but also private rooms. Free WiFi, kitchen, and a communal outside area with hammocks. Warm hospitality and a delicious Peruvian lunch are available. **$–$$**

Los Portales Hotel
Libertad 875, Piura
Tel: 073-321-161
www.hotelportalespiura.com
Historic building right on the main square, with restaurant, nice pool, casino, and business center. The bar offers live shows and karaoke. It is often used for big receptions, so ask when booking if you want to ensure your nights are not disturbed. **$$$$**

Punta Sal Club Hotel
Crta. Sullana, km 173, Tumbes
Tel: 072-540-088
www.puntasal.com.pe
Situated right on the beach, this resort hotel offers smart beach bungalows for larger groups as well as simple rooms in the central building. Deep-sea fishing trips are also offered here. **$$$$**

Cajamarca

Hostal Los Balcones de la Recoleta
Jr. Amalia Puga 1050
Tel: 076-369-217/363-302
Built around a central garden, this atmospheric old building is a clean, friendly, and welcoming place to stay. There's a good restaurant, too. One of the nicest *hostales* in Cajamarca, and great value. **$$**

Hotel Costa del Sol
Jr. Cruz de Piedra 707
Tel: 076-362-472
www.costadelsolperu.com
A well-located, comfortable new hotel in the center of town, just next to the cathedral. It has WiFi, a restaurant, spa, gym, and heated pool. Airport pickup is also available. **$$$$$**

Hotel El Portal del Marques
Jr. del Comercio 644
Tel: 076-368-464/343-339
Reservations in Lima: 01-988-805-440
www.portaldelmarques.com
Pleasant hotel just a block away from the Plaza de Armas. Staff are friendly and efficient, and there's an excellent restaurant on site. Happy hour runs from 7–9pm in the hotel's bar. **$$$$**

Posada del Puruay
Crta. Porcon–Hualgayoc, km 4.5
Tel: 076-367-928/028
Reservations in Lima: 01-336-7869
www.posadapuruay.com.pe
This superbly renovated hacienda just outside Cajamarca has a lovely central courtyard, with a fountain, acres of terracotta tiles, and beautifully decorated rooms. A peaceful place to stay, close to the hot springs of the Baños del Inca. **$$$$**

RESTAURANTS

Peru's north coast (Piura in particular) is famous for its cuisine, with its sharp flavors and elaborate preparation. Dishes include *seco de chavelo* (mashed plantains with pork), *majado de yucca con chicharrón* (mashed manioc with pork), *chifles* (fried plantain), and *natilla* (molasses made from goats' milk and sugar cane). Cajamarca, meanwhile, cooks up traditional Andean food.

Restaurant price categories

Prices are for a three-course menu including juice but no wine or coffee

$ = below US$2
$$ = US$2–5
$$$ = US$6–10
$$$$ = over US$10

Trujillo

El Cuatrero
Francisco Borja 187, Urb. La Merced
Tel: 044-222-690
Good, inexpensive meat grills in this restaurant that is renowned among locals as the best *parrilla* place in town. It also does an excellent roast chicken. The restaurant is a bit small, but it is highly recommended. **$**

Mar Picante
Av. America Sur 2199
Tel: 044-221-544
This restaurant serves wonderful seafood, including excellent *ceviche*, at low prices. It tends to fill up quickly, so it's worth going before the hordes of locals, or booking. **$$$**

El Mochica
Jr. Bolivar 462
Tel: 044-244-401
www.elmochica.com.pe
Well-prepared *criollo* fare at reasonable prices, El Mochica specializes in fish and seafood. It has occasional live music and is popular with locals, so it is advisable to book in advance. **$$$$**

Romano Rincón Criollo
Estados Unidos 162, Urb. El Recreo
Tel: 044-244-207
www.romanogroup.net/criollo
Specialized in northern Peruvian cuisine, this lively restaurant is where many locals come for the good-value set menu. *Tacu tacu* (traditionally prepared with rice and beans) is a specialty here – try it in a shrimp sauce. **$$$$**

Clams in Chiclayo

Il Valentino
Jr. Orbegoso 224
Tel: 044-246-643
If you have had your fill of Peruvian food, Il Valentino is the place for you. This popular eatery serves good-value Italian food – including pizzas, pasta, and good salads. **$$$**

North coast

Club Colonial
Av. La Rivera 514, Huanchaco
Tel: 044-461-015
Located in a beautiful mansion in a quiet square, this restaurant is very elegant. The menu offers a mix of Peruvian and Franco-Belgian dishes, including *ceviche*, some homemade pastas, and cordon bleu. **$$$$**

El Huaralino
Libertad 155, Urb. Santa Victoria, Chiclayo
Tel: 074-270-330
This is one of Chiclayo's best and most upscale restaurants. It serves great Peruvian food (including good *papas a la huancaína*, boiled potatoes in a spicy cheese sauce), international fare, and local specialties. **$$$**

Otra Cosa
Av. Victor Larco 921, Urb. El Boquerón, Huanchaco
Tel: 044-461-346
www.otracosa.nl
This vegetarian restaurant is owned by a Dutch-Peruvian couple who also run volunteer projects in the area. Food is mostly organic, the yoghurt is local, and portions are large. It also serves up a great breakfast. **$$**

Restaurant Big Ben
Av. Larco 1182, Urb. El Boquerón, Huanchaco
Tel: 044-461-869
www.bigbenhuanchaco.com
Wonderful fresh seafood is served here daily, with both Peruvian and international dishes on offer. Pick a table overlooking the sea, and enjoy a long, slow lunch to the sound of the waves. **$$$$**

Romana
Balta 512, Chiclayo
Tel: 074-223-598
A popular place serving a great variety of dishes, all of which are local favorites. If you're feeling brave, try the *chirimpico* for breakfast; it's stewed goat tripe and organs, and is guaranteed to either cure a hangover or give you one. Otherwise, you can choose between pastas, steaks, seafood, chicken or pork *chicharrones* with yucca. **$$$**

La Santitos
Libertad 1014, Piura
Tel: 073-309-475
This restaurant is very popular with locals, and it is often full on account of its tasty, simple fare. The eatery provides a full-on *costeña* (coastal) experience, with local music and waiters dressed in traditional clothing. **$$–$$$**

Cajamarca

El Batán
Jr. del Batán 369
Tel: 076-366-025
A beautiful restaurant that is spacious and has a patio. It offers good local and international food, and there is live music on Friday and Saturday nights. After dinner you can also explore the art gallery which is attached to the restaurant. **$$$$**

Sunset on Huanchaco Beach

Tasty lobster soup

El Cajamarqués
Amazonas 770
Tel: 076-362-128/822-128
Situated in a colonial building, with high ceilings and white walls, this is the most elegant and traditional restaurant in town. Despite the fancy setting, it has great-value good food and cheap set menus for lunch. **$$$$**

Carpa Bruja
Jr. Amalia Puga 519
Tel: 076-506-175
The 'witches' tent' conjures up tasty international dishes, with lots of salad and vegetables, and tasty sandwiches on wholemeal bread from its kitchen. Perfect for vegetarians. There is a happy hour in the evening. **$**

El Querubino
Jr. Amalia Puga 589
Tel: 076-340-900
Just off the Plaza de Armas, this has become a hip hangout and it is quite popular among locals. It has a diverse menu, and modern art is displayed on the walls. There is often a live band. **$$**

Restaurante Salas
Jr. Amalia Puga 637
Tel: 076-362-867
This Cajamarca institution, centrally located, has been around since the 1940s. It is very popular with locals, although some say the food used to be better. It offers inexpensive regional dishes. **$$$**

NIGHTLIFE AND ENTERTAINMENT

As befits the ocean setting, much of the nightlife in the north is focused on the beach, but the inland cities also have many bars and *peñas* with live music. Traditional festivities liven up the evenings in cities like Cajamarca and Trujillo.

Trujillo

El Estribo Internacional
San Martín 809
Tel: 044-224-641
www.elestribointernacional.com
Open from Wednesday to Sunday, El Estribo is Trujillo's most popular *peña*. Food available, live music every night.

Luna Rota Pub
Av. America Sur 2119
Tel: 044-242-182/221-488
This is a lively bar, only open during the weekend, with snacks and live *criollo* music.

North coast

La Mamacha
Túpac Amaru 117, Huanchaco
Tel: 044-462-347
This bar, adjacent to a restaurant with the same name, is a popular local hangout, and a great place to kick back and enjoy a relaxed drink. Time your visit for happy hour.

Queen's
Av. Guardia Civil D1–D2, Piura
Open Thursday to Saturday, this disco is popular among locals and gringos.

Solid Gold
Av. Federico Villarreal 115, Chiclayo
Tel: 074-234-911
www.granhotelchiclayo.com.pe
This casino and karaoke bar is one of Chiclayo's most popular nighttime destinations. Located inside the Gran Hotel Chiclayo.

Tribal Lounge & Bar
Alfredo Lapoint 682, Chiclayo
As this is such a nice place to hang out, Tribal has become particularly popular among travelers. There is occasionally live music. Free WiFi.

Cajamarca

Club Los Frailones
Av. Perú 701
Tel: 076-364-113
This club is very lively during the weekends, when it is a popular destination with locals and tourists alike.

Peña Usha Usha
Amalia Puga 320
Tel: 076-997-4514
If you want to catch some live music, this bar is the best place in town. Local music and lively jam sessions are amongst the offerings here.

SPORTS, ACTIVITIES, AND TOURS

There is plenty to keep one busy in northern Peru – from archeological sites to wonderful surfing beaches. Tours to any of the major archeological sites (Huacas del Sol y de la Luna, Huaca del Dragón, and Chan Chan) can be arranged in Trujillo, while tours of Cajamarca include numerous colonial churches, the thermal baths at Baños del Inca, and the Ventanillas de Otuzco, and can be arranged with numerous agencies.

Trujillo

Contunor
Jr. Francisco Pizarro 478, Of. 101
Tel: 044-200-412
www.contunor.com
Offers a city tour of the region that includes the mud city of Chan Chan, Huacas del Sol y de la Luna, and a visit to Huanchaco beach.

Guía Tours
Jr. Independencia 580
Tel: 044-245-170
Two- or three-day tours take in Chan Chan. A city tour of Trujillo, where travelers also visit local museums, is also offered.

Trujillo Tours
Jr. Diego de Almagro 301
Tel: 044-233-069
www.trujillotours.com
Runs a three-day tour which takes in archeological sites including Chan Chan.

North coast

Octopus Surf Tours
Tel: 099-400-5518
Email: info@octopussurftours.com
www.octopussurftours.com
Operated by Marco Antonio Ravizza, known

Exploring the Huacas del Sol y de la Luna

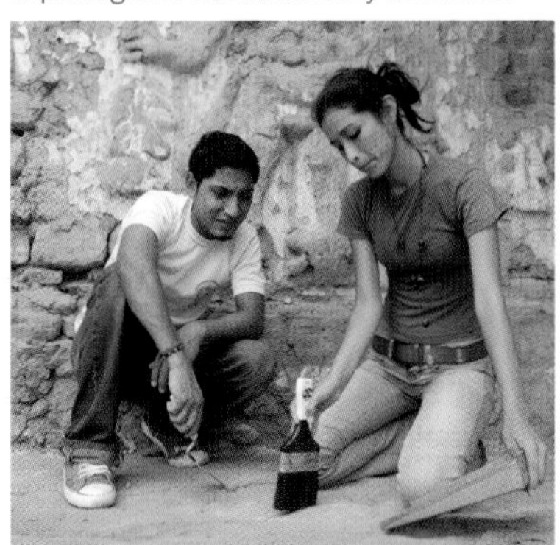

locally as 'Pulpo' (Octopus) and who has over 20 years' experience in surfing, this company offers surf tours out of Máncora to most of Peru's northern beaches, including places off the beaten track. Ideal for surfers of all abilities. Also includes trips to ruins and local museums.

Cajamarca

Cumbe Mayo Tours
Jr. Amalia Puga 635
Tel: 076-362-938
This company organises a good selection of short tours in and around Cajamarca.

Clarín Tours
Jr. Del Batán 161
Tel: 076-366-829
www.clarintours.com
Offers cultural tours, including an expedition to the Inca baths in Cajamarca.

Chachapoyas

Vilaya Tours
Jr. Amazonas 261
Tel: 041-477-506
www.vilayatours.com
Runs tours and treks in the Northern Sierra, including trips to the Kuélap ruins.

FESTIVALS AND EVENTS

With an extraordinary range of influences from coast, Andes, and Amazon, festivities in the north are the most varied in Peru.

January

Festival de la Marinera
Trujillo
At the end of January hundreds of couples compete in this traditional dance competition.

February

Cruz de Chalpon
Motupe
From February 1–15 this handicraft and commercial fair takes place in the pilgrimage center of Motupe, close to Chiclayo.

Carnival
Cajamarca
Cajamarca is known as the capital of the Peruvian Carnival. Every mid-February each neighborhood participates with its own queen; costumes are prepared months in advance.

March

Festival of the Captive Lord of Monsefú
Monsefú
On March 14 a vibrant festival with processions, a textiles fair, flower decorations, dances and music takes place in Monsefú, near Chiclayo.

June

Festival of the Divine Child of the Miracle of Etén
It is believed that the image of Jesus Christ appeared twice within one month in the town of Etén, close to Chiclayo, in the 17th century. The event is celebrated with a big fair on June 22 (and repeated on July 22 for four days).

September

International Festival of Spring
Trujillo
Concerts, show horses, and parades make September 20–30 one of the most fun times to be in Trujillo.

Dancer at the Festival de la Marinera

The Amazon Basin

Taking up more than half of Peru's landmass, the vast Amazon Basin is home to innumerable plant and animal species, but just 11 percent of the Peruvian population. Yet despite its remoteness, it offers many exhilarating experiences. Track forest creatures great and small in preserves around Iquitos, or in Manu National Park, one of the most pristine sections of rainforest in South America.

Iquitos

Population: 406,340

Local dialing code: 065

Local tourist office: Loreto 201, corner Raimondi; tel: 065-236-144

Main police station: Comisaría de Morona de Iquitos, Morona 120; tel: 065-231-123. Tourist police: Sargento Lores 834; tel: 065-242-081

Main post office: Serpost: Av. Arica 402; tel: 065-223-812/234-091

Hospitals: Hospital Regional de Loreto; Av. 28 de Julio s/n, Punchana; tel: 065-252-004/252-733. Clínica Ana Stahl; Av. la Marina 28, tel: 065-252-535

Local newspapers: *La Región*; *Crónicas*; *Iquitos Times*

Viewed from the air, Peru's Amazon looks like an endless sea of lumpy green sponges, stretching in all directions to the horizon. It is this thick umbrella of trees that creates the millions of homes below in which animals and plants live. The upper canopy is virtually a desert. The crowns of the trees are exposed both to the fierce tropical sun and to winds that frequently snap and topple the tallest of them. To reduce evaporation, the leaves at this level are quite small. Beneath the canopy is a very different world of reduced light, protected from direct sun and wind, where the leaves are larger and struggle for light. Toward the jungle floor, the air is calm even in strong storms, and at times completely still. The sound of insects is overpowering, as millions of unseen little creatures call to one another. At the bottom-most level the leaves are very large; less than 5 percent of the sun's light actually reaches the jungle's floor. It is this enormous variation of light, wind, and temperature that, together with the thousands of different species of plants, affords millions of different homes for animal and plant species. Whole communities of insects, birds, and other animals are specialized and adapted to different levels of the rainforest, so it is not surprising that it contains the highest species diversity in the world.

A good way to become acquainted quickly with the jungle is to visit one of a number of lodges that have been set up on rivers in the vicinity of Iquitos. Although many of the two- or three-day lodge tours can be booked through a travel agent in Lima, they are much cheaper if arranged in Iquitos itself.

A commercial riverboat traveling either upriver toward Pucallpa or downriver toward Brazil is another great way to experience the Amazon, but for those who have a lot more time and want to get off the beaten path, it is a good idea to hire a small boat and guide of your own. As with the commercial riverboats, the best way to locate a small boat and guide in Iquitos is simply to ask about on the wharves. With a boat, the entire Amazon suddenly opens up for your exploration. *See Unique Experience on Amazon Adventures, pp.30–35.*

Riverboat on the Amazon

Iquitos from above

Iquitos

Some 3,200km (1,990 miles) upriver from the Amazon's mouth lies the jungle-locked city of **Iquitos ❶**, which has long been a center for excursions into the surrounding jungle. The capital of the department of Loreto, it is home to more than 400,000 people, and is linked to the exterior world only by air

Iquitos cuisine

The local dish is *paiche a la loretana*, a fillet of a primitive fish *(Arapaima gigas)*, served with fried manioc (a tropical tuber) and vegetables. Ask where the *paiche*, at up to 100 kg (220lbs) one of the world's biggest freshwater fishes, has been caught: overfishing has taken its toll and breeding programs are underway to protect it. Laguna Quistacocha, 15km (9 miles) from Iquitos, has a hatchery and restaurants, and is worth an outing.

The astounding variety of fruit is another salient feature of Amazonian food. In Iquitos, exotic fruit juices are sold on the street corners, as are ice creams flavored with mango, papaya, *granadilla* (passion fruit), and many other fruits.

and riverboats. At one time the clearing-house for the millions of tons of rubber shipped to Europe, Iquitos still displays the vestiges of its former status as one of the most important rubber capitals in the world. Houses both near the main plaza and the river are still faced with *azulejos* (glazed tiles), which at the height of the rubber boom were originally shipped from Italy and Portugal along with other luxury goods such as early 20th-century ironwork from England, glass chandeliers, caviar, and fine wines.

City center

On the **Plaza de Armas** stands the Casa de Fierro, or Iron House, which was designed by Gustave Eiffel for the Paris Exhibition in 1898 and now houses a good restaurant upstairs called the Amazon Café. It is said to be the first prefabricated house in the Americas and was transported unassembled from Paris by a local rubber baron. It is entirely constructed of iron trusses and bolted iron sheets. This sounds more impressive than it looks, and it is more interesting as a symbol of the town's short-lived affluence than architecturally.

Also on the plaza is the house of Carlos Fitzcarrald, the Peruvian rubber baron who dragged a steamship over the pass that bears his name, thus opening up the department of Madre de Dios. The German director Werner Herzog shot part of his film *Fitzcarraldo* here, and several of the refurbished steamships that he used are still in port. Hundreds of *iquiteños* were used as extras in the movie, which created a brief mini-boom of its own.

Wooden carving of tropical birds in Iquitos

Plaza de Armas

Iquitos today is a colorful, friendly city that seems to have a monopoly not on rubber but on three-wheeled taxis (charging approximately S./0.5 a ride); motor scooters, with the consequent din as they are continually revved up; Amazon views; and a very special atmosphere. It is located some 80km (50 miles) downriver from where the **Marañón** and **Ucayali** rivers join to create the Amazon River.

You can take a taxi or simply walk down from the main plaza to the picturesque waterfront district of **Belén**, to the southeast of the town, where the houses float on rafts in the water. A primitive Venetian-style labyrinth of canals, canoes, and stores, Belén is the center for an incredible variety of Amazon products: exotic fruits, fish, edible frogs, herbal medicines, and waterfowl.

Iquitos transport

 **Airport:** Aeropuerto Internacional Francisco Secada Vignetta (IQT); Av. Abelardo Quiñónez km 6.5; tel: 065-260-147/260-151. Taxis from the airport to the center of Iquitos take 20 minutes and cost around S./15

 **Combis** (minibuses) charge S./3 to S./6 up to km 80 on the road to Nauta (the only town reachable by road from Iquitos)

 **River port:** Terminal Portuario de Iquitos; Av. La Marina 1383; tel: 065-252-275; destinations include Pucallpa (Ucayali), Yurimaguas (Loreto), Santa Rosa (border with Colombia and Brazil)

 **Car rental:** Iquitos Rent a Car; Morona 368; tel: 065-235-633

 **Taxis:** Taxis charge S./20 for by-the-hour transport in the city. Radio taxis include Fono Taxi; tel: 065-232-014; cell: 065-965-611-311. Taxi Aeropuerto; tel: 065-241-284; cell: 065-965-612-639. Negotiate fares in advance and insist that taxis take you to your destination, as they will often seek to take customers to hotels where they receive commissions. **Mototaxis** charge S./8 to S./10 per hour – a journey in the center usually costs S./2 to S./3 and to the airport S./6 to S./8. Recommended is MOSEG (Mototaxi Seguro); cell: 065-965-626-720

Plowing the waterways are a plethora of small canoe-taxis paddled by *iquiteños*, some as young as five years old. A canoe tour of one of the most unusual waterfronts in the world costs just a few dollars.

Around Iquitos

If you are spending a few days in Iquitos, it is worth taking a day trip to **Pilpintuwasi Butterfly Farm** (www.amazonanimalorphanage.org; Tue–Sun 9am–4pm; charge) just outside the city at Padre Cocha. On the banks of the Nanay River is a huge walk-through butterfly enclosure, with exhibits that explain the fascinating lifecycle of the butterfly. It is a delight to walk around surrounded by drifts of the colorful creatures. Located on the same site is the **Amazon Animal Orphanage**, a refuge for injured or previously caged animals. There is a magnificent jaguar and a giant anteater, as well as monkeys, tapirs, parrots, sloths, and a number of other denizens of the jungle, all rescued from unhappy captivity or recuperating from maltreatment.

The Butterfly Farm and the Animal Orphanage are a 20-minute boat ride from the Bella Vista sector in Iquitos (ask for Pilpintuwasi). In the dry season, there is a 15-minute walk from where the boat leaves you; in the wet, you are brought right to the front gate.

Some 15km (9 miles) south of the city is the beautiful **Lago Quistacocha**, set in lush tropical jungle, which can be reached by bus. There is a small zoo, the Parque Zoológico de Quistacocha (closed Monday; charge), where jaguars, ocelots, parrots, and anacondas can be seen, as well as the giant *paiche* fish – the one that features in the local dish *(see box p.231)* – which are bred here in hatcheries.

Consider a day trip to Pilpintuwasi Butterfly Farm

The long and winding Amazon

Only 100km (62 miles) from Iquitos is the biggest national park in Peru, the 2 million-hectare (5 million-acre) **Reserva Nacional Pacaya-Samiria** ❷, a wildlife-packed lowland jungle area that can be reached by hiring a boat and a guide, in either Iquitos or the village of Lagunas, and staging your own expedition, or joining a tour.

The central Amazon

Although it is still well off the beaten track, access to the central Amazon is improving. Pucallpa can be reached by road from Lima, and infrastructure for visitors is improving fast. The descent to the Amazon is via narrow and spectacular roads lined with waterfalls and tropical trees, and eco-lodges provide some of the world's best birding opportunities.

The Amazon Rim

German-speaking immigrants colonized the area around **Oxopampa** and **Pozuzo**, which along with **La Merced** offers a convenient base for exploring tropical areas when arriving from the Central Sierra or Lima by road. It's an area of coffee-growing, steeply forested ravines, cascading rivers, and adventure sports. **Satipo** is a gateway to explore remote Amazon parks like Otishi and a town where many Asháninka indigenous people shop for supplies. The road through **Tingo María** is more easy to travel to head down into the flat Amazon Basin. Near the city, the **Cueva de las Lechuzas** in Tingo María National Park has oilbirds (mistakenly called *lechuzas*, or owls, by the locals) and unusual nocturnal parrots.

Deforestation

Jungles have existed for hundreds of millions of years, but it is only within the past 100 years that they have been on the decline. The trend is in direct relation to the population of human beings. In the course of the past century humans have destroyed half of the world's rainforests. At the present rate of destruction, only 40 percent of the original Amazon rainforest will remain by 2025 or thereabouts.

AYAHUASCA AND COCA

Nothing more intimately and controversially links ancient pre-Hispanic rituals with the present than the use of ayahuasca and coca, used in shamanic rituals and for healing for thousands of years. Industrialization and criminalization, particularly of coca, have led to much suffering in Latin America, yet many a foreign visitor has felt the benefits of coca when dealing with the discomfort of altitude sickness.

Among the many Amazon herbal remedies, ayahuasca and coca are both the most famous and infamous.

Ayahuasca *(Banisteriopsis caapi)* is a rainforest vine with hallucinogenic properties that is used to promote knowledge and healing under the guidance of a shaman. The vine has been used for centuries by Amazon tribes as part of traditional celebrations and initiations. It has also been used to make predictions, in decision-making, and to aid the resolution of interfamilial and intertribal conflicts. Today, it is principally used as a key to self-knowledge and expanded consciousness.

Extract of the vine is prepared as a bitter-tasting drink which is administered by the shaman. After some time, this promotes vomiting – part of the cleansing process – and then a state in which visions are experienced, leading to a mental state of clarity, certainty, and self-awareness.

Courses of ayahuasca are used in some Amazon clinics to treat alcoholism and drug addiction, and, in

Picking coca leaves

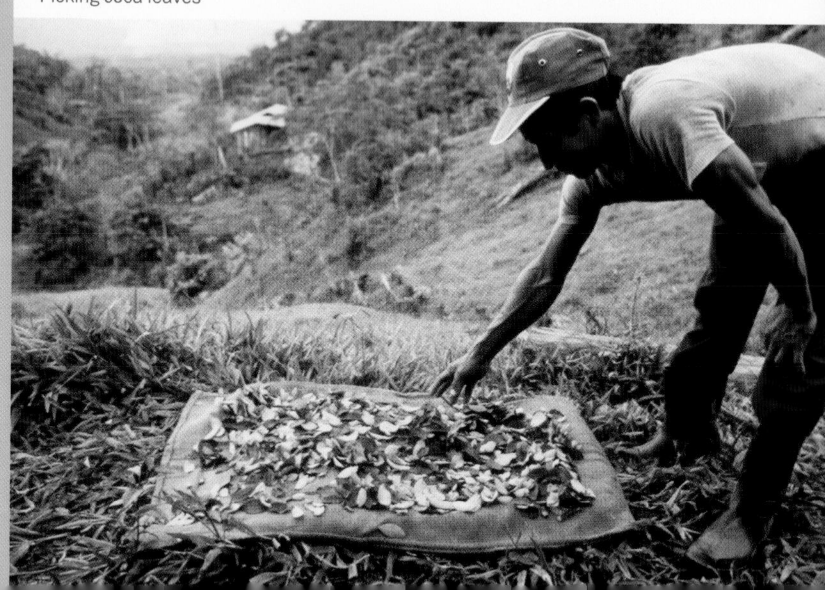

recent years, drinking ayahuasca has become a popular activity for tourists. Some shamans conduct ayahuasca ceremonies for groups, but if you are attracted by the idea, do your research carefully. While at its best, ayahuasca is said to be profoundly enlightening, a bad experience can be very frightening.

Coca, while better known, in fact is much less of an issue in its leaf form. Many visitors to high-altitude destinations like Cusco or Juliaca may get a cup of coca tea as soon as they step off the plane. The plant's alkaloids, however, contain the potent stimulant cocaine.

Some 3 million South Americans chew coca regularly, adding a little bicarbonate of soda or lime to get the saliva going and sucking its juices. It gives energy and dulls the senses against cold. In Peru, coca is mostly cultivated in the Huallaga Valley – definitely an area to avoid, as even though some coca is produced legally in the country, much goes to the global cocaine trade. Besides leaves and tea, coca goes into cookies, granola bars, and some soft drinks, including, apparently, Coca-Cola. Scientists agree that there are no dangers in chewing the leaf, nor is it addictive, but because of its association with cocaine, coca leaves are banned in most countries. Taking home just a strip of coca leaf chewing gum or a coca teabag could get you into trouble. Irrespective of the international prohibition, cocaine trafficking remains widespread and highly problematic.

Coca leaf tea

Preparing ayahuasca

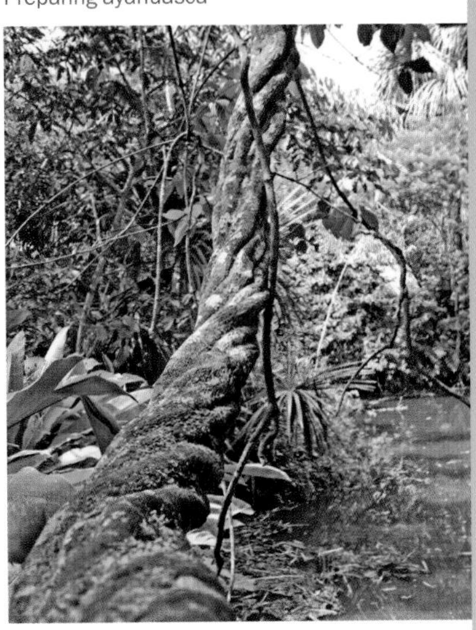

Ayahuasca vine

Pucallpa

Seven days' travel upriver from Iquitos on the Río Ucayali is **Pucallpa** ❸, a rapidly growing city of 250,000 that can be reached from Lima by air – there are several flights daily – or on a 20-hour bus journey. The trip is best done by day due to security concerns. Most people arriving in the city prefer to stay at Puerto Callao on the nearby **Lago Yarinacocha**, a 20-minute bus journey from the city, which is the main tourist attraction of the area.

In **Puerto Callao** you can visit the fascinating artisanal cooperative **Maroti Shobo**, where high-quality ceramics and weavings made by the Shipibo people from the surrounding villages are displayed and sold, and are sent to museums all over the world.

The Shipibo people have inhabited the area for at least the past 1,000 years, and trips can be arranged to some of their villages. There are a couple of lodges on the lake, and more wildlife than you might expect, considering the nearby population. The lodges will also organize jungle excursions, and private excursions by motor canoe into the surrounding jungle and canals are easy to arrange from Puerto Callao. While traveling on the canals, you may see numerous piranhas, caiman, and the occasional monkey.

The southern Amazon

The traditional hopping-off point for Peru's southern jungle is the city of Cusco *(see pp.123–33)*, where a variety of tours is available, along with a wealth of information on some of the national parks in the southern region, but the area has been included in this section of the book to offer continuity to readers who are interested in all aspects of travel in the Peruvian Amazon.

Hammocks at a market in Pucallpa

There are 13 different species of monkey at Parque Nacional del Manu

Birdwatching tours

The forests of Amazonian Peru offer the finest birdwatching experience. However, identifying all the different species, and finding elusive birds in the forest undergrowth, can prove overwhelming for an ornithologist inexperienced in tropical forests, which is why an expert guide is invaluable. Birdwatching tours also help to support local families, who will conserve rainforest birds, as their livelihoods depend on it. Local people won't hunt macaws for trade or feathers if they can make more money by taking visitors to see them. By choosing such tours, visitors can make a positive conservation impact. Contact **Kolibri Expeditions** in Miraflores, Lima (tel: 01-273-7246; www.kolibriexpeditions.com) or **Manu Expeditions** in Cusco (tel: 084-225-990; www.birding-in-peru.com).

Pongo de Manique

The adventurous traveler can go from Cusco by rail and truck to **Quillabamba** and **Kiteni** and from there hire a boat through the **Pongo de Manique**, a narrow gorge surrounded by lush jungle and waterfalls on the upper **Río Urubamba**, a journey described in Peter Matthiessen's 1962 classic, *Cloud Forest*. It must be emphasized that transport is infrequent in this area, and you should be extremely flexible, or take a tour.

Manu National Park

Also accessible from Cusco is one of the most bio-diverse rainforest parks in the world, located in Peru's southernmost jungle department of **Madre de Dios**. At 1.8 million hectares (4.5 million acres), the **Parque Nacional del Manu** ❹, one of the few truly pristine regions of the tropics, is perhaps the best area in the Amazon rainforest for watching wildlife. In many other jungle areas, because of the proximity of humans, you may be lucky to see anything other than birds, insects, or an occasional large animal, but in Manu you will see so many monkeys (there are 13 different species) that you may grow tired of them. Besides an abundance of turtles, you'll have a great opportunity to see giant otters, peccaries, capybaras, tapirs, and if very lucky the elusive jaguar.

A catamaran canoe glides across Lago Sandoval

Manu is also an unparalleled place for birdwatching. Founded in 1973, the park was declared a Biosphere Reserve in 1977, and a Unesco World Natural Heritage Site 10 years later. It harbors over 1,000 species of bird – 300 more species than are found in the USA and Canada combined. The world record for the number of species seen and heard in one day was set in Manu in 1982, when 331 species were recorded in just a few square miles of forest.

By far the easiest way to visit Manu is with one of the local tour operators *(see pp.246–7)* who will arrange all permits, transport, equipment, gasoline, and food supplies for the trip. It can take up to two days to reach this isolated area by traveling overland from Cusco, down through the cloud forest, and later transferring to a boat – an unforgettable experience. There is also the option of chartering a small plane, which can fly to the junction of the Madre de Dios and Manu rivers. This is much more expensive, but a good idea if your time is limited. Prices depend on the number of passengers.

Reserva Nacional Tambopata

There are yet more chances to see birds in Peru's second-largest reserve: the **Reserva Nacional Tambopata** ❺. Created by the Peruvian government in 1989, this 1.5 million-hectare (3.8 million-acre) zone has been set up both as an extractive reserve (for rubber, Brazil nuts, and other products) and for eco-tourism. The reserve encompasses the entire watershed of the **Río Tambopata**, one of Peru's most beautiful and least disturbed areas.

The river begins high in the Andean department of Puno; several tour companies lead kayak expeditions down the Tambopata, which offers a spectacular transition from the Andes to the low jungle. The reserve protects the largest macaw lick in South America, the **Colpa de Guacamayos**.

Here birdwatchers can view one of the world's phenomenal avian spectacles, as hundreds of red, blue, and green parrots and macaws gather at the lick daily. Squawking raucously, they wheel through the air before landing together on the riverbank to eat clay. This breathtaking display can only be seen where there is undisturbed rainforest with healthy populations of wild macaws, as in southeast Peru. Trails around the macaw lick offer birding in both floodplain and high-ground forest. Orinoco geese and large horned screamers can also be seen along clear streams near the Andean foothills.

Macaws gathering at a clay lick

Puerto Maldonado

From Cusco you can reach **Puerto Maldonado** ❻, the capital of the department of Madre de Dios, either by air or along the 500km (310-mile) road, a trip that takes two and a half days; it's a bit uncomfortable, but worth it for the scenery. Long cut off from the rest of the world both by rapids on the **Río Madeira** and by the Andes, Puerto Maldonado, a thriving rubber town at the turn of the 20th century, lapsed into anonymity again until the discovery of gold in the 1970s, and the building of an airport in the early 1980s turned the city into a gold-rush boom town.

Set on a bluff overlooking the Madre de Dios and Tambopata rivers, Puerto Maldonado has a pleasant **Plaza de Armas**, and numerous hotels for miners on brief trips to town, but not much to see or do. Buy a bag or two of Brazil nuts while you are here. These rich, abundant, and inexpensive nuts will help encourage the preservation of Madre de Dios's rainforest, where around 30 percent of the population is employed in nut extraction.

Only an hour south of Puerto Maldonado is **Lago Sandoval**, a beautiful jungle lake that can be reached by boat from Puerto Maldonado's port. Three hours farther downriver, and well worth an overnight fishing expedition, is **Lago Valencia**, which is quite remote and relatively free of tourists. A several-day expedition can be mounted to the 100,000-hectare (250,000-acre) **Reserva Nacional Pampas de Río Heath**, a wild area of plains and swamps located on the Río Heath bordering Bolivia.

ACCOMMODATIONS

Hotel options in the Amazon are mostly limited to the few towns and the jungle lodge options, of which there are plenty. The latter are more expensive, but by far the better option to observe Amazon wildlife. Mosquito nets and insect repellent are a basic necessity, and in a pinch can be bought in many places.

Accommodations price categories

Prices are for one night's accommodation in a standard double room (unless otherwise specified); price categories have not been included for jungle lodges, where rates are always based on multi-day packages

$ = below US$20
$$ = US$20–40
$$$ = US$40–60
$$$$ = US$60–100
$$$$$ = over US$100

Iquitos

El Dorado Plaza Hotel
Jr. Napo 254, Plaza de Armas
Tel: 065-222-555
Reservations in Lima: tel: 01-255-7736
Email: info@Grupo-Dorado.com
www.grupo-dorado.com
This amazing, glitzy place looks straight out of Las Vegas. Good food, good rooms, good service, good cocktails, and above all, air-conditioned to positively Arctic degrees. It has a swimming pool. **$$$$$**

Hobo Hideout
Putumayo 437
Tel: 065-234-099
http://hobohideouthostel.minihostels.com
With cheap dorm beds, as well as private rooms with shared bathrooms, this is a popular place for backpackers. Rooms have fans, but no air conditioning. There is a shared kitchen. **$**

Explorama Lodges

Hospedaje La Pascana
Pevas 133
Tel: 065-235-581
www.pascana.com
This simple little place is set around a quiet garden. The rooms have cold water and powerful fans. An excellent in-house agency, Pascana Amazon Services, arranges off-the-beaten-track Amazon adventures and visits to lodges. **$**

Hostal El Colibri
Jr. Nauta 172
Tel: 065-244-018
Email: hostalelcolibri@hotmail.com
http://hostalelcolibri.com
A short distance from the boulevard which runs along the Amazon waterfront, this simple hotel has comfortable rooms with fans, private bathrooms, and cable TV. The rooms overlooking the street can be noisy. **$$**

Hotel La Casona
Av. Fitzcarrald 147
Tel: 065-234-394
www.hotellacasonaiquitos.com
This may be a classic backpacker place, but if you're after peace, its lower-level rooms on the inner courtyard are possibly the quietest in the city. A quaint little hotel that will also help you arrange jungle trips. **$**

Hotel Marañón
Fitzcarrald and Nauta 285–289
Tel: 065-242-673
Email: reservas@hotelmaranon.com

www.hotelmaranon.com
This cool, air-conditioned place is efficient, friendly, and very close to the Plaza de Armas. It can suffer from street noise, so ask for the quietest room or pack earplugs. **$**

Northern Amazon

Amazonia Expeditions
Reservations in the US: tel: 800-262-9669
www.perujungle.com
Amazonia Expeditions runs Tahuayo Lodge, close to the Tamshiyacu-Tahuayo Reserve, comprised of 15 suitably rustic but comfortable cabins right on the Tahuayo River. Many researchers choose to visit this beautiful, remote lodge; consequently the guides are top-rate. The area that constitutes the Tamshiyacu-Tahuayo reserve is thought to be a Pleistocene refugia (an area that remained forested during the last Ice Age, when most of the Amazon was dry savanna); many of the species here exist nowhere else in the world.

Explorama Lodges
Av. La Marina 340, Iquitos
Tel: 065-252-530
Reservations in the US/Canada:
tel: 1800-707-5275
www.explorama.com
One of the best-known tour operators, around for over 45 years. They now run four lodges as well as the renowned Canopy Walkway that allows guests to walk above the tops of the rainforest trees. Guests can also visit Renuperu ethnobotanical medicinal plant garden, where the secrets of the Amazon's healing plants are studied.

Paseos Amazónicos
Pevas 246, Iquitos
Tel: 065-231-618
Reservations in Lima:
Tel: 01-241-7576
www.paseosamazonicos.com
Three lodges, 32, 60, and 185km (20, 38, and 115 miles) from Iquitos. Sinchicuy Lodge (the closest to Iquitos) is adapted for wheelchair access. Various excursions offered, including three suitable for disabled travelers and a 'shamanism program.'

A simian resident of Yarapa River Lodge

Yacumama Lodge
Reservations in the US:
Eco-Expeditions, 12973 SW 112th Street, Miami, FL 33186
Email: info@yacumamalodge.com
www.yacumamalodge.com
Comfortable lodge on the Río Yarapa, 177km (110 miles) upriver from Iquitos; three-night/four-day and one-week itineraries. Emphasis on the ecological side of things, with composting, organic gardening, and solar power.

Yarapa River Lodge
Reservations in Iquitos:
Av. La Marina 124
Tel: 065-993-1172
Reservations in the US: tel: 315-952-6771
Email: reservations@yarapa.com
www.yarapa.com
This beautiful award-winning lodge on the Yarapa River offers three-night and longer itineraries, with activities that include wildlife spotting, piranha fishing, rainforest walks, lake swimming (not where you fish for piranhas), and visits to local villages. Excellent food, and guides that know the rainforest inside out. Accommodations in fully mosquito-netted rooms. There are rescued and orphaned animals that choose to stay close to the lodge, making this feel at times like a wonderful open-air zoo.

Parque Nacional del Manu

Manu Expeditions
Reservations in Cusco:
Tel: 084-225-990/224-235
Email: manuexpedition@terra.com.pe
www.manuexpeditions.com
Run by British ornithologist Barry Walker and his Peruvian wife Rosario, who offer camping trips into the reserve, led by knowledgeable guides. There are also customized trips into other areas/lodges in the southern jungle.

Manu Nature Tours
Reservations in Cusco: tel: 084-252-721
Email: info@manunaturetours.com
www.manuperu.com
Manu Lodge is the only lodge inside the Parque Nacional del Manu; Manu Cloud Forest Lodge is also available. More expensive than some of the lodges, but it's comfortable, and an excellent spot for birdwatching.

Reserva Nacional Tambopata

Eco Amazonia Lodge
Bajo Río Madre de Dios, km 30
Jr. Lambayeque 774, Puerto Maldonado
Tel: 082-573-491
Reservations in Cusco: tel: 084-236-159/242-244
Reservations in Lima: tel: 01-242-2708
www.ecoamazonia.com.pe
This lodge is two hours downriver from Puerto Maldonado, with oxbow lakes and tree canopy access. Choose from one-night/two-day to one-week itineraries. You get to sleep on hammocks in the lodge's bungalows, protected by nets, but proper beds are also available.

Explorers' Inn
Reservations in Lima: tel: 01-447-8888
www.peruviansafaris.com
About 60km (38 miles) from Puerto Maldonado on the Tambopata River, with a good chance of observing wildlife. Up to six biologists work as resident naturalists on the premises and, besides working on their research project, they also function as tour guides.

Libertador Tambopata Lodge
Reservations in Puerto Maldonado:
tel: 082-571-726
Reservations in Cusco: tel: 084-245-695
www.tambopatalodge.com
Offers a good chance of observing wildlife for smaller groups. Situated four hours upriver from Puerto Maldonado, this lodge is relatively small, with a capacity of 59. Tours start from three days/two nights.

RESTAURANTS

Jungle food is truly exotic for outside palates, with flavorful fruits and tasty yucca making it entirely different from the cuisine of the Andes or the coast. Sadly, it's also stocked with wildlife meats and fish of uncontrolled origin, most likely shot by poachers. It's best to avoid any odd mammals and reptiles and make sure your *paiche* is farmed.

Restaurant price categories

Prices are for a three-course menu including juice but no wine or coffee

$ = below US$2
$$ = US$2–5
$$$ = US$6–10
$$$$ = over US$10

Iquitos

Al Frio y al Fuego
Restaurant departure point: Av. La Marina, cuadra 1
Tel: 065-224-862
Email: reservas@alfrioyalfuego.com
www.alfrioyalfuego.com
This restaurant is a breezy, floating, palm-roofed pavilion in the middle of the Río Itaya. You are ferried there by a lamplit boat and offered a menu cooked by Iquitos's only cordon bleu chef, Cesar Moran. Try

the *patarashca*, a river fish called *doncella* cooked in a palm leaf with fried or steamed yucca. **$$$**

Blanquita
Bolognesi 1181
Tel: 065-266-015
This is the place to eat for Iquitos locals in the know. Run by a group of *iquiteña* ladies, it serves up classic homely cooking. Try the *juanes* (rice, chicken, olive, and hardboiled egg, all wrapped in the leaf of a *bijao* plant), *humitas* (corn dumplings steamed in a corn leaf), empanadas, and fish cooked in jungle leaves. **$$**

Chifa Long Fung
Jr. San Martín 454
Tel: 065-233-649
There are tons of Chinese restaurants in Iquitos, but this is definitely the best. This huge place is often full and you may have to queue for a seat, but the food is certainly worth it. **$**

Huasai
Av. Fitzcarrald 131
Tel: 065-242-222
www.huasairestaurant.com
Very popular with locals, this unpretentious eatery serves *juanes*, Iquitos chorizo with fried plantains, jungle-style fish, and some vegetarian plates. It does breakfast and lunch every day except for Saturday. **$$**

El Mesón
Malecón Maldonado 153
Tel: 065-231-857
www.restaurantelmeson.com
Right on the Iquitos waterfront, this popular place serves all the Iquitos specialties. You can take a table on the pedestrian boulevard outside and eat your meal only a stone's throw from the Amazon. **$$**

Puerto Maldonado

El Califa
Jr. Piura 266
Tel: 082-571-119
This restaurant does all the jungle specialties like fried bananas, yucca, *ensalada de chonta* (palm-heart salad), and tasty BBQ meats. It has a variety of fresh juices with all the local fruit available. **$$**

El Tigre
Jr. Tacna 456
Tel: 082-572-286
This simple place makes the best *ceviche* in Puerto Maldonado. Open only for lunch every day except for Mondays, it is very popular with locals. Delivery and takeaway available. **$$**

Wasai
Jr. Billinghurst s/n (on the corner with Plaza Grau)
Tel: 082-572-290
This restaurant is very small, but it is worth a visit for its well-prepared local dishes, for which it's very popular with locals. Tables are in a patio overlooking the Madre de Dios River. **$$$**

Mugs of coca leaf tea

NIGHTLIFE AND ENTERTAINMENT

Hot days mean people in the Amazon love going out at night, making for a friendly, lively atmosphere, particularly in the big city of Iquitos. Beers and refreshing pisco sours abound. Many places are outdoors or have air conditioning, but don't forget your insect repellent.

Iquitos

Arandú Bar
Malecón Maldonado 113
Tel: 065-243-434
This bar sits in a privileged spot from which you can catch the sunset and Iquitos's street performers. Popular among travelers.

Café-Teatro Amauta
Amauta 250
Tel: 065-233-109
Live performances and local music every night in this hip café.

Noa Noa
Av. Fitzcarrald 258
The best-known disco in town plays *cumbia* (a Colombian music style) as well as rock. Open until late Wednesday to Saturday.

Puerto Maldonado

Karambola
Jr. Arequipa 162
Tel: 098-274-1682
http://karamboladiscoteca.com
Modern club with air conditioning; it is also a tavern and a restaurant.

T-Saica
Loreto 335
A good bar to have a relaxed drink, with live music during the weekend.

SPORTS, ACTIVITIES, AND TOURS

Most sporting activities are tied to trips to lodges. Visitors can count on hiking in calf-length rubber boots, fishing, swimming, and canoeing during their stays in the rainforest. Target-shooting at fruit through blowguns is also a fun – and often funny – activity. You can also swing on a vine and enjoy a relaxed float down rivers on innertubes.

Parque Nacional del Manu

The following tour companies organize trips into Manu National Park from Cusco.

Manu Expeditions
Clorinda Matto de Turner 330, Urb. Magisterial Primera Etapa, Cusco
Tel: 084-225-990/224-235
Email: manuexpedition@terra.com.pe
www.manuexpeditions.com
This company uses a variety of lodges ranging in prices and luxuriousness. Departure dates are Sundays, Mondays, and Fridays, depending on the length of the trip.

Pilpintuwasi Butterfly Farm

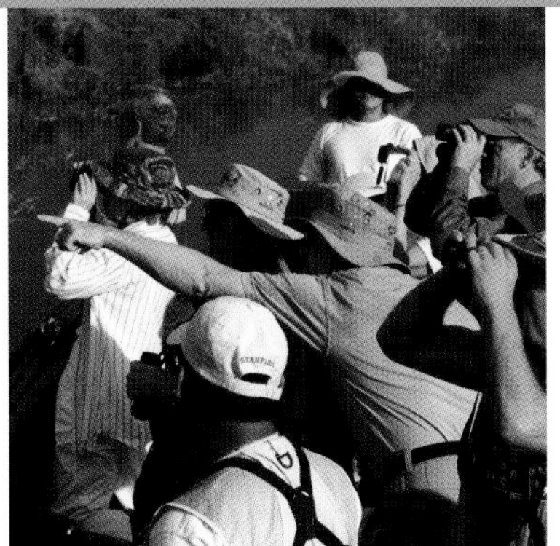

Exploring the Amazon by riverboat

Manu Nature Tours
Av. Pardo 1046, Cusco
Tel: 084-252-721/521
www.manuperu.com
As well as wildlife tours, this agency also offers exhilarating activities such as white-water rafting, mountain biking, trekking, and canopy walking.

Pantiacolla Tours (Manu Biosphere Reserve)
Saphy 554, Cusco
Tel: 084-238-323
www.pantiacolla.com
This agency has an emphasis on bird-watching and can organize tailored trips for those interested.

Reserva Nacional Tambopata

The following companies based in Lima organize trips into Tambopata National Reserve from Puerto Maldonado.

Peruvian Safaris
Alcanflores 459, Miraflores, Lima
Tel: 01-447-8888
www.peruviansafaris.com
This is a large tour agency that organizes tours across the whole of Peru.

Rainforest Expeditions
Av. Aramburú 166, Dep. 4B, Miraflores, Lima
Tel: 01-421-8347
Tel in US: 877-870-0578
www.perunature.com
This agency is part of the Tambopata Research Center and operates from their simple but comfortable lodge.

FESTIVALS AND EVENTS

Festivals in the Amazon region are much newer and less traditional than those of the Andes and coast that mostly commemorate municipal anniversaries. They are spirited affairs nonetheless, with balmy temperatures ensuring that most revelry happens outdoors.

January

Anniversary of Iquitos
The city celebrates its anniversary in the first week of the month, with local dances and music.

June

Festival of San Juan
This festival is celebrated all around the region every June 24, but it's particularly big in Iquitos. People prepare *juanes* (stuffed leaves) and dance and drink by the river all night long.

July

Anniversary of Puerto Maldonado
The residents of Puerto Maldonado celebrate July 12 with social and cultural activities.

August

Santa Clara Crafts Festival
The town of Santa Clara, 14km (9 miles) from Iquitos, celebrates this festival along the banks of the Nanay River during the dry season in mid-August, when beautiful white-sand beaches appear.

PRACTICAL ADVICE

Accommodations

Accommodations in Peru can be as sophisticated or as simple as you wish. There's everything from the smartest five-star hotels imaginable to village home-stays where your bed is nothing more than a mattress on an earthen floor. In between there's a plethora of sleeping options, from colonial mansions to simple and welcoming hostels. Some of the loveliest places to stay are the country haciendas and lodges. These often offer activities such as trekking and horseback riding, and are sometimes built near hot springs. Hotels tend to remain open throughout the year, but should be booked several weeks ahead for Easter Week (Semana Santa) and independence celebrations (Fiestas Patrias).

HOTELS

Hotels are plentiful in most cities, and options among all categories are readily available. Places that offer overnight stays must by law sport an outside plaque indicating whether they are hotels (H), hostels (Hs), residence hotels (HR), or guesthouses (*pensión*; P). These indications are, however, of little use as more than anything else they are a way of determining the size of the hotel. Good quality can be found at any range, although those near bus stations will most likely be sub-standard in quality and safety.

The majority of rooms offer two single beds, so if you want a double bed you'll need to specify a *cama matrimonial*. One common problem is street noise, so it is a good idea to ask for *la habitación más tranquila* (the quietest room) when booking.

Most hotels include continental breakfasts in their rates and many, particularly in Lima and Cusco, offer a free airport pickup. Though security is not a great problem in the more upmarket hotels, it's best to

Lima hotel bar

hide your valuables inside lockable luggage, or make use of the hotel safe, if there is one.

Most hotels in Peru are clean, efficient, friendly, and good value. Excluding the most budget variety, the majority have en suite bathrooms, comfortable beds, and are serviced every day. Hot water is not always reliable, however, so it's worth checking whether the taps run warm water 24 hours a day. Foreign residents shouldn't pay the 19 percent value-added tax (IGV). Also note that *moteles* are rent-by-the hour facilities on the outskirts of cities rather than motor hotels.

Budget accommodations

Peru's firm place on the South American backpackers' route has led to increasing numbers of good-quality hostels – run by both locals and foreigners – to stay in and meet fellow travelers. There are also similarly inexpensive places catering to Peruvian travelers, but these often have less relevant information for foreign tourists and staff are less likely to speak English. Hostels can have single or double rooms, with or without baths, and single-sex dorm rooms without a bath. A computer terminal with internet and/or WiFi is common and normally free, as well as lockers to store belongings. Expect to pay anywhere between $12 and $30 a night for your own room and $6 to $20 for a bed in a dorm. Cheaper places will likely be very low quality. Peru has a hostelling association, Av. Casimiro Ulloa 328, Miraflores, Lima; tel: 01-446-5488; www.hostellingperu.com.pe.

Jungle lodges are a key part of the Amazon experience

Other accommodations

Outside the cities and towns, there are many other options that can provide both activities like horseback riding or mountain biking, as well as trips to nearby archeological sites. After a period of decay, many of Peru's stately estates – haciendas – have become converted into beautiful rural luxury hotels. Some new rural hotels with spas have also sprung up to cater to visitors looking for relaxation outside the cities, with prices starting at $70 per night. Most rural hotels are in the Sacred Valley, near Arequipa, and in the northern Sierra, although more are being developed all the time. There are also expensive resorts near or on beaches like Punta Sal in the north and Paracas in the south. Like the above, luxurious Amazon River cruises charge northward of $150 per night. Jungle lodges may also enter the luxury

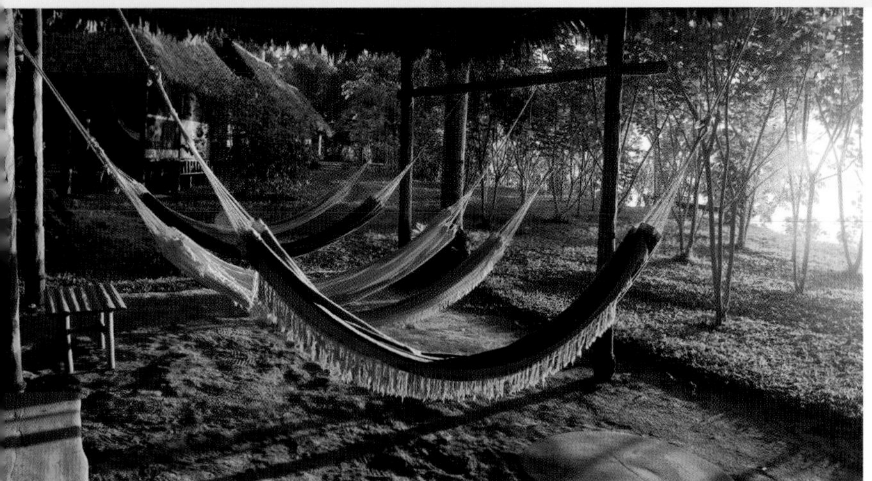

You'll be able to relax in style at many Peru hotels

category, although there are also less expensive options and they are generally the only way to experience the rainforest closely. Due to their remoteness, they are booked in packages, with last-minute, off-season deals available in places like Cusco, Lima, Iquitos, or Puerto Maldonado. Rural tourism in indigenous communities is an inexpensive alternative, and generally basic but clean and comfortable, even if warm running water may not always be available. Peru's iPerú travel office (www.turismoruralperu.gob.pe) has information, although details are only available online in Spanish.

CAMPING

Camping is uncommon in Peru but possible in many areas. Camping in tents is most popular along the main Andean trekking routes, and equipment hire is possible at agencies in Huaraz or Cusco. Porters with llamas or mules are also available in trekking hubs. Contact Peru's Club de Exploradores, Urb. Papa Juan XXIII A. 17b, San Borja, Lima; tel: 01-799-6678; www.clubdeexploradores.org (in Spanish) for recommendations on appropriate rural camping sites throughout the country. Some campsites with limited services are available in protected areas. Robberies can be a problem near inhabited places, so tents should never be left unattended and even gear worth little should be kept inside. Ask permission before camping from a local official or churchman, or from a farmer to use his field. Do not presume that because other groups are camping that it is fine to pitch up your own tent.

Take sturdy trash bags along with you so you can take any garbage with you when you leave.

Dozens of foreign travelers head down the Panamericana Highway in recreational vehicles each year, but there are no facilities, and many park outside hostels or other closed places for safety overnight.

Transportation

GETTING TO PERU

By air

Long-haul international flights land exclusively at Lima's Jorge Chávez airport (LIM; tel: 01-511-6055; www.lap.com.pe), 16km (10 miles) west of downtown, which is also the dominant hub for domestic flights. From North America, several airlines fly to Lima from a series of airports including Atlanta (7hrs), Dallas (7hrs), Houston (7hrs), Los Angeles (9hrs), New York (8hrs), and Miami (6hrs), allowing for daily connections from most places. US airlines flying to Lima include American Airlines (www.aa.com), Continental (www.continental.com), and Delta (www.delta.com), while good Latin American options include LAN (www.lan.com) and TACA (www.taca.com). Air Canada (www.aircanada.com) flies several times a week from Toronto (8hrs).

Getting around Lake Titicaca

Direct European flights to Lima depart from Amsterdam (13hrs) and Madrid (12hrs), with flights from Paris on Air France (12hrs; www.airfrance.com) scheduled to begin in the second half of 2011.

Travelers from Australia and New Zealand can fly via Santiago, Chile on LAN, or via Los Angeles.

From South Africa, Malaysia Airlines (www.malaysiaairlines.com) has direct flights from Cape Town to Buenos Aires, from where direct connections to Lima are available.

Low-season flights are substantially cheaper. For the Christmas and Northern Hemisphere summer travel periods, book well ahead. The best way to find flights is online, with multi-stop options on www.despegar.com often cheaper than direct flights. Lima's airport charges a $31 departure tax, payable in dollars or soles, which is rarely included in the price of international airfare.

Very few other airports receive infrequent international flights from neighboring countries, including Piura and Chiclayo from Ecuador and Cusco from Bolivia.

GETTING AROUND PERU

Narrow roads and the Andes Range make getting around Peru a relatively slow affair. Major investments in highways are going ahead, but many towns lack bypasses, slowing down long-distance traffic on the coastal Pan-American Highway.

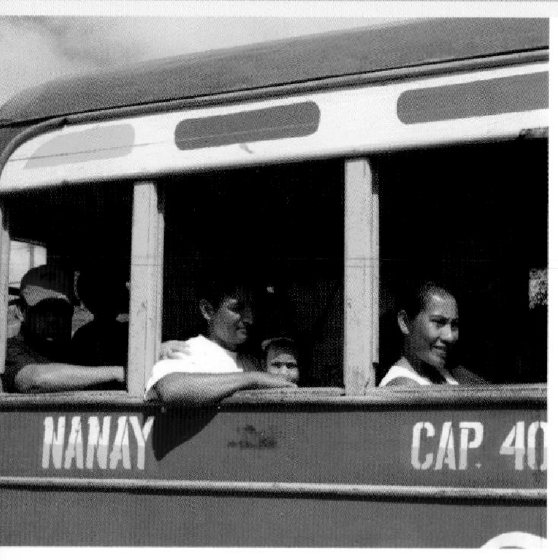

A packed bus makes the commute through Lima

Rain from October through March can also cause serious delays in the Andes and the Amazon Basin. The country's vast size will often make it necessary to book a local flight, which, though more expensive than in Europe or the US, tend to be reasonable. Most travelers will either fly or travel overland by bus. Adventurers will travel the Amazon Basin rivers by boat as they are often the only option in the central and northern Amazon.

Domestic flights

Peru has numerous domestic airports. Prices for domestic flights aren't exorbitant, but the cheapest options tend to be reserved for Peruvian citizens. Safety has improved dramatically, but domestic operators have suffered from financial problems, hamstringing the longevity of national carriers and handing the biggest share of the market to Chile's LAN (tel: 01-213-8200; www.lan.com). Lima is relatively centrally located and the dominant hub. This, however, means that flights from one city to another often require stopping over in the capital, an exception being the Tarapoto to Iquitos route, which isn't flown daily. LAN, TACA (tel: 01-511-8222; www.taca.com), and Peruvian Airlines (tel: 01-716-6000; www.peruvianairlines.pe) serve the larger domestic cities. Smaller cities in the north and central Andes are served by LC Busre (tel: 01-619-1300; www.lcbusre.com.pe), while Star Perú (tel: 01-705-9000; www.starperu.com) has the largest overall domestic network. The airlines often have special discounts advertised on their websites. Note, however, that domestic return flights must be reconfirmed and that overbooking is common. If you need to travel on a certain date, arrive at the airport early. Late arrivers may be bumped from a flight in favor of people on waiting lists. Flights to Iquitos and Tacna are the furthest from Lima and take a little less than two hours.

Trains

A luxury option in Peru is to travel by rail on the few remaining passenger routes between Cusco and Machu Picchu and Cusco and Puno, as well as the 'Train to the Skies' from Lima to Huancayo. They are comfortable and have increased in number, but they're also expensive. Trains from Poroy near Cusco are run by Perurail (www.perurail.com), including the *Vistadome* ($75 one way), *Expedition* ($59 one way), and *Hiram*

Bingham ($349 one way). From Ollantaytambo, prices are $31–43 (depending on when you go) for the *Expedition*, $43–89 for the *Vistadome*, and $270 for the *Hiram Bingham*.

Inca Rail (Av. Sol 611, Cusco; tel: 01-613-5288/084-233-030; Incarail.com.pe) makes the round-trip voyage from Ollantaytambo to Machu Picchu every day, charging $100 standard class and $220 first class; children go half-price. Machu Picchu Train (Av. Sol 576, Cusco; tel: 084-221-199; www.machupicchutrain.com) runs six daily round-trip trains, including the $59 *Lost City Traveller*. Tickets are available at stations and at travel agencies, and the companies are rolling out online booking.

Perurail's *Andean Explorer* train makes the 10-hour journey between Cusco and Puno and vice versa four times a week in the April to October dry season and three times during the rest of the year. A one-way ticket costs $220.

The roughly twice-monthly, 12-hour Lima to Huancayo 'Train to the Skies' run by Ferrocarril Central Andino (José Gálvez Berrenechea 566, San Isidro, Lima; tel: 01-226-6363 ext. 222 and 235; www.ferrocarrilcentral.com.pe) costs $80 one way and $114 return, or $40 one way and $62.65 return in the cheaper *clásico* car. Tickets are also available online.

The 10-hour *Tren Macho* runs twice daily between Huancay and Huancavelica, and is open to both locals and foreigners at inexpensive rates. It's necessary to get in line by 6am on the day of travel, however.

Intercity coaches

Private buses travel the length and breadth of Peru, but quality varies widely. It's best among well-traveled routes between major cities. Journeys to remote destinations are possible but should be made only during daylight hours for safety. The quality of bus terminals varies, and only some cities have official terminals. The better companies have their own terminals in Lima, including CIVA (tel: 01-418-1111; www.civa.com.pe), Cruz del Sur (tel: 01-431-5125; www.cruzdelsur.com.pe), Ormeño (tel: 01-427-5679; www.grupo-ormeno.com.pe), and TEPSA (tel: 01-427-5624; www.tepsa.com.pe). Tickets for these companies can often be ordered over the phone. Book well ahead of popular holidays, during which prices can rise 60 percent to 100 percent. With long distances, factor in long hours – 19hrs from Lima to Cusco or Arequipa, 8hrs to Trujillo.

Roads can be busy in Peru

Taxi in Lima

Cycling

In Lima and on main overland routes, cycling is challenging, to say the least, due to lack of infrastructure or respect from motorized traffic. There are numerous tours available, however, even in the capital, and major tourism hubs rent bikes. Check them carefully for quality. Up-to-the-minute is available from South American Explorers and, in Spanish, from Ciclismo Peru (www.ciclismoperu.com). Cicloturismo Perú (tel: 01-433-7981; www.cicloturismoperu.com) has tours in the capital and the rest of the country.

DRIVING

Driving in Peru can be bewildering and even a bit scary, particularly in the Lima free-for-all. With a bit of patience, however, it's not much of a problem – just expect the unexpected and drive defensively. Paved highways are being expanded so while conditions are improving, expect delays due to construction sites on major routes. Driving can give you more flexibility in reaching smaller towns not served that often by public transportation.

Road conditions

Despite much new surfacing, most of the 70,000km (43,750 miles) of Peruvian roads are still gravel and dirt, and should be driven with caution, especially at night. The rainy season threatens road closures due to landslides. This is compounded by poor driving skills, particularly a lack of respect by many bus drivers. The Pan-American Highway along the coast is generally in good condition, as are the connections to Huaraz and from Chiclayo to Tarapoto across the Andes as well as the route to Cajamarca. From Lima to Pucallpa, also across the Andes, the road is mostly asphalt, as are the Nazca to Cusco and Pisco to Ayacucho routes and Cusco to Puno and onward to Arequipa. Check ahead for the distance between service stations as they can be a stretch. Consider taking fuel in canisters for long trips in rural areas.

Regulations

You must have an international driver's license to drive in Peru. Driving is on the right, and look for stop signs which indicate right of way; don't assume another driver will obey signs, however. Low tolls apply on some parts of the Pan-American Highway, and some municipalities in Lima charge tolls for expressways.

The speed limit is 100km/h (62mph) on the Panamericana and generally 35km/h (22mph) in urban areas, with the maximum speed posted in major arteries. It is a good idea to slow down when entering a town, as police may be waiting to ticket you. Seat belts are compulsory, and 50mg per 100 milliliters is the limit for alcohol consumption, although this limit may be cut due to high accident rates.

Motoring associations

If you break down, telephone the agency from which you rented the car. In an emergency dial the police, tel: 105.

Vehicle hire

Car rental in Peru is possible for those aged 25 and older, provided you can present your home driver's license, passport, and a credit card for deposits. Inspect the car carefully to make sure there is no debate over scratches, dings, or other damages when you return it. It is best to book ahead of important domestic holidays. Prices are steep due to high costs and, particularly, accident rates, and will easily set you back $60 to $80 a day, plus insurance. Drivers with their own car – best recommended by hotels or tour agencies – will likely be slightly cheaper, including fuel. Hotel and tour agencies may also be able to recommend less expensive local rental agencies, but these generally have lower-quality cars. International agencies include Avis (tel: 01-444-0450; www.avis.com.pe), Budget (tel: 01-442-8703/442-8706; www.budgetperu.com); Dollar (tel: 01-444-4920; www.dollar-rentacar.com.pe), and National (tel: 01-575-1111; www.nationalcar.com).

A busy road through Lima's Barranco neighborhood

Approximate driving times	
Lima–Arequipa	16hrs
Lima–Cusco	18hrs
Lima–Huaraz	7hrs
Lima–Trujillo	10hrs
Arequipa–Cusco	8hrs

ACCESSIBILITY

While people with disabilities are protected under Peruvian law, the reality is starkly different, and traveling without a companion is quite difficult as access ramps and other facilities are rare luxuries. At some sites, like Machu Picchu, staff may be on hand to assist disabled travelers; check with iPerú (01-574-8000; www.peru.travel) for current availability. In general, sites around the coast are more accessible.

Pro Peru Travel (tel: 01-221-0110; www.properutravel.com.pe) and Lima Tours (tel: 01-619-6900; www.limatours.com.pe) and Mosoq Huayra in Cusco (tel: 084-261-133) offer tours for disabled travelers.

Health and safety

Peru's beaches are great for swimming, but beware of stingrays and the strong sun

MEDICAL CARE

Health care in Peru varies widely from developed urban centers and tourism hubs to more remote areas, where quality service is rare. The most serious illnesses to guard against are yellow fever and malaria, which both occur in jungle areas of the north and south Amazon, and malaria on parts of the coast. Visitors are advised to consult their physician about anti-malarial drugs before leaving home and have a yellow fever shot at least 10 days before traveling to a jungle area. Cholera is not a great threat to tourists. The best protection is to take hygiene precautions such as avoiding unclean water and raw or poorly cooked food (particularly seafood), and steering clear of dirty accommodations and swimming pools.

Two shots taken six months apart should protect against hepatitis A for 10 years (one shot works for six months). A much more common condition for travelers in Peru is upset stomach and diarrhea. In most cases, the symptoms will improve after a day or so of fasting and drinking plenty of fluids (hot tea without milk is ideal). If the more serious condition of dysentery develops (i.e. any blood or pus in the stool), you should see a doctor.

Don't be surprised if your exultation at flying into Andean mountain cities is followed by a less pleasant sensation called *soroche* or altitude sickness. In most cases the symptoms are mild – fatigue, shortness of breath, slight nausea, and headache. The best prevention and cure is to lie down for a few hours upon arrival at your hotel and then slowly introduce yourself to physical activity. Coca tea, available in all highland hotels and restaurants, also helps. If it doesn't, medication (which among other things includes aspirin and caffeine) is available without prescription at pharmacies. If the symptoms are severe – i.e. vomiting, rapid irregular pulse, insomnia – take it very seriously and descend immediately to a lower altitude. Travel insurance which covers the cost of an air ambulance should be taken out before you start your trip.

HOSPITALS

Clínica Anglo Americana, San Isidro; tel: 01-616-8900; www.angloamericana.com.pe.

Clínica Internacional, downtown Lima; tel: 01-619-6161; www.clinicainternacional.com.pe.
Instituto de Medicina Tropical in the Cayetano Heredia Hospital; tel: 01-482-3903; www.upch.edu.pe/tropicales.
Clínica Padre Luis Tezza; tel: 01-610-5050; www.clinicatezza.com.pe.
Clínica Ricardo Palma; tel: 01-224-2224; www.crp.com.pe.
International Health Department, at Jorge Chávez airport; tel: 01-517-1845; open 24hrs a day for vaccinations.

NATURAL HAZARDS

The strong tropical sun means you can burn quite badly. Ultraviolet rays are particularly powerful at high altitudes; wearing a brimmed hat as well as sunglasses, and using a high-factor sunscreen will all help protect you from the glare. High humidity can dehydrate the body. It is important to drink plenty of liquids and add salt to your food.

On the northern and Paracas beaches, ask locals about the risk of stingrays. Sandflies are common on some beaches and parts of the Amazon after dusk. Raising your fist will normally frighten away stray dogs anywhere – they'll think you might have a rock. It is also advisable to wear calf-length boots while hiking in the rain forest.

Peru is at risk of earthquakes and associated tsunamis. During a quake, leave the building as quickly as possible if this can be done in a few seconds, otherwise, stay clear of windows and shelves, preferably seek shelter under a doorway, staircase or a heavy table. Note evacuation routes in the event of a tsunami. Flash flooding can happen along rivers in the rainy season, as well as landslides, so avoid remote rural roads during heavy rainfall.

Emergency contacts

Police emergency: 105
Tourist police (more likely to have an English-speaker):

- Lima tel: 01-243-2190
- Cusco tel: 084-249-654
- Arequipa tel: 054-201-258
- Iquitos tel: 065-242-081

Ambulance (SAMU): 117
Fire service: 116

FOOD AND DRINK

Impure drinking water and ice will cause stomach problems, so it's best to buy or order bottled water. For the same reason, make sure salads have been properly washed and avoid unpasteurized dairy products. For

Make sure salads have been properly washed

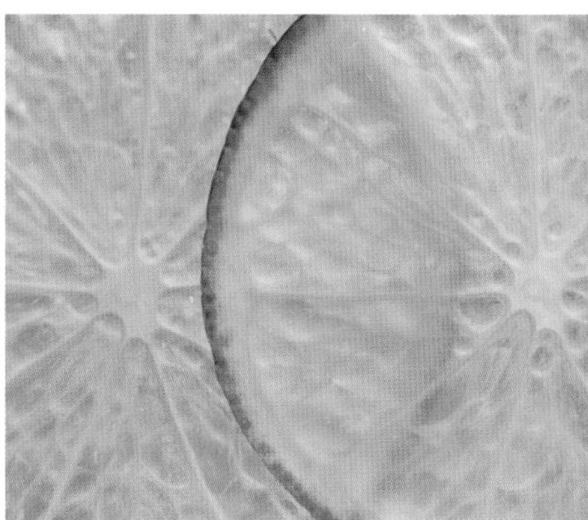

Avoid wearing flashy jewelry when out and about in Lima

long overland trips, buy your own food as roadside stops may not be at quality restaurants.

CRIME

As Peru's urban centers have swollen, so has petty crime. Pickpockets and thieves have become more and more common in Lima and Cusco. It is recommended that tourists do not wear costly jewelry and that watches be covered by a sleeve. Thieves are amazingly adept at slitting open shoulder bags, camera cases, and knapsacks; keep an eye on your belongings.

All kind of confidence tricksters pull ever more imaginative ruses; some pose as policemen, others work together with bus and taxi drivers or use diversionary tactics to get hold of your valuables. Special care is needed at railway stations and airports. Should you have anything stolen, you will need to fill out a report with the tourist police. Go out at night in small groups if possible.

Officials also warn against dealing with anyone calling your hotel room or approaching you in the lobby or on the street, claiming to represent a travel agency or specialty shop. Avoid contact with over-friendly strangers who may want to get you involved in criminal deals. Be aware that drug dealing is a crime that results in a long prison sentence. Police corruption is a problem. Don't hitchhike. For journeys overland choose only well-known and established bus companies, and take care that you are always able to identify yourself: carry your passport at all times.

There is little activity by rebel groups these days, and incidents of violence involving foreign tourists are few and far between. There is army activity in the coca-growing regions of the Andes, which should be avoided.

FOREIGN EMBASSIES IN LIMA

Australia: Víctor A. Belaúnde 147, Edificio Real 3, Of. 1301, San Isidro; tel: 01-222-8281
Canada: Bolognesi 228, Miraflores; tel: 01-319-3200
Ireland: Av. Paseo de la República 5757 B, Urb. San Antonio, Miraflores; tel: 01-242-9516
South Africa: Víctor A. Belaúnde 147, Edificio Real 3, Of. 801, San Isidro; tel: 01-440-9996
UK: Av. José Larco 1301, Torre Parque-Mar, 22nd floor, Miraflores; tel: 01-617-3000; British Consulate, Cusco; tel: 084-239-974
US: Av. La Encalada s/n, cuadra 17, Santiago de Surco; tel: 01-618-2000; US Consulate, Cusco; tel: 084-231-474

Money and budgeting

Peru's currency is the nuevo sol – normally just called the sol, abbreviated to S./, and divided into 100 céntimos; coins under 10 céntimos are rarely in circulation, and it's a good idea to keep small change handy to pay fares and other expenses, as there is often a lack of change available. Notes exist in S./10, 20, 50, 100, and 200 denominations; coins in S./1, 2, and 5, and 1, 5, 10, 20, and 50 céntimos.

Foreign currency in excess of $10,000 must be declared on entry. No other restrictions apply.

At press time, exchange rates were US$1=2.75; GB£1=4.45; €1=3.92.

CASH AND CARDS

The proliferation of ATMs has made accessing cash a lot easier. The most convenient way to get soles is on arrival at Jorge Chávez airport in Lima. ATMs usually dispense both soles and US dollars, which in small denominations can be exchanged for soles or used as payment in a pinch. It is also worth checking any notes you receive for forgeries. Travelers cheques have lost popularity, and exchanging them can be slow outside Lima.

Local currency can be obtained using Visa, Cirrus, Plus, and MasterCard at the ATMs of most banks. Banking hours are generally 9am–6pm, but they often close for lunch until 3pm outside Lima and Cusco. Exchange bureaus *(casas de cambio)* often have better rates, but they do prefer dollars or euros.

TIPPING

At some of the smartest hotels and restaurants, service charges are sometimes included, and this will be stated on the bill. Otherwise tipping is up to the customer. Peruvians themselves rarely leave tips in restaurants, and tipping is not routinely expected, but you can leave a few soles. Tipping is most customary in Cusco, where there are the most tourists. Tip people who help you with your luggage. If you stay any length of time in a hotel, you can leave a tip for the people who have serviced your room. On the conclusion of outdoor adventure activities, it's common to leave a generous tip for your guide.

TAX

A value-added tax (VAT; Spanish IGV) of 19 percent is applied to the cost of all goods and services and is generally included in all prices. VAT is added to accommodations and restaurants,

Money-saving tips

- Buy set lunches in small restaurants and covered markets
- Ask locals for current prices before negotiating taxi fares
- Organize your trip so you can make full use of the Sacred Valley site ticket
- Take small bills and be ready to bargain over prices in crafts and food markets, and for off-season hotel prices – ask for a *rebajita* (little discount)
- International student discount cards are often accepted

A selection of antique coins

sometimes together with a 10 percent service fee. During the second half of 2011, there are plans to implement a VAT return policy for foreign visitors for some services, including hotels and transportation. Airports collect a departure tax; passengers traveling abroad from Lima must pay a $30.25 departure tax, payable in soles. The fee is $7 for domestic flights.

BUDGETING FOR YOUR TRIP

Peru is cheaper than most Western countries, especially outside Lima. However, imported electronic and other manufactured goods and travel gear are expensive. Peruvian food is delicious and inexpensive.

Low season, economy return flights from New York to Lima are $750–950 (£450–570), high season from $1,000–1,300 (£600–780); business class from $3,300 (£1,975), high and low season.

Low season, economy return flights from London to Lima are $1,200–1,900 (£830–1,615), high season from $1,800–2,700 (£1,100–1,650); business class from $5,500 (£3,300), high and low season.

For a (very) budget holiday, set aside S./340 (£70/US$125) per person per week. A standard family holiday for four will cost around S./2,800 (£600/US$1,000) per week. A luxury break can cost over S./25,000 (£5,400/US$9,000) per person per week.

Budgeting Costs

Top-class/boutique hotel: S./555–1,100 for a double
Standard hotel: S./129–182 for a double
Bed & breakfast: S./86–125 for a double
Youth hostel: S./33–56 per person

Domestic flight: $350 Lima–Cusco–Lima
Intercity ticket: S./79–142 Lima–Máncora
Car hire: S./160–225 per day
Gasoline: S./15 a gallon for 98 Octane
10-minute taxi ride: S./7 in Lima
Short bus ride: S./1

Breakfast: S./5–7
Set lunch: S./8–10
Coffee/tea in a café: S./4
Main course, budget restaurant: S./7–15
Main course, moderate restaurant: S./16–30
Main course, expensive restaurant: S./31–100
A bottle of wine in a restaurant: S./70–160
Beer in a pub: S./3–9

Museum admission: Free–S./25
Two-hour surf course: S./70
Movie theatre ticket: S./14
Theatre/concert ticket: S./35–1,000
Nightclub entry: S./12–30

Responsible travel

GETTING THERE

Carbon Footprint (www.carbon footprint.com) has several suggestions for ways to offset your journey, including reforestation and renewable energy initiatives, or donate to Climate Care, www.CO2.org. A return flight from London to Lima leaves a carbon footprint of 1.85 metric tons of carbon dioxide. To offset this amount would cost £13.50. A return flight from New York to Lima leaves a footprint of 1.07 metric tons of carbon dioxide and would cost $13.10 to offset.

ECOTOURISM

Ecotourism is growing in importance in Peru, given the fragility of many natural areas and indigenous traditions. Before booking, review how lodges, in particular, treat refuse and effluence, and whether they manage illegal zoos. Peru Verde (www.peruverde), a non-governmental organization, has managed several projects and owns the Inka-Natura green travel agency (www.inkanatura.com), which operates five lodges in the southeast Amazon area. In Cusco, Peru Treks (www.perutreks.com) is heavily involved in community support and organizes local home-stays in the Sacred Valley.

ETHICAL TOURISM

Sustainable travel means that local people should feel the need – and pride – of protecting their heritage. Consider buying goods from local producers and using small local businesses, including restaurants, and home-stay options. This is easily possible even without contacting non-governmental organizations and charities.

VOLUNTEERING/CHARITIES

There are numerous opportunities to volunteer throughout Peru. The South American Explorers Club (www.saexplorers.org), a non-profit organization, maintains a database of reputable organizations. US-based Earthwatch Institute (www.earth watch.org) and UK-based Cross-Cultural Solutions (www.cross culturalsolutions.org) provide information on projects in Peru.

THINGS TO AVOID

There is a significant problem with alcoholism in Peru. It is best to avoid drinking in public, and some tourism operators also recommend that tourists do not drink alcohol with locals, especially in indigenous communities, so as not to contribute to problems with alcoholism.

Begging is a problem, and informal labor and begging by children shouldn't be rewarded. Indiscriminate fishing and hunting is a threat to wildlife in the Amazon. Don't eat turtle or caiman meat or buy things made with the bright feathers of birds, or purchase 'orphaned' young animals. Don't take pictures of people without permission.

Family holidays

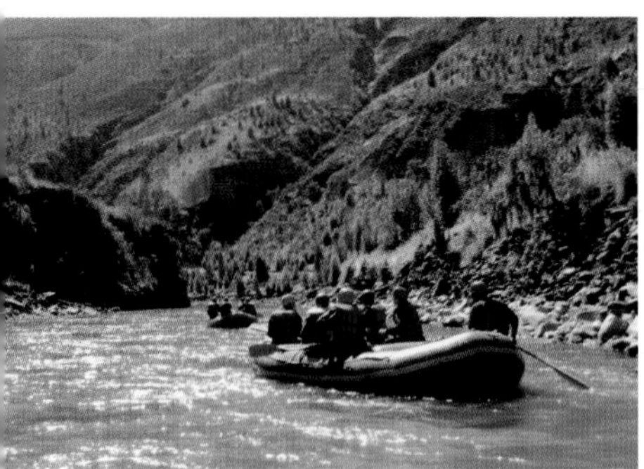

Rafting on the Amazon

PRACTICALITIES

Peruvians love children, and are likely to make a fuss of your child while you travel in Peru. Even officials in uniform tend to be captivated by small children, particularly if they've learned a smattering of Spanish. In Lima and the bigger cities there are parks with children's playgrounds, and older children will enjoy many of the regular tourist attractions.

Stores sell babies' diapers (nappies), baby food, and milk formula all over the country. Changing facilities, however, are less common, limited mostly to shopping malls. Strollers are quite a convenience, especially in the high-altitude Sierra, but they are not available for rent. As friendly as Peruvians are towards children, their cities aren't. Rabid drivers and cracked sidewalks can make negotiating narrow streets with small children a chore. A very sturdy stroller from home is thus recommended. Child seats are also in short supply with car rentals.

ACCOMMODATIONS

The obvious choice for stays in Peru are the beach resorts in the north, which benefit from warmer ocean water and have numerous activities for children of all ages and active teenagers anxious to try out surfing or kite surfing. Paracas resorts, too, are attractive, with the added draw of nearby wildlife tours. Peruvian families tend to flock to these resorts as well, so children should find no trouble mixing with local kids, and many have activities specifically geared towards children.

Family trips aren't limited to the beach, however. Many hotels in the main cities have two to three beds to a room, easily accommodating families. Tour operators have also developed multi-day programs that include activities designed for children and adolescents in rural adventures.

In the southeast Amazon, Rainforest Expeditions (www.perunature.com) organises 4–6-day programs in the Tambopata reserve for families with young children or teenagers. Aimed at being both entertaining and educational, the company offers activities specifically designed to entertain children, and nighttime caiman-seeking expeditions. In the Sacred Valley, Urubamba-based Cusco For You (www.cuscoforyou.com) has multiple-day outings on horseback for children as young as five on gentle paso horses.

FOOD AND DRINK

While Peruvian cuisine is, justly, the talk of the international cuisine scene, it may well be problematic for children who have trouble adapting to an exotic palate. Many types of fruit common in non-tropical areas, such as bananas and oranges, are available. It is best to avoid uncooked vegetables, salads, and unpeeled fruit. Children are normally quite welcome, with better restaurants providing high chairs. Many restaurants offer children's portions, or can offer a half-serving *(media porción)*.

Children can become particularly tired at high altitude: take it easy and make sure they remain hydrated. Ensure all water is bottled, filtered, or at least boiled, before they drink it.

There are plenty of things for children to see and do in Peru

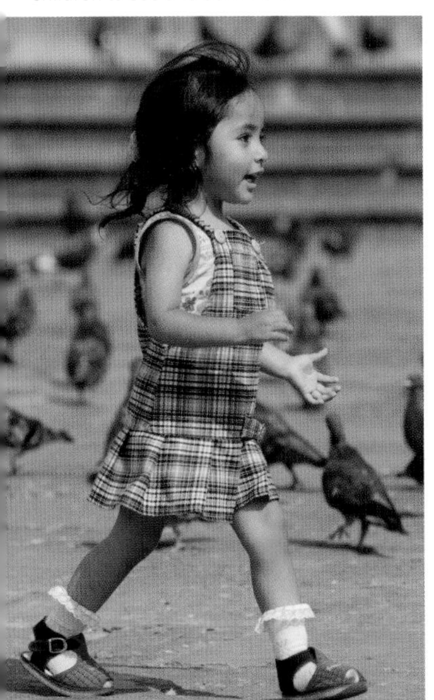

If all else fails, Italian and fast food is available all over the country, and supermarkets have international food brands.

ATTRACTIONS AND ACTIVITIES

Tourism hubs around Peru have attractions that children will like, from train rides to beach games. Lima has its share of interesting places. Children will love the giant fountain display at the Circuito Mágico del Agua (www.circuitomagicodelagua.com.pe), both during the day and during the illuminated evening show. The city also has two zoological gardens, Parque de las Leyendas (www.leyendas.gob.pe), which also has a botanical garden, and the Huachipa zoo (www.zoohuachipa.com.pe). Minimundo (www.minimundo.pe) in the Jesús María district has miniature displays of Lima landmarks in models and a few rides. Daytona Park in Lima is a fairly large amusement center with traditional rides like carrousels, miniature trains, boat rides, and bumper cars for children and video games for adolescents.

Larcomar shopping center (www.larcomar.com) offers movie theaters and bowling, and its surf and parasailing schools nearby provide daytime entertainment. La Tarumba (www.laturamba.com) is a theater-circus project mostly focused on entertaining children, with juggling displays and other acts.

Outside Lima, many of the cultural landmarks are short distances away from adventure tourism spots, including the sand dunes near Nazca.

SETTING THE SCENE

History

Written records go back only a few centuries, but Peru's history is a long one, filled with the marvels of ancient civilizations that fed multitudes by irrigating deserts, wove textiles so fine they cannot be reproduced even today, and built adobe cities that have survived millennia of earthquakes. Some, like the Chimú, Moche, Nazca, Wari, and Chavín, left remains that have allowed archeologists to reconstruct pieces of their societies. Others may always remain nameless and obscure. No group is as well known, or perhaps as astounding, as the Inca – the magnificent culture dominating much of the continent when the Spanish conquistadors arrived.

In little more than 50 years, Inca domination was extended as far north as modern Colombia and south into present-day Chile and Argentina. Groups that resisted were summarily vanquished and relocated as punishment. Others, through peaceful negotiations, joined the kingdom with little loss of regional control provided that they were prepared to worship Inti, the sun, as their supreme god, and paid homage to the Inca leaders.

By the time the Spanish arrived, Cusco, the Inca capital, was a magnificent urban gem; irrigated deserts and terraced mountainsides were producing bountiful crops, storehouses of food had eliminated hunger, and Inca military might had become legendary.

It was no match, however, for the gold-hungry and battle-hardened crack troops that swooped in from Spain in the early 16th century. After plundering Peru for native gold and silver, they established a new civilization, under which downtrodden indigenous cultures survived and even influenced the Spanish colonial elite in art and language. Slaves from Africa, too, managed to preserve and adapt their culture. Lima, meanwhile, became the capital of Spain's South American colonies. Based at the seat of power, Peruvian elites hesitated to join the cause of freedom, imposed by troops from the north and south only at the end of the wars of independence. Peru, however, then fell to the same vices of political instability, internal wars, and strongman rule that marred post-colonial societies in Latin

A gold artifact dating from the Moche civilization

America. Dictatorships and guerrilla warfare stunted growth, and the illicit narcotics trade continues to infuse violence. Yet Peru has recovered from violence to become one of the fastest-growing economies of the world, helped by exporting the very natural resources its ancients used to create exquisite works of art.

EARLY CIVILIZATIONS

The first traces of permanent settlements in Peru have been found along the coast, where river valleys running off the western slope of the Andes slice through the desert, creating fertile oases. Small communities thrived along the coast, harvesting the rich Pacific Ocean for its bounty. On river floodplains they cultivated cotton and gourds and hunted for deer. In the *lomas*, lush belts of fog vegetation located a few miles inland, they gathered wild plants. Before the introduction of true weaving, they created twined and looped textiles of cotton and sedge, some decorated with intricate designs that attest to technological and esthetic skills. Continuous discoveries in the early 21st century have revealed that agriculture and complex societies existed much earlier than previously thought. As early as 3000BC – at the same time as in ancient Egypt and Mesopotamia – the first major urban settlements emerged at Caral and nearby sites north of Lima, forming the first towns in the Americas. Caral, encompassing some 60 hectares (150 acres) and more than a dozen pyramids, was inhabited for about 600 years.

Although the majority of sites

The Chan Chan archeological site

documented from this time average only 20km (12 miles) from the coast, they were far enough up-valley to tap the rivers and construct irrigation canals, substantially increasing the ancient Peruvians' subsistence base. Other early sites include Moxeke-Pampa de las Llamas and Sechín in the Casma Valley.

GREAT CULTURES

A succession of cultures sprang up in different areas around the country, only to disappear through changes in the environment and war. In the highlands, construction began around 800 BC at the ceremonial center of Chavín de Huantar *(see pp.194–5)*.

On an arid plain near the southern coast, the Nazca (AD200–600) etched giant images by brushing away surface soil and stones to reveal the lighter-colored soil beneath *(see pp.105–6)*. Around the same time, the Moche

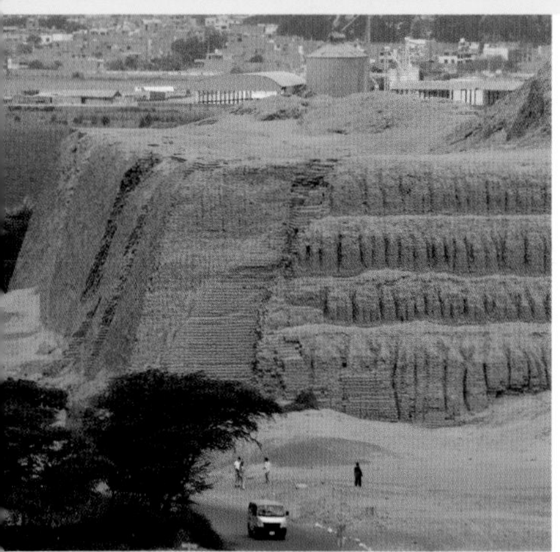

The unexcavated sun temple as seen from the moon temple, near Trujillo

people flourished near present-day Trujillo. Their Temple of the Sun, one of the most imposing adobe structures ever built in the New World, was composed of over 100 million mud-bricks, and they reached the pinnacle of pre-Hispanic metalsmithing. Sometime in AD650–700, the Moche Kingdom came to an end. An El Niño phenomenon may have produced torrential rains and destroyed irrigation canals, causing famine.

With the fall of Moche in the north and the decline of Nazca, the powerful Andean Wari (or Huari) kingdom exerted its architectural and artistic influence over large areas of Peru between AD600 and 1000. The Wari style is strongly reminiscent of the ceramics and sculpture from the Bolivian Altiplano site of Tiahuanaco (200BC–AD1200).

With its decline, regional cultures again flourished in the coastal valleys. The Sicán and Chimú cultures developed on the north coast. Around 1300, construction began at Chan Chan, the Chimú capital, which fell to the powerful Inca armies of Tupac Yupanqui about 1464. Today the sprawling mud-brick capital of Chan Chan is a bewildering labyrinth of ruined adobe walls, some 7.5m (25ft) high and stretching for 60m (200ft). Remains of adobe friezes showing patterns of waves, fish, seabirds, and fishing nets, all vital to the survival of these coastal people, can still be seen adorning some of the walls. In the northern Andes, the Chachapoyas built the great Kuélap fortress, but vanished in the 15th century.

THE INCA EMPIRE

The Inca were at first a small regional culture based in the south-central highlands. In the early 1400s, under the reign of Pachacutec, they began one of the greatest and most rapid expansions ever, based on a foundation of efficient agriculture. The Inca's great food surpluses enabled them to divert labor to a variety of enterprises. They created a vast road network and built astonishing structures of stone, so finely worked and of blocks so large that they required staggering amounts of time and effort. They also raised great armies, able to march thousands of miles without carrying provisions, so extensive was their network of storehouses. As each regional culture fell, Inca teachers, weavers, builders, and metallurgists studied the conquered people's textile techniques, architecture, gold-working, irrigation, pottery, and healing methods.

The system that made these works possible was called *mita*. It was a kind of community tax, paid in labor. Every community sent some of its able-bodied young men and women for a limited period into the service of the state.

A combination of techniques sustained the growth of the Inca Empire. Military conquest played a part, but so did skillful diplomacy; some of the most important territories may have been allied confederates rather than subordinate domains. The glue holding the empire together was the practice of reciprocity: ritual generosity and favors to local rulers on a huge scale, in exchange for loyalty, labors, and military levies, women for the Inca nobility, products specific to the region, and so on.

As the Inca extended farther from their center, they confronted groups with ideas and identities increasingly different from their own. Thus, continued expansion increasingly required the use of force. Many opponents surrendered without a fight when they saw the size of the army sent against them. The Inca still preferred to cut off an enemy's water supply, or starve him into submission, rather than confront him directly in battle. They fought with clubs, stones, and all-wooden spears. Even the bow and arrow, though known to them, was not widely used in battle. The gulf between their fighting capacity and that of the steely Spanish conquistadors was tragically wide.

In the years just before the Spanish invasion, Pachacutec's grandson, Huayna Capac, was far from his homeland, fighting in the mountains along the present northern frontier of Ecuador. Quito, the base from which the campaigns were launched, had become a de facto second capital, and a northern aristocracy had formed. On the death of Huayna Capac the two groups fell into violent conflict, resulting in civil war between Huascar and Atahualpa, the victor. This left the empire open to attack.

Bas-relief depicting human sacrifice at the moon temple

CONQUEST AND COLONIZATION

Although only a handful in number, the invading Spaniards had on their side an astonishing streak of good luck, complete technological superiority, and a lack of principle that would have made Machiavelli shudder. Apparently experiencing no emotions other than greed and fear, they were repeatedly able to trick their way into the confidence of the Inca rulers and nobility, only to betray them. By the time the Inca

Cusco cathedral

realized the ruthlessness of their foes, it was too late. Capturing Atahualpa in an ambush in Cajamarca, they quickly decapitated the empire. Atahualpa's eventual murder incensed even the king of Spain, but the arriving gold quickly quaffed the scandal. Priceless art and sculpture of the great Inca Empire went straight to the smelters of Seville. A group of Inca under Manco Cápac II rebelled and held on until Túpac Amaru was captured and executed in 1572.

After a period of looting and anarchy, Spain imposed order under its viceroys. Conquistadors who had received land and the right to native labor under the *encomienda* system became the elite of the new colony. They extorted tribute in the form of grain, livestock, and labor, and forced the native peoples into a brutal form of feudalism. Via an adaptation of the *mita*, indigenous people were forced to work in the equally lucrative and deadly silver mines. In *reducciones*, they had to resettle into Spanish-style towns complete with a central plaza, church, town hall, and prison – the symbols of Spanish authority. *Reducciones* facilitated the collection of tribute from the Indians and their conversion to Christianity.

The early 1600s saw a far-flung campaign against idolatry, spurred on by a revival of native religion. The renewed religious zeal of the Catholic Church led to a push to stamp out native beliefs once and for all. Priests visited outlying provinces, collecting information on cults and sometimes torturing villagers to reveal the whereabouts of idols and *huacas*. In many ways, the Catholic campaign entrenched native faiths; Christianity simply formed a veneer over traditional cults and beliefs, many of which still exist today.

Under the prevailing system of mercantilism, which promoted exports and restricted imports and goods produced for local consumption, the elite grew rich, while the mass of people remained impoverished. Spain decreed that all trade from South America should pass through Lima, ensuring a massive influx of taxes. Lima, the opulent 'City of Kings,' was crammed with magnificent churches and mansions.

In Spain, meanwhile, the end of the War of the Spanish Succession (1700–13) saw the Habsburg dynasty replaced by the Bourbons, who reigned until Napoleon occupied Madrid in 1808. Efforts by Bourbon monarchs to improve the colonial economy and stem corruption were to little avail but disaffected creole subjects. Indigenous rebellions also multiplied.

INDEPENDENCE AND TROUBLED DEVELOPMENT

On the eve of Napoleon's march on the Iberian peninsula, Spain's hold on its colonies was already waning. When Napoleon forced Charles IV to abdicate in 1808, and then placed his own brother Joseph on the Spanish throne, there were rebellions in many parts of Latin America. Declarations of independence in Upper Peru (now Bolivia) and Quito (Ecuador) in 1809 were followed by uprisings in the Peruvian cities of Huánuco and Cusco. But freedom from Spain had to be won in bloody wars waged for the next 15 years. Many Peruvians supported the colonial system since Lima was still its wealthy administrative capital. Peru became the strongest bastion of pro-Spanish feeling, and other newly independent countries could not feel secure until it, too, was liberated. This was imposed by Argentine General José de San Martín and Venezuelan General Simón Bolívar, who stamped out the last royalist troops at Ayacucho in 1824.

The Battle of Ayacucho established Peruvian independence from Spain in 1824

Post-independence turmoil eased somewhat from 1845 under the influence of President Ramón Castillo, under whom exports of nitrates from the guano islands funded modernization, including railroad construction. By 1877, however, guano deposits ran out and Peru became bankrupt. Worse came in the War of the Pacific (1879–83; *see p.114*), which found the armed forces of Peru and Bolivia woefully unprepared against Chile. Chilean troops invaded southern Peru and then bombarded Callao, occupying Lima and cutting off the capital from the hinterland. Following the peace treaty of 1883, Peru ceded Tarapacá to Chile.

It took decades to recover. When industry grew, workers in the mines, coastal factories, and urban sweatshops began to form unions as poverty remained widespread under intermittent Conservative and military rule. A first, cautiously progressive government of Fernando Belaúnde (1963–8) failed, and yet another coup occurred. General Juan Velasco, the new president, however, championed many of the radical APRA demands, including sweeping agrarian reform, nationalization of the oil, mining, and fishing industries, as well as food subsidies for city dwellers. Poorly thought out, the reforms sent the economy reeling even before the 1973 oil crisis. Subsequent military governments proved similarly incompetent. Democracy returned in 1980, when President Belaúnde won

Lima police officer

office a second time. Natural disasters and the Latin American debt crises, however, kept the economy on its back. The populist Alan García presidency ended in economic disaster, while unrest grew, particularly from the Sendero Luminoso (Shining Path) terrorist group. Voters turned to an outsider, Alberto Fujimori, in 1990, who stabilized the economy and stamped out the guerrilla. This, however, occurred with numerous human rights violations, an interruption of democratic rule, and massive corruption that only ended with his forced resignation in 2000. Elections won by Alfredo Toledo, Peru's first indigenous president, and a matured Alan García kept economic stability, while Peru has sent Fujimori to jail for his crimes until 2049.

Alejandro Toledo, the shoeshine boy who went on to graduate from Stanford and Harvard, took office in 2001. Despite his reforms aimed at reducing poverty and restoring faith in the country's corrupt institutions, his presidency was marked by strikes and scandals. In the mountain town of Andahuaylas, an insurrection led by Antauro Humala, brother and cohort of the ultra-nationalist politician Ollanta Humala, claimed five lives and rocked the government.

Nevertheless, in 2006 Toledo presided over orderly elections and handed over a buoyant economy to the new president, a resurgent Alan García. García's first term in the 1980s had taken Peru into economic meltdown, but his main opponent, Ollanta Humala, was seen by most as an even riskier choice. Humala's political strength came from the impoverished and rebellious highlands where many were seeing little benefit from the country's economic success.

A major earthquake on the south coast in August 2007 became a political scandal, owing to the slow pace of reconstruction. And a maritime border dispute with Chile has inflamed nationalist anti-Chilean grievances dating back to the 19th century. The US–Peru free-trade treaty, negotiated under Toledo and ratified in 2007, has been controversial and divisive. While coastal regions and mining enclaves thrive, poverty and social unrest persists in the mountains. Peru has also been rattled by numerous protests because its fast economic growth has not led to vast improvements for the majority of citizens. In Bagua on the upper Amazon, dozens of people were killed in protests against mining and oil development in mid-2009. Soaring growth also failed to eliminate poverty, and discontent helped populist Ollanta Humala win the 2011 elections.

Historical landmarks

FROM 3000 BC
A civilization emerges at Caral, the oldest known city of the Americas.

800 BC–AD300
The Chavín de Huantar culture dominates the north-central Andes.

1ST–7TH CENTURY AD
Nazca culture blooms, making irrigation canals and mysterious lines in the desert.

7TH–11TH CENTURY AD
Two related cultures, Huari and Tiahuanaco, control the central Andes and Lake Titicaca.

1250–1470
The Chimú culture rules much of northwest Peru from its great capital at Chan Chan.

1200–1532
The Inca Empire emerges from Cusco to conquer much of the Andes and Pacific coast of South America.

1532–3
Spanish adventurer Francisco Pizarro conquers the Inca Empire.

1542
Spain founds its viceroyalty in Peru, with Lima as its capital.

1782
José Gabriel Condorcanqui claims Inca heritage as Túpac Amarao II and leads an unsuccessful indigenous rebellion.

1819–24
Generals José de San Martín and Simón Bolívar defeat Spanish colonial armies and impose independence.

1879–83
Peru loses its southernmost provinces to Chile in the War of the Pacific.

1932
Massacre of around 1,000 followers of the leftwing APRA party near Trujillo.

1941–2
Peru wins its northwest Amazon territories by invading Ecuador.

1963–8
Fernando Belaúnde antagonizes the US by trying to nationalize Standard Oil's Peruvian subsidiary and attempting land reform.

1968–75
Leftwing dictator Juan Velasco Alvarado nationalizes Peruvian industry, carries out a land reform, and censors the media.

1980–5
Belaúnde returns Peru to democracy. Peru's foreign debt rises and hundreds of human rights violations are reported.

1985–90
Alan García of the APRA party tries to boost the economy by populist spending and refusing to repay debt. The experiment causes hyperinflation and terrorism by the "Shining Path" and other guerrillas.

1990–2000
Alberto Fujimori adopts a conservative economic course that ends inflation. He defeats the guerrillas at a cost of massive human rights violations. In his third term he resigns amid corruption allegations.

2001–06
Alfredo Toledo, the first indigenous president of Peru, steers a pro-business economic course amid corruption scandals.

2006–11
Alan García defeats ultra-nationalist Ollanta Humala. He oversees fast economic growth but corruption accusations mar his record.

2009
Fujimori is sentenced to 25 years in jail for organizing death squads.

2011
Humala wins the presidency, triggering fears of another populist experiment.

Culture

PERUVIANS

Almost 500 years of foreign settlement and interracial mixing have produced a complex blend of indigenous Peruvian, European, African, and East Asian cultures. Almost half of Peruvians live in the narrow coastal region, some 8 million of them in the capital, Lima. It is a city of extremes, with the richest and most Europeanized Peruvians living not far from the poorest shantytowns, where migrants from the provinces have come in search of work or to escape the violence that has marked Peru in recent years.

For the modern nation state, geography poses major problems for development and integration into a single society. The huge natural barrier of the Andes severely limits the penetration of motorized transport and telecommunication, while frequent earthquakes and landslides further complicate the already arduous terrain. The result is dramatic regional diversity, and considerable inequalities in services and living standards. Health, education, and law enforcement are very unevenly distributed across Peru. Discrimination against Peruvians of indigenous and African origin continues to be difficult to overcome, and fragile native societies in the Amazon are massively threatened by immigration, logging, oil, and mining.

MULTIETHNIC SOCIETY

Over the past 470 years, there has been a long process of intercultural mixing, creating the mestizo – a mixture of indigenous and European heritage. Today the majority of Peruvians fall into this category, and it is possible to become mestizo by choice as well as by birth. Anyone assuming Western dress in the rural highlands is usually referred to as mestizo or – derisively – *cholo*. Peruvian social divisions are culturally, as much as racially, defined, although the overwhelming majority of people speak Spanish and are at least nominally Catholic.

Beyond these broad distinctions, other complexities arise. There are 'white' ethnic groups, like the Morochucos of Pampa Cangallo (Ayacucho), who have light-colored eyes and hair, speak Quechua, and see themselves

Local Peruvian girls pose in colorful traditional dress

as *campesinos* (subsitence farmers). The *misti*, the dominant social class in the Andes, speak Quechua and share other cultural traits, but enjoy access to education and some of the luxuries of modern life. To the east, the Andes mountains fall away to the Amazon river system. The *selva alta* (highland forest) was colonized by *campesinos* only in the second half of the 20th century. The lower foothills of the Andes gradually give way to the vast Amazon river system and its *selva baja* (low-lying jungle). It is here that the 53 ethno-linguistic indigenous groups (only some 5 percent of Peru's population) live.

Until the trade was banned in the 19th century, landowners brought in black Africans to serve as slaves on their haciendas and frequently used them to repress the local Indians. Despite being only a small, discriminated minority today, Afro-Peruvians' influence on music, dance, and sport has been extensive and has also made an impact on the country's cuisine.

THE URBAN–RURAL DIVIDE

Peruvian culture is sharply divided between indigenous and colonial societies, between the mountains and the city. There are the elite, white *criollos*, most of whom live in Lima, who can trace their bloodlines back to the Spanish conquest of 1536. They are joined by arrivals from Italy, Spain, and other European countries. A number of politicians have Arabic surnames: there was an influx of Palestinian refugees to Peru after 1948. The *criollos* are thought to enjoy the cultural legacy of colonialism, and

Young Peruvian women hanging out in the sunshine

their eyes are firmly fixed on Europe and the United States. International mass culture, from Reebok to Disneyland, is an integral part of their children's upbringing, and shopping trips to Miami for clothes and consumer goods are quite common among those who can afford it. Most of these products, however, can now be found in the mega shopping centers of Lima, although they do come at a higher price, and visitors from Europe or the USA will feel a comfortable familiarity in Lima's cafés, department stores, and supermarkets.

Rural communities now also aspire to ownership of modern produce, but this comes into conflict with their traditional values. Heirs to awe-inspiring pre-Columbian cultures, the people of the Andes are fighting to keep the traditional practices of their ancestors alive in a rapidly changing world. Their livelihood continues to

Young dancers at Trujillo's Festival de la Marinera

be based on family-owned fields, or *chacras*, which are farmed by hand or with the help of draft animals.

The social organization of communities in the Andes differs greatly from that of Europeanized *criollo* culture. Work, marriage, and land ownership are centered on a complex extended family organization – called the *ayllu* in Quechua – which dates back at least to Inca times. One of the main functions of *ayllus* is to organize reciprocal work exchanges. These often take the form of group projects like roof raising or potato harvesting, which are usually made more festive and enjoyable by communal meals and plentiful supplies of *chicha* (homemade corn beer).

The Quechua- and Aymara-speaking peoples of Peru inhabit some 5,000 peasant communities located throughout the Andean Sierra. These communities are based on an agricultural economy, but families frequently supplement their incomes with labor-intensive cottage industries in which they produce the distinctive handicrafts found on the tourist trail, in addition to foodstuffs such as bread, cheese, and honey.

A large majority of highland people live a marginal and impoverished existence. Fiercely loyal to their ancestral heritage, the poor people of the Andes are nonetheless eager to share in the benefits of a modern lifestyle, which include educational opportunities, electricity, sewage systems, and clean water.

MIDDLE-CLASS PERU

The most difficult social area to define is that of the middle classes. Until the 1960s, it was the poor cousin of the oligarchy, providing clerks, merchants, and civil servants. Once modernization started in earnest in the 1970s, the middle class came into its own, both in Lima and in provincial cities. This was due to the diversification of the economy and to the expansion of the Peruvian state, both as a purveyor of public services and as an employer. However, middle-class prosperity was short-lived, as these were the very same people who suffered most under García in the 1980s, when hyperinflation wiped out their savings and reduced the buying power of their salaries. Many professionals, teachers among them, were forced to eke out a hand-to-mouth existence. Their situation is somewhat better now, but, as recent history has demonstrated, the middle class is vulnerable because it depends on a disposable income to maintain its lifestyle.

A WOMAN'S PLACE

The shakeup of Peruvian society that came with the terror of the Sendero Luminoso years in the 1980s brought a sudden change in the role of women. Although in pre-conquest Andean Peru women had rights and obligations on a more equal footing than in the colonial era, that standing had gradually been eroded in a society best described as *machista*, where women generally took a traditional wife-and-mother role. In many ways, the 1980s marked a shift. In the Andes, and later in the Amazon, the disruption of normal life by the Sendero Luminoso attacks and migrations often left the women in charge of reorganizing life; some 78 percent of migrant families had a woman head of household at one point. In Lima shantytowns, where economic chaos left many impoverished, it was women who were the backbone of daily life, holding the family together with the *vaso de leche* (glass of milk) breakfast clubs and the ubiquitous *clubes de madres* (mothers' clubs). The community soup kitchens the women organized were vital to feed their families, and the work of organization brought forward many female community leaders at a time when other popular organizations like trade unions and local political parties were falling apart because of rebel and military threats.

Divorce is not uncommon, but can be hard to obtain. Many married men openly take lovers, and in this predominantly *machista* society this is accepted without much fuss. In many rural communities the attitude toward women is still extremely traditional: in societies like that of the Ashaninka in the central Amazon jungle, men still take two or more

Customs and etiquette tips

- Don't take pictures of someone without asking for permission
- Peruvians of all groups of society tend to be quite formal. Make contact with '*Disculpe, buenos días*' or '*Disculpe, buenas tardes*' (Pardon, good morning/Pardon, good afternoon)
- Peruvians shake hands liberally. Women greet and are often greeted with a kiss on the right cheek, but this is less formal and should only be done if initiated by the Peruvian woman
- Visitors who don't want to stick out like sore thumbs should avoid wearing trekking gear off the trail or indigenous woolens
- Punctuality is rare. Expect events to start at least 30 minutes after their official time

Family life in Peru

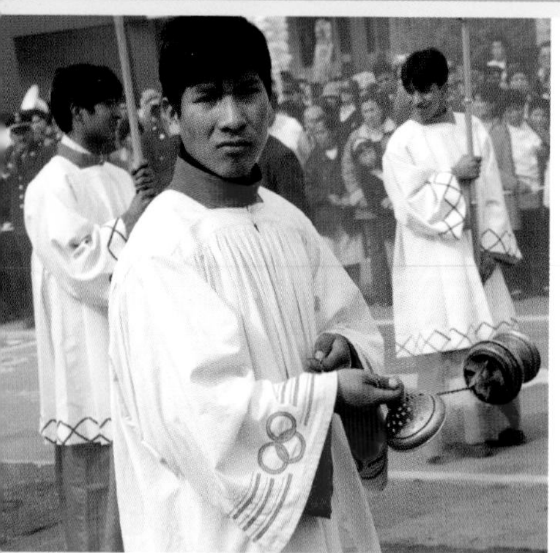

Religious procession at La Virgen de la Candelaria festival, Puno

wives. Women do most of the work in the fields, while men restrict themselves to hunting and fishing. In rural Peru illiteracy rates are much higher among women (43 percent) than among men (30 percent).

In urban Peru, women are shaking off the restrictions of the *machista* society, with students going to university now almost equally split between the genders, and women starting to have a presence in professional ranks as judges, academics, and bankers. In public life, women occupy ministerial posts, and a prominent political party is led by Lourdes Flores Nano, who has been a viable candidate in two presidential elections.

RELIGION

Even the Roman Catholic Church, a pillar of the old order, has changed tremendously in recent decades, with consequences for Peru's predominantly Catholic population. Since the late 1960s, there has been increasing tension between the conservative Catholic Church hierarchy and the so-called 'liberation theologists' who argue that the Church must fight to reduce poverty and injustice in this world. They have encouraged Masses in Quechua, Aymara, and other languages, and helped lead social protest movements.

But today the counter-revolution championed by leaders calling for the Church to focus on its spiritual message has been largely won, with the archbishop of Lima and most other Peruvian bishops now belonging to the ultra-conservative Opus Dei movement. In recent years there has also been a major rise of evangelical sects, particularly among the groups newly arrived in the cities from the country areas.

MUSIC AND DANCE

Peru has an extraordinary variety of dances, some typical Andean, others influenced by African traditions, still others adapted from Spanish dances and closely related to dances in neighboring countries.

Ethnologists and musicologists have registered more than 200 dances in Peru's Andes, grouped more broadly in six regional styles – the Altiplano, Ayacucho, the Callejón de Huaylas, Cusco, the Mantaro Valley, and Parinacochas. These are the ones visitors most closely associate with Peru. One dominant dance is the Huayno, which has become wildly popular throughout the Andes, although it can't be traced to Inca origins. Diabladas are characteristic of the Altiplano on both sides of the Peru–Bolivia border.

With mass immigration to Lima, many Andean dances can be seen Sundays at dance *coliseos* in the capital. *Chicha* and *tecnocumbia* are ubiquitous, popularized versions of Andean music with electronic instruments like synthesizers and drum machines.

Along the coast, both Spanish and Afro-Peruvian dances are popular. The dominant dance, more popular than waltzes and polkas, is the Marinera, a courtship dance akin to Chile's Cueca. African music has influenced its sister dance, the Tondero, along the north coast, but it continues to stand out on its own in dances including the Festejo and Alcatraz that will remind listeners of the Salsa and Son of the Caribbean.

See the Festivals and music Unique experience, pp.42–7.

LITERATURE

Without a written language, the oral traditions of indigenous languages were crippled by the Spanish dominance, although it is known that epic and lyric poems existed. Early chroniclers, especially Inca Garcilaso de la Vega, and Guamán Poma de Ayala, however, rescued some fragments for posterity. The anonymously authored play *Apu Ollantay*, commonly performed in Cusco in the 18th century, is entirely Quechua, though heavily influenced by Spanish drama.

Lima had South America's first printing press from 1583, helping the spread of literature, though limited mostly to the rich and powerful and religious orders. Early works copied Spanish styles but also showed an interest for the native societies encountered by the colonists.

Dance is an integral part of Peruvian culture

Examples of traditional Peruvian art

Independence and the crisis of the War of the Pacific strongly influenced Peruvian literature, leading first to Romanticism and later to Modernism with José Santos Chocano and José María Eguren. In the first half of the 20th century, poets like César Vallejo and Xavier Abril embraced the avant-garde, while Indigenism – appreciation of indigenous cultures – found protagonists in Ciro Alegría and José María Arguedas.

Julio Ramón Ribeyro, Alfredo Bryce Echenique and the 2010 Nobel Prize winner Mario Vargas Llosa *(see p. 106)* are the main representatives of the Urban Realism novelists who emerged starting in the 1950s. While Vargas Llosa's fame and popularity outshines all other contemporary Peruvian writers, Jaime Bayly, who also hosts an irreverent televised talk show, became popular with his 1994 novel *No se lo digas a nadie (Don't Tell Anyone)*. Other recent authors are Carlos Yushimito, Santiago Roncagliolo and Daniel Alarcón.

ART

Indigenous roots continue to play an important role in Peru's contemporary arts. The government has instituted prizes for traditional artists working in metals like gold and silver, as well as ceramics and weaving *(see p.54–9)*, but also painting. Like elsewhere in Latin America, muralists – above all Teodoro Núñez Ureta – created works celebrating workers and history, influenced by Mexicans Diego Rivera and David Alfaro Siqueiros. Peruvian painting's main claim to fame is painting in the style of its Mannerist and Baroque Cusco School *(see pp. 130–1)*. Among the more notable modern and contemporary artists are Francisco González Gamarra, Alejandro Alayza, and Julia Codesido.

FILM

Slow to grow under the dominance of the Hollywood film industry, Peruvian cinema took an additional hit amid the 1980s economic crisis and political violence. Adaptations of the country's literary greats, particularly Vargas Llosa, helped to win over local viewers. Francisco José Lombardi was one of the first directors to embark on this strategy. Like much of contemporary Latin American cinema, more recent films have focused on the social issues and review the late 20th-century turmoil suffered by Peru. Newer directors include Josué Méndez, Aldo Salvini, Edwin Cavello, and Claudia Llosa. Her movie *La Teta Asustada* (translated as *The Milk of Sorrow*), dealing with the trauma of women raped by the army and police during the repression of the Shining Path and the suffering of their children, in 2009 won the Berlin Festival's Golden Bear and became the first Peruvian film to be nominated for an Oscar as the Best Foreign Language Picture. The Lima cinema festival, an annual event launched in 1997 by the Catholic University, has become the country's main showcase for new independent films. Film piracy, however, visibly affects not only deep-pocketed foreign studios but also the nascent local industry that faces many more difficulties in finding financial support.

A group of revelers enjoying the festival atmosphere

SPORTS

Peruvians go wild over soccer (football), and the country has produced several stars, the best of which – including 1970s legend Teófilo Cubillas – played or still play in top European leagues. The most popular clubs are Lima's three greats, Alianza Lima, Sporting Cristal, and Universitario de Deportes. International glory, however, has belonged to Cusco's Cienciano alone, which won two South American championships in the early 2000s.

The national team, unfortunately, has been a bottom-dweller in international tournaments, failing to qualify for the World Cup since 1982. Other major spectator sports are horse racing and the seasonal bullfighting events.

The sport where Peru has had the most international success is surfing, with the male world champion Felipe Pomar in 1965 and Sofia Mulánovich winning the women's title in 2004.

Food and drink

A woman showing off her catch of the day

South America's most exiting cuisine is based on the myriad ingredients provided by Peru's many climates. Although regionally very varied, most towns of significant size will nowadays offer at least classic national dishes from the coast and the Andes, along with local specialties. In fact, surprisingly good food can be found even in small eateries throughout the country, from the *cevicherías* along the coast to rustic market stalls in the Sierra and the exotic fruit juice stands along the shores of the Amazon.

Created by Peru's many native and immigrant traditions, the country's cuisine has been refined by a generation of chefs since the 1980s, some of whom – like Gastón Acurio – have now gained celebrity status. A fine experiment for visitors is to sample both the folksy little eateries, which are also great places to talk to the locals, as well as to splurge on some of the trendiest restaurants in the Western hemisphere in Lima or Arequipa. Your tastebuds will thank you. Take care with some of the spiciest foods, though, if you're not accustomed to Peru's red-hot chili peppers.

FRUITS OF THE SEA

The most typically Peruvian dish is *ceviche*, a plate of raw white fish in a spicy marinade of lemon juice, onion, and hot peppers. Each restaurant has its own marinade recipe, and when the fish is freshly caught, *ceviche* can be delicious. It is healthier to avoid buying the cheaper versions of this dish sold in the street. *Ceviche* is traditionally served with corn and sweet potato, and there are many variations on the basic formula, often with the addition of shellfish in *ceviche mixto.* Another cold fish recipe is *escabeche de pescado*, cold fried fish in an onion, hot pepper and garlic sauce, adorned with olives and hard-boiled eggs.

Among the best shellfish are *camarones* (shrimp), *calamares* (squid), and *choros* (mussels), all prepared in various ways. Any dish listed as *a lo macho* means it comes with a shellfish sauce.

The king of fresh sea fish is the *corvina* or white sea bass, together with another excellent white fish, the *chita,* and the *lenguado* or sole. These are usually served *a la plancha* (grilled) or with any number of sauces.

In the highlands, farmed *trucha* or rainbow trout is plentiful. Less common but more distinctive is *pejerrey* or kingfish.

HEARTY PLATTERS

As well as the seafood, the cities and towns of the coastal desert region offer hearty dishes with chicken, duck, or goat. A favorite on the northern coast is *seco de cabrito* (roasted kid goat), often cooked with fermented *chicha* and served with beans and rice. A similar recipe is used to cook lamb, which becomes *seco de cordero*. A popular way of serving chicken is *ají de gallina,* a rich concoction of creamed chicken and a touch of hot peppers, served on boiled potatoes.

Limeños (people from Lima) often prepare a thick vegetable stew called *sancochado* served with meat. Another hearty meal common in the capital is *cau cau*, tripe cooked with beans and potatoes, served with rice.

Restaurants in Arequipa vie with each other to serve their version of *rocoto relleno* (stuffed peppers), which is delicious with fresh local cheese. Visitors unaccustomed to hot spices should be cautious when sampling the most fiery *ají.*

Every street corner and many restaurants offer *anticuchos* – skewers of meat which were originally grilled cattle and pig hearts, but can now include tuna or vegetables. Around Cusco, a choice delicacy is the *cuy* or guinea pig. It is often deep-fried, and tastes somewhere between chicken and rabbit.

Dining out

Mealtimes tend to be about an hour later than in the US and UK, with dinner generally eaten after 8pm. Restaurant menus can sometimes fail to spell out 19 percent value-added taxes and 10 percent mandatory service charges – and even a 20 percent *selectivo* tax for imported wine. Expensive restaurants may add on a charge for bread or other snacks served ahead of the meal.

A WORLD STAPLE

Potatoes are an essential part of most of the filling one-pot dishes common in highland cuisine. A famous dish named after them is *papas a la huancaína,* a creamy concoction of potatoes, peppers, and boiled eggs. Or they can be served with a peanut sauce in *papa ocopa,* or simply stuffed with meat, onions, boiled eggs, and raisins for *papa rellena*. They also take their place in *estofado* (a stew of chicken, corn, carrots, and tomatoes) as well as the ever-present *lomo saltado* (strips of beef with onions, tomatoes, and fried potatoes). The *papa amarilla* (yellow potato) is considered the best.

Women in traditional dress selling fresh fruit and vegetables at a Sunday market

The distinctive skin of an *olluco*, similar in taste to a new potato

Peru's highlands also produce other tubers. The *olluco*, which can range in color from red to orange, tastes like new potatoes. It is often shredded and served with dried llama meat or *charquí* (beef jerky) in a stew. In a few places you may find *oca* or *arracacha* served instead of the usual potato. The sweet potato or *camote* is also plentiful and full of taste.

Choclo, boiled large-grained ears of corn, are sold on every street corner, usually with slices of cheese and *picante* sauce. Fried corn kernels called *cancha* are also a common snack, served before meals or to nibble with beer or pisco. Other grains, including the purple-flowered *kiwicha* and the golden quinoa – both kinds of amaranth – are being rediscovered as healthier variants to the potato and these are now being used in breads, cookies, soups, and salads.

JUNGLE FARE

As well as the plentiful fish of the Amazon and other tropical rivers in Peru, the jungle area offers many other culinary delights: peccary or wild boar, and other game, as well as *juanes*, a kind of *tamal* stuffed with chicken and rice. Bananas, of many different kinds, can be fried, boiled, or eaten fresh, and yucca (also called manioc or cassava) accompanies most meals. Both serve as good replacements for the potato in the Amazon.

WHERE TO EAT

Street corner snacks are common, but not necessarily the safest bet for unaccustomed stomachs. For cheap local cuisine, it's best to head to the covered markets for quality eateries, or *picanterías*, at rock-bottom prices. You should ask at your local hotel for a guide to the best places.

Set lunches *(menú del día)* are cheaper than à la carte meals and dinners. They include a soup, non-alcoholic drink, main course, and often a small dessert. Popular *chifas* and *pollo a la brasa* (chicken on a spit) are also good places for inexpensive meals. Lima's culinary highlights meanwhile are best booked ahead, especially for Friday and Saturday nights and Sunday lunches, when they tend to be full.

SWEET TEETH

Peruvians love to finish a meal with a sweet dessert. Often this will be something that is part of the culinary tradition brought over from Spain. Favorites include *manjar blanco*, a kind of fudge made from boiled milk and sugar; *cocadas* (coconut macaroons); or the typically Spanish *churros*, pastry dough similar to donuts fried and eaten with honey or chocolate. *Manjar blanco* and meringue, along with a dash of port and a sprinkling of cinnamon, are used to make Peru's most famous dessert, *suspiro limeño* ('Lima sigh'). Other common sweets include *yuquitas*, which is deep-fried yucca-dough balls rolled in sugar; *picarones*, which are donuts coated in honey; and *tejas*, a sweet biscuit filled with *manjar blanco*.

Inca Kola is the most popular soft drink in Peru

Tropical fruit and vegetables

Peru is a tropical country, so seasons don't vary much. The main summer growing season runs October through March, but most fruits and vegetables are available throughout the year. Specialty foods are prepared for religious festivals, like *turrones* for Lima's October Señor de los Milagros celebration.

THIRST QUENCHERS

Most of Peru's grapes are used for making pisco, which in turn is the basic ingredient for the Peruvian national drink, pisco sour *(see pp.98–9)*. Wine is less common, with a few noteworthy vineyards around Ica – which produce the Tacama, Tabernero, and Ocucaje brands. Exotic fruit juices are common, with *maracuya* (passion fruit) and papaya just two of many on offer.

Soft drinks are called *gaseosas*; extremely popular is the local Inca Kola. Beyond common beers, the fermented corn drink *chicha* is made into a cloudy and extremely strong beer for the harvest festivals. Purple corn is also converted into a refreshing non-alcoholic drink known as *chicha morada*.

Mate de coca, tea made from coca leaves, is served throughout the highland region as an antidote to altitude sickness. Coffee usually comes as a concentrated liquid known as *esencia*, which is then diluted with boiled water. Peru grows high-quality coffee; the best is from Chanchamayo, and one of the best brands is Britt.

PHRASE BOOK

HABICH
JOSE GRANDE

Phrase book

Behind Mandarin Chinese and English, Spanish is the world's third-most commonly spoken tongue, and the official language of 21 nations. Spanish and Peruvians often drop the 's' before a consonant, pronouncing it like the 'h' in house, but otherwise, Peruvian Spanish is among the clearest, easiest kinds of Spanish to understand. Among native languages, 14 percent speak Quechua, mainly in rural areas, and Aymara is spoken near Lake Titicaca. Only in more remote areas do people fail to speak at least some Spanish. Outside hotels, better restaurants, and tour companies, English is rarely spoken, so the learning of basic terms is helpful – and much appreciated.

PRONUNCIATION

This section is designed to make you familiar with the sounds of Spanish using our simplified phonetic transcription. You'll find the pronunciation of the Spanish letters and sounds explained below, together with their 'imitated' equivalents. This system is used throughout the phrase book; simply read the pronunciation as if it were English, noting any special rules below.

Underlined letters indicate that that syllable should be stressed. The acute accent ´ indicates stress, e.g. **río**, ree•oh. Some Spanish words have more than one meaning. In these instances, the accent mark is also used to distinguish between them, e.g. **él** (he) and **el** (the); **sí** (yes) and **si** (if).

There are some differences in vocabulary and pronunciation between the Spanish spoken in Spain and that in the Americas, although each is easily understood by the other. This phrase book is specifically geared to travelers in Latin America.

Consonants

Letter	*Approximate Pronunciation*	*Symbol*	*Example*	*Pronunciation*
b	1. as in English	b	**bueno**	*bweh • noh*
	2. between vowels as in English, but softer	b	**bebida**	beh•bee•dah
c	1. before e and i like s in same	s	**centro**	sehn•troh
	2. otherwise like k in kit	k	**como**	koh•moh
ch	as in English	ch	**mucho**	moo•choh
d	as in English	d	**donde**	dohn•deh
g	1. before e and i, like ch in Scottish loch	kh	**urgente**	oor•khehn•teh
	2. otherwise, like g in get	g	**ninguno**	neen•goo•noh
h	always silent		**hombre**	ohm•breh

j	like ch in Scottish loch	kh	**bajo**	bah•khoh
ll	like y in yellow	y	**lleno**	yeh•noh
ñ	like ni in onion	ny	**señor**	seh•nyohr
q	like k in kick	k	**quince**	keen•seh
r	trilled, especially at the beginning of a word	r	**río**	ree•oh
rr	strongly trilled	rr	**arriba**	ah•rree•bah
s	1. like s in same	s	**sus**	soos
	2. before b, d, g, l, m, n, like s in rose	z	**mismo**	meez•moh
v	like b in bad, but softer	b	**viejo**	beeyeh•khoh
z	like s in same	s	**brazo**	brah•soh

Letters f, k, l, m, n, p, t, w, x and y are pronounced as in English.

Vowels

Letter	*Approximate Pronunciation*	*Symbol*	*Example*	*Pronunciation*
a	like the a in father	ah	**gracias**	grah•seeyahs
e	like e in get	eh	**esta**	ehs•tah
i	like ee in meet	ee	**sí**	see
o	like o in rope	oh	**dos**	dohs
u	1. like oo in food	oo	**uno**	oo•noh
	2. silent after g and q		**que**	keh
	3. when marked ü, like we in well	w	**antigüedad**	ahn•tee•gweh•dahd
y	1. like y in yellow	y	**hoy**	oy
	2. when alone, like ee in meet	ee	**y**	ee
	3. when preceded by an a, sounds like y + ee, with ee faintly pronounced	aye	**hay**	aye

English	Spanish	Pronunciation
How much?	**¿Cuánto?**	*kwahn • toh*

Spanish words and phrases appear in bold. A simplified pronunciation guide follows each Spanish phrase; read it as if it were English, giving the underlined letters more stress than the others. Among English phrases, you will find some words included in square brackets; these are the British English equivalents of American English expressions.

General

0	**cero** *seh • roh*	100	**cien** *seeyehn*
1	**uno** *oo • noh*	500	**quinientos** *kee • neeyehn • tohs*
2	**dos** *dohs*	1,000	**mil** *meel*
3	**tres** *trehs*	1,000,000	**un millón** *oon mee • yohn*
4	**cuatro** *kwah • troh*	Monday	**lunes** *loo • nehs*
5	**cinco** *seen • koh*	Tuesday	**martes** *mahr • tehs*
6	**seis** *seyees*	Wednesday	**miércoles** *meeyehr • koh • lehs*
7	**siete** *seeyeh • teh*	Thursday	**jueves** *khweh • behs*
8	**ocho** *oh • choh*	Friday	**viernes** *beeyehr • nehs*
9	**nueve** *nweh • beh*	Saturday	**sábado** *sah • bah • doh*
10	**diez** *deeyehs*	Sunday	**domingo** *doh • meen • goh*

Hello.	**Hola**. *oh • lah*
Goodbye.	**Adiós**. *ah • deeyohs*
See you later.	**Hasta luego**. *ah • stah lweh • goh*
Yes.	**Sí**. *see*
No.	**No**. *noh*
OK.	**De acuerdo**. *deh ah • kwehr • doh*
Excuse me! (to get attention)	**¡Disculpe!** *dees • kool • peh*
Excuse me. (to get past)	**Perdón**. *pehr • dohn*
I'm sorry.	**Lo siento**. *loh seeyehn • toh*
How are you?	**¿Cómo está?** *koh • moh ehs • tah*
Fine, thanks.	**Bien, gracias**. *beeyehn grah • seeyahs*
I'd like…	**Quiero…** *keeyeh • roh…*
How much?	**¿Cuánto?** *kwahn • toh*
Where is…?	**¿Dónde está…?** *dohn • deh ehs • tah…*
Please.	**Por favor**. *pohr fah • bohr*
Thank you.	**Gracias**. *grah • seeyahs*
You're welcome.	**De nada**. *deh nah • dah*
Please speak slowly.	**Hable más despacio, por favor**. *ah • bleh mahs dehs • pah • seeyoh pohr fah • bohr*
Can you repeat that?	**¿Podría repetir eso?** *poh • dree • ah reh • peh • teer eh • soh*
I don't understand.	**No entiendo**. *noh ehn • teeyehn • doh*
Do you speak English?	**¿Habla usted inglés?** *ah • blah oos • ted een • glehs*
I don't speak Spanish.	**No hablo español**. *noh ah • bloh ehs • pah • nyohl*
What's your name?	**Cómo se llama?** *koh • moh seh yah • ma*
My name is…	**Me llamo…** *meh yah • moh…*
Nice to meet you.	**Encantado/Encantada**. *ehn • kahn • tah • doh/ ehn • kahn • tah • dah*
Where's the restroom [toilet]?	**¿Dónde están los servicios?** *dohn • deh ehs • tahn lohs sehr • bee • seeyohs*
Help!	¡Socorro! *soh • koh • rroh*

Arrival and departure

I'm on vacation [holiday]/business.	**Estoy aqui de vacaciones/en viaje de negocios**. *ehs • toy ah • kee deh bah • kah • seeyohn • ehs/ehn beeyah • kheh deh neh • goh • seeyohs*
I'm going to…	**Voy a ...** *boy ah…*
I'm staying at the Hotel…	**Me alojo en el Hotel...** *meh ah • loh • khoh ehn ehl oh • tehl…*

Money and banking

Where's…?	**¿Dónde está...?** *dohn • deh ehs • tah…*
– the ATM	**– el cajero automático** *ehl kah • kheh • roh awtoh • mah • tee • koh*
– the bank	**– el banco** *ehl bahn • koh*
– the currency exchange office	**– la casa de cambio** *lah kah • sah deh kahm • beeyoh*
When does the bank open/close?	**¿A qué hora abre/cierra el banco?** *ah keh oh • rah ah • breh/seeyeh • rrah ehl bahn • koh*
I'd like to change pounds/dollars into…	**Quiero cambiar libras/dólares a...** *keeyeh • roh kahm • beeyahr lee • brahs/doh • lah • rehs ah*

Transport

How do I get to town?	**¿Cómo se llega a la ciudad?** *koh • moh seh yeh • gah ah lah seew • dahd*
Where's…?	**¿Dónde está...?** *dohn • deh ehs • tah…*
– the airport	**– el aeropuerto** *ehl ah • eh • roh • pwehr • toh*
– the train [railway] station	**– la estación de tren** *lah ehs • tah • seeyohn deh trehn*
– the bus station	**– la estación de autobuses** *lah ehs • tah • seeyohn deh awtoh • boo • ses*
– the subway [underground] station	**– la estación de metro** *lah ehs • tah • seeyohn deh meh • troh*
How far is it?	**¿A qué distancia está?** *ah keh dees • tahn • seeyah ehs • tah*
Where do I buy a ticket?	**¿Dónde se compra el boleto?** *dohn • deh seh kohm • prah ehl boh • leh • toh*
A one-way [single]/round-trip [return] ticket to…	**Un boleto de ida/ida y vuelta a...** *oon boh • leh • toh deh ee • dah/ee • dah ee bwehl • tah ah…*
How much?	**¿Cuánto es?** *kwahn • toh ehs*
From which…?	**¿De qué...?** *deh keh…*
– gate	**– puerta de embarque** *pwehr • tah deh ehm • bahr • keh*
– line	**– línea** *lee • neh • ah*
– platform	**– andén** *ahn • dehn*
Where can I get a taxi?	**¿Dónde puedo tomar un taxi?** *dohn • deh pweh • doh toh • mahr oon tah • xee*
Take me to this address	**Lléveme a esta dirección**. *yeh • beh • meh ah ehs • tah dee • rehk • seeyohn*
Where's the car rental?	**¿Dónde está el alquiler de autos?** *dohn • deh ehs • tah ehl ahl • kee • lehr deh ahoo • tohs*
Can I have a map?	**¿Podría darme un mapa?** *poh • dree • ah dahr • meh oon mah • pah*

Accommodations

I have a reservation.	**Tengo una reserva**. *tehn • goh oo • nah reh • sehr • bah*
My name is…	**Me llamo...** *meh yah • moh…*
Do you have a room…?	**¿Tienen habitaciones...?** *teeyeh • nehn ah • bee • tah • seeyoh • nehs…*
– for one/two	**– individuales/dobles** *een • dee • bee • doo • ah • lehs/ doh • blehs*
– with a bathroom	**– con baño** *kohn bah • nyoh*
– with air conditioning	**– con aire acondicionado** *kohn ayee • reh ah • kohn • dee • seeyoh • nah • doh*
For…	**Para...** *pah • rah…*
– tonight	**– esta noche** *ehs • tah noh • cheh*
– two nights	**– dos noches** *dohs noh • chehs*
– one week	**– una semana** *oo • nah seh • mah • nah*
How much?	**¿Cuánto es?** *kwahn • toh ehs*
Is there anything cheaper?	**¿Hay alguna tarifa más barata?** *aye ahl • goo • nah tah • ree • fah mahs bah • rah • tah*

Internet and communications

Can I access the internet/check email?	**¿Puedo acceder a Internet/revisar el correo electrónico?** *pweh • doh ahk • seh • dehr ah een • tehr • neht/reh • bee • sahr ehl koh • rreh • oh eh • lehk • troh • nee • koh*
How do I connect/log on?	**¿Cómo entro al sistema/inicio la sesión?** *koh • moh ehn • troh ahl sees • teh • mah/ee • nee • seeyoh lah seh • seeyohn*
A phone card please.	**Una tarjeta telefónica, por favor**. *oo • nah tahr • kheh • tah teh • leh • foh • nee • kah pohr fah • bohr*
Hello. This is…	**Hola. Soy...** *oh • lah soy…*
Can I speak to…?	**¿Puedo hablar con...?** *pweh • doh ah • blahr kohn…*
Can you repeat that ?	**¿Puede repetir eso?** *pweh • deh reh • peh • teer eh • soh*
I'll call back later.	**Llamaré más tarde**. *yah • mah • reh mahs tahr • deh*
Where's the post office?	**¿Dónde está la oficina de correos?** *dohn • deh ehs • tah lah oh • fee • see • nah deh koh • rreh • ohs*
I'd like to send this to…	**Quiero mandar esto a...** *keeyeh • roh mahn • dahr ehs • toh ah…*

Sightseeing

Where's the tourist information office?	**¿Dónde está la oficina de turismo?** *dohn • deh ehs • tah lah oh • fee • see • nah deh too • reez • moh*
What are the main attractions?	**¿Dónde están los principales sitios de interés?** *dohn • deh ehs • tahn lohs preen • see • pah • lehs see • teeyohs deh een • teh • rehs*
Do you have tours in English?	**¿Hay visitas en inglés?** *aye bee • see • tahs ehn een • glehs*
Can I have a map/guide?	**¿Puede darme un mapa/una guía?** *pweh • deh dahr • meh oon mah • pah/oo • nah gee • ah*

Shopping

Where's the market/mall [shopping centre]?	**¿Dónde está el mercado/centro comercial?** *dohn • deh ehs • tah ehl mehr • kah • doh/sen • troh koh • mehr • seeyahl*
Can you help me?	**¿Puede ayudarme?** *pweh • deh ah • yoo • dahr • meh*
How much?	**¿Cuánto es?** *kwahn • toh ehs*
That one please.	**Ése/Ésa, por favor**. *eh • seh/eh • sah pohr fah • bohr*
Where can I pay?	**¿Dónde se paga?** *dohn • deh seh pah • gah*
I'll pay in cash/by credit card.	**Voy a pagar en efectivo/con tarjeta de crédito**. *boy ah pah • gahr ehn eh • fehk • tee • boh /kohn tahr • kheh • tah deh kreh • dee • toh*
A receipt, please.	**Un recibo, por favor**. *oon reh • see • boh pohr fah • bohr*

Culture and nightlife

What's there to do at night?	**¿Qué se puede hacer por las noches?** *keh seh pweh • deh ah • sehr pohr lahs noh • chehs*
What's playing tonight?	**¿Qué hay en cartelera esta noche?** *keh aye ehn kahr • teh • leh • rah ehs • tah noh • cheh ehl sehn • troh*
Where's...?	**¿Dónde está...?** *dohn • deh ehs • tah...*
– the downtown area [city centre]	**– el centro** *ehl sehn • troh*
– the bar	**– el bar** *ehl bahr*
– the dance club	**– la discoteca** *lah dees • koh • teh • kah*
Is there a cover charge?	**¿Hay que pagar entrada?** *aye keh pah • gahr ehn • trah • dah*

Business travel

I'm here on business.	**Estoy aquí en viaje de negocios**. *ehs • toy ah • kee ehn beeyah • kheh deh neh • goh • seeyohs*
Here's my business card.	**Aquí tiene mi tarjeta**. *ah • kee teeyeh • neh mee tahr • kheh • tah*
Can I have your card?	**¿Puede darme su tarjeta?** *pweh • deh dahr • meh soo tahr • kheh • tah*
I have a meeting with...	**Tengo una reunión con...** *tehn • goh oo • nah rewoo • neeyohn kohn...*
Where's...?	**¿Dónde está...?** *dohn • deh ehs • tah...*
– the business centre	**el centro de negocios** *ehl sehn • troh deh neh • goh • seeyohs*
– the convention hall	**el salón de congresos** *ehl sah • lohn deh kohn • greh • sohs*
– the meeting room	**la sala de reuniones** *lah sah • lah deh rewoo • neeyohn • ehs*

Travel with children

Is there a discount for children?	**¿Hacen descuento a niños?** *ah • sen dehs • kwehn • toh ah nee • nyohs*
Can you recommend a babysitter?	**¿Puede recomendarme una niñera?** *pweh • deh reh • koh • mehn • dahr • meh oo • nah neeh • nyeh • rah*
Do you have a child seat/highchair?	**¿Tienen una silla para niños/alta?** teeyeh • nehn oo • nah see • yah pah • rah nee • nyohs/ahl • tah
Where can I change the baby?	**¿Dónde puedo cambiar al bebé?** dohn • deh pweh • doh kahm • beeyahr ahl beh • beh

Disabled travelers

Is there…?	**¿Hay...?** *aye…*
– access for the disabled	**– acceso para los discapacitados** *ahk • seh • soh pah • rah lohs dees • kah • pah • see • tah • dohs*
– a wheelchair ramp	**una rampa para sillas de ruedas** *oo • nah rahm • pah pah • rah see • yahs deh rweh • dahs*
– a disabled accessible restroom [toilet]	**– un baño con acceso para discapacitados** *oon bah • nyoh kohn ahk • seh • soh pah • rah dees • kah • pah • see • tah • dohs*
I need…	**Necesito...** *neh • seh • see • toh…*
– assistance	**– ayuda** *ah • yoo • dah*
– an elevator [a lift]	**– un ascensor** *oon ah • sehn • sohr*

Emergencies

Help!	**¡Socorro!** *soh • koh • rroh*
Get a doctor!	**¡Llame a un médico!** *yah • meh ah oon meh • dee • koh*
Call the police!	**¡Llame a la policía!** *yah • meh ah lah poh • lee • see • ah*
Where's the police station?	**¿Dónde está la comisaría?** *dohn • deh ehs • tah lah koh • mee • sah • ree • ah*
There was an accident/attack.	**Hubo un accidente/asalto.** *ooh • boh oon ahk • see • dehn • teh/ah • sahl • toh*

Health

I'm sick [ill].	**Me siento mal**. *meh seeyehn • toh mahl*
I need an English-speaking doctor.	**Necesito un médico que hable inglés**. *neh • seh • see • toh oon meh • dee • koh keh ah • bleh een • glehs*
It hurts here.	**Me duele aquí**. *meh dweh • leh ah • kee*
I have a stomach-ache.	**Tengo dolor de estómago**. *tehn • goh doh • lohr deh ehs • toh • mah • goh*
Where's the pharmacy [chemist]?	**¿Dónde está la farmacia?** *dohn • deh ehs • tah lah fahr • mah • seeyah*
What time does it open/close?	**¿A qué hora abre/cierra?** *ah keh oh • rah ah • breh/ seeyeh • rrah*
Can you make up this prescription?	**¿Puede darme este medicamento?** *pweh • deh dahr • meh ehs • teh meh • dee • kah • mehn • toh*

Eating out

Can you recommend a good restaurant/ bar?	**¿Puede recomendarme un buen restaurante/bar?** *pweh • deh reh • koh • mehn • dahr • meh oon bwehn rehs • taw • rahn • teh/bahr*
A table for…, please.	**Una mesa para..., por favor**. *oo • nah meh • sah pah • rah… pohr fah • bohr*
A menu, please.	**Una carta, por favor**. *oo • nah kahr • tah pohr fah • bohr*
I'd like…	**Quiero...** *keeyeh • roh…*
The check [bill], please.	**La cuenta, por favor**. *lah kwen • tah pohr fah • bohr*
Is service included?	**¿Está incluido el servicio?** *ehs • tah een • kloo • ee • doh ehl sehr • bee • seeyoh*

Menu reader

Spanish		English
el aceite	*ehl ah • seyee • teh*	oil
la aceituna	*lah ah • seyee • too • nah*	olive
el agua	*ehl ah • gwah*	water
el arroz	*ehl ah • rrohs*	rice
el asado	*ehl ah • sah • doh*	roast
el atún	*ehl ah • toon*	tuna
el azúcar	*ehl ah • soo • kahr*	sugar
el bacalao	*bah • kah • lao*	salted, dried cod
la berenjena	*lah beh • rehn • kheh • nah*	eggplant [aubergine]
el café	*ehl kah • feh*	coffee
el café solo	*ehl kah • feh soh • loh*	espresso
la carne	*lah kahr • neh*	meat
la carne de cerdo	*lah kahr • neh deh sehr • doh*	pork
la carne de res	*lah kahr • neh deh rehs*	beef
la cebolla	*lah seh • boh • yah*	onion
la cerveza	*lah sehr • beh • sah*	beer
el cordero	*ehl kohr • deh • roh*	lamb
descafeinado	*dehs • kah • feyee • nah • doh*	decaffeinated
el durazno	*ehl duh • rahs • noh*	peach
la empanada	*lah ehm • pah • nah • dah*	pastry filled with meat or vegetables
la ensalada	*lah ehn • sah • lah • dah*	salad
los fiambres	*lohs feeyahm • brehs*	charcuterie [cold cuts]
el filete	*ehl fee • leh • teh*	steak
la frambuesa	*lah frahm • bweh • sah*	raspberry
la fresa	*lah freh • sah*	strawberry
la fruta	*lah froo • tah*	fruit
el gazpacho	*ehl gahs • pah • choh*	cold tomato-based soup
el helado	*ehl eh • lah • doh*	ice cream
el huevo	*ehl weh • boh*	egg
el jamón	*ehl khah • mohn*	ham
el jugo	*ehl khoo • goh*	juice

Spanish		English
la leche	*lah leh • cheh*	milk
los macarrones	*lohs mah • kah • rrohn • ehs*	macaroni
el maíz	*ehl mah • ees*	sweet corn
la mantequilla	*lah mahn • teh • kee • yah*	butter
la manzana	*lah mahn • sah • nah*	apple
el marisco	*ehl mah • rees • koh*	shellfish
la mermelada	*lah mehr • meh • lah • dah*	marmalade/jam
la mostaza	*lah mohs • tah • sah*	mustard
la naranja	*lah nah • rahn • khah*	orange
el pan	*ehl pahn*	bread
la papa/las papas fritas	*lah pah • pah/pah • pahs free • tahs*	potato/French fries [chips]
el pastel	*ehl pahs • tehl*	pie
el pescado	*ehl pehs • kah • doh*	fish
la pimienta	*lah pee • meeyen • tah*	pepper
el pollo	*ehl poh • yoh*	chicken
el queso	*ehl keh • soh*	cheese
la sal	*lah sahl*	salt
la salchicha	*lah sahl • chee • chah*	sausage
la sopa	*lah soh • pah*	soup
el té	*ehl teh*	tea
la ternera	*lah tehr • neh • rah*	veal
tinto	*teen • toh*	red (wine)
el tocino	*ehl toh • see • noh*	bacon
la torta	*lah tohr • tah*	cake
la tortilla	*lah tohr • tee • yah*	omelette
la tostada	*lah tohs • tah • dah*	toast
las uvas	*lahs oo • bahs*	grapes
la verdura	*lah behr • doo • rah*	vegetable
el vinagre	*ehl bee • nah • greh*	vinegar
el vino	*ehl bee • noh*	wine
la zanahoria	*lah sah • nah • oh • reeyah*	carrot

Index

Accommodation Index

Credits for Berlitz Handbook Peru

Written by: Stephan Küffner
Series Editor: Tom Stainer
Map Production: Phoenix Mapping and Apa Cartography Department
Production: Linton Donaldson, Rebeka Ellam
Picture Manager: Steven Lawrence
Art Editor: Tom Smyth
Photography: Alamy 5C, 7CR, 9BL, 42, 44, 47, 83T&B, 112, 182, 187B, 193B, 196, 238, 264, 273; Mitch Aidelbaum 88; Martin St Antal 131B; Paul Ark 152; AWL Images 187T, 233, 241; Bar Lima 250; Mark Bowler/ Nature Picture Library 8T, 30; Brooklyn Museum 131T; ferro carril 177; Caitlin Childs 105; Choco Museum 126; Corbis 9CL, 192; Marcos Ferro/Aurora/SpecialistStock 215T; Fotolia 183; Martin Garcia 76; Ica R Geisel 95; Getty Images 32, 72, 173T, 174, 176, 185, 194; Jorge Gobbi 177T; Gringo Bills 150; Robert Harding Picture Library 3TR, 9BR, 218; Inkaterra Lodge 33, 251, 252; iStockphoto.com 2TL, 5BR, 9BR, 16, 17, 25, 37, 57, 91, 92, 95T, 100, 119, 120, 142, 145, 173B, 191, 198, 200, 213, 214, 216, 221, 222; Latitude Pictures 113; Markus Leupold-Löwenthal 287; Paul Lowry 91; Machu Sanctuary Lodge 149; Manu Wonderland Tours 246; Kari Medig/ Aurora/SpecialistStock 215B; Miraflores Hotel 86; Museo Larco 75; Novalima Press 46; Pete Oxford/Nature Picture Library 239; Photolibrary 3TL, 5TR, 6BL, 6BR, 6TR, 7TL, 9TR, 24, 27, 53, 74, 84, 85, 99B, 104, 121, 147, 155, 166, 175, 179, 180, 189, 195, 212, 217, 220, 231T&B, 232, 235, 286; Peru Hotel Libertador 168; Mike Presser 146; Olivier Renck/Aurora/ SpecialistStock 7TR; Wendorf Rodríguez 114; Jeff Rotman/Nature Picture Library 31; Second Home Peru 87; South American Pictures 181; Jon Spaull/Panos 82; Still Pictures 34, 35, 41, 101, 132, 190, 236; SuperStock 234, 245, 247, 254; Tambo Colorado 102; Carlos Tanner 237M; Adriana Torres 103; R. Tyler Gross/ Aurora/SpecialistStock 240 Yarapa Lodge 243
Cover: front: AWL Images; back left and middle: Fotolia.co.uk; back right: iStockphoto.com

Printed by: CTPS-China

First Edition 2012

Contacting Us

At Berlitz we strive to keep our guides as accurate and up to date as possible, but if you find anything that has changed, or if you have any suggestions on ways to improve this guide, then we would be delighted to hear from you. Write to Berlitz Publishing, PO Box 7910, London SE1 1WE, UK or email: berlitz@apaguide.co.uk

Worldwide: APA Publications GmbH & Co. Verlag KG (Singapore branch), 7030 Ang Mo Kio Ave 5, 08-65 Northstar @ AMK, Singapore 569880; tel: (65) 570 1051; email: apasin@singnet.com.sg
UK and Ireland: Dorling Kindersley Ltd, a Penguin Group company 80 Strand, London, WC2R 0RL, UK; email: customerservice@dk.com
United States: Ingram Publisher Services, 1 Ingram Boulevard, PO Box 3006, La Vergne, TN 37086-1986; email: customer.service@ingrampublisherservices.com
Australia: Universal Publishers, 1 Waterloo Road, Macquarie Park, NSW 2113; tel: (61) 2-9857 3700; email: sales@universalpublishers.com.au

www.berlitzpublishing.com